Teaching and Learning in the Elementary School

Teaching and Learning in the Elementary School

THIRD EDITION

JOHN JAROLIMEK
CLIFFORD D. FOSTER
University of Washington, Seattle

MACMILLAN   PUBLISHING   COMPANY / New York

COLLIER MACMILLAN PUBLISHERS / London

Cover photo by Patricia Rush, Gig Harbor, Washington 98335

Copyright © 1985, Macmillan Publishing Company, a division of Macmillan, Inc.
Printed in the United States of America

Macmillan Publishing Company
866 Third Avenue, New York, New York 10022

Collier Macmillan Canada, Inc.

Library of Congress Cataloging in Publication Data

Jarolimek, John.
   Teaching and learning in the elementary school.

   Includes index.
   1. Elementary school teaching. 2. Lesson planning.
I. Foster, Clifford Donald, 1923–   . II. Title.
LB1555.J34 1985   372.11′02   84–3927
ISBN 0–02–360340–2

Printing: 5 6 7 8   Year: 6 7 8 9 0 1 2 3

ISBN: ISBN 0-02-360340-2

Preface

The news media and some of the literature of education may leave the impression that we are now in the midst of a revolutionary transformation in the way children are taught in schools. The introduction of new technologies to education has prompted some speculation about what the role of the teacher should be in a school equipped with microcomputers, information processors, and other electronic devices.

If past experience is any guide to what is likely to happen in the future, those entering the field of teaching might be reassured—or disappointed—in knowing that there is much about the work of the elementary school teacher that has not changed appreciably in the past one hundred fifty years. Teachers still encourage and inspire all children to do their best work; seek and groom the latent talents of each individual. Teachers still hold children's hands on the playground, comfort them when their bodies—or feelings—have been hurt, arbitrate conflicts between them, correct their papers, place grades on their report cards, and decide which of the children are going to "pass." Teachers still become annoyed with tattletales and with children who visit or chew gum in class. In other words, elementary school teaching remains primarily a helping profession, and to do it well, one must be a deeply sensitive person who cares about children, who is committed to providing human service, and who is professionally competent. Those requirements are not likely to change much in the foreseeable future.

If society expects teachers to sow the seeds of a civilized humanity and subsequently hopes to enjoy a bountiful harvest, the elementary school curriculum must concern itself with the achievement of broad educational goals. To embrace broad goals does not, of course, minimize the importance of basic skills. It suggests, rather, that the school be concerned about developing the social, emotional, and physical maturity of children as well as their intellectual capabilities. We are learning that development of the sensory system through the arts actually facilitates learning in the "academics." A commitment to broad educational goals has many implications for the arrangement of the classroom environment and how teaching takes place in it. Classrooms should not be entirely adult centered but should allow children to develop some sense of ownership in what goes on there. Peer learning and the social dynamics of the classroom are critical to the achievement of broad educational goals.

The position taken in this text is that it is the teacher's responsibility to provide a classroom environment—a learning "context"—that will enable children to engage in those tasks that are essential for them to perform if they are to learn what the school curriculum offers. This means that teachers will need to do extensive planning—including some cooperative planning with the children—in order to have a systematic, and in some sense, sequential program of instruction. It means, too, that the teacher has to be well grounded in such teaching skills as classroom management, lesson preparation and presentation, setting objectives, using various modes of teaching, selecting and using appropriate instructional materials, selecting and implementing learning activities, asking questions and responding to children's answers, and evaluating their learning.

The primary focus of this text is on *generic* teaching skills. Generic teaching skills are defined as those general, universal skills that can be applied in a wide range of subjects, skills, and instructional contexts. Once learned, generic teaching skills can be transferred to, and applied in, many different settings. The generic teaching skills developed in this text can be inferred from the statements of competencies and related performance criteria found at the beginning of each chapter. The competencies and performance criteria have come from several sources, including current educational literature and research. Many of the ideas and suggestions presented in the text have been field tested with hundreds of students in teacher education programs across the country.

The authors are indebted to Patricia A. Conrard, Bellevue Public Schools; Kay F. Engelsen, Tacoma School District; and Terri Malinowski, Northshore School District, all of Washington State, for their assistance in securing photographs for the text. We wish to express our sincere thanks and appreciation to them for that contribution.

We also acknowledge our gratitude to our wives, Mildred Fleming Jarolimek and Margie Osborn Foster, for their expert technical assistance with the preparation of the manuscript and for their thoughtful and constructive comments regarding the substance of the text.

John Jarolimek
Clifford D. Foster

Contents

5

MODES OF TEACHING   119

6

ORGANIZING GROUPS OF LEARNERS   147
FOR INSTRUCTION

The Challenge of Teaching in the Elementary School

THE QUALIFIED AND COMPETENT TEACHER . . .

1. Is familiar with some of the social realities that elementary school children confront in their daily lives.

2. Knows how teacher behavior affects the achievement and aspirations of children.

3. Cares about children and is personally and professionally committed to their education.

Performance Criteria

As a result of the serious study of this chapter, the student should be able to . . .

1. Identify major goals and purposes of elementary education.

2. Identify factors in and out of school that relate to a child's success in school.

3. Identify conditions that stand in the way of achieving equality of educational opportunity for all children.

4. Provide examples of institutionalized racism and sexism and develop strategies for promoting race and sex equity.

5. Describe the role of the classroom teacher in providing instruction for children with handicapping conditions.

6. Discuss some of the emerging developments and concerns affecting elementary education.

Excellence in education, high achievement expectations, quality school programs, effective teaching, and the application of new technologies appear to be the social conditions that are giving direction to American education in the decade of the 1980s. Virtually every educational journal, every educational conference, and every book written on education illustrates how these developments seem to be motivating much that is being said and written about education today. Moreover, these directions in education are enjoying strong public support. The current situation provides an excellent example of how schools respond to the social conditions of the times.

Whereas American parents in the 1980s are likely to think of their children's education in terms of high quality and high "tech," the early New England colonists had different things in mind for the education of their children. The colonists thought about education within a religious context. It was important they thought for one to be literate in order to read the Bible, an essential requirement for the salvation of one's soul. Additionally, they wanted their children to grow up embracing the moral principles to which the community was committed and to respect and obey its laws. The colonists also wanted their children to learn a trade so they would be able to support themselves, thus not becoming indigents and paupers who would require public assistance.

An immigrant family at the turn of the last century thought of education in terms of seeing its children assimilated in American society. The family wanted to see its children "get ahead" in the new world, to "make something of themselves." They perceived a good education as one that helped their children achieve goals that were related to social mobility.

Similarly, a black family in the 1960s viewed education as a means of achieving equality of opportunity for its children. Failure to have a good education meant that opportunities for equal consideration in the social, political, and economic worlds were simply foreclosed to them. In a society in which the status positions are occupied by people with good educations, the undereducated remain forever outside the circle of influence.

Thus far we have been describing education in terms of *private* purposes. That is, individuals and families usually evaluate the quality of a school program in terms of what it will do for *them.* Education as an institution of society, however, was established to serve *public* purposes. Individual citizens may indeed benefit from having an education, but it is the larger society that is the chief beneficiary of having a population of educated, literate, politically knowledgeable citizens.

In modern times, education has been viewed as a vehicle for the achievement of certain social goals of the larger society, such as equality of opportunity. Although this may be viewed as a means of achieving the private purposes of individuals from disenfranchised groups, the main purpose is a broader one. It represents a public concern over civil rights, racism, discrimination, and inequality.

The concern for excellence in education in the 1980s is clearly a call for the schools to be more cognizant of their need to serve public purposes. The Report of the Commission on Excellence in Education, issued in April 1983, speaks of education as undergirding "American prosperity, security, and civility."

(Top photo courtesy of Patricia A. Conrard. Bottom photo courtesy of Kay F. Engelsen.)

Imagine the hopes and aspirations the parents of these children have for them as they begin their elementary school experience! In what ways can the school help these children fulfill the dreams their parents have for them?

The report quotes President Reagan, "Certainly there are few areas of American life as important to our society, to our people, and to our families as our schools and colleges,"[1] a view expressed in one form or another by many of his predecessors in the White House.

It is the responsibility of the elementary school teacher to see that the school serves the public purposes for which it was established. Let us illustrate this with an example from the field of reading. The teacher is not primarily concerned about teaching each child to read because being a skillful reader will help the child succeed in school and eventually qualify him or her for a job. More importantly, the teacher wants each child to learn to read because, as a society, we cannot risk having a large population of illiterate citizens. A nation with a poorly or marginally educated citizenry is indeed "a nation at risk."[2]

Purposes of Elementary Education—Then and Now

LITERACY

Since colonial times, schools have had responsibility to develop basic literacy in children. Often the colonial schools were little more than schools for reading, a skill that was taught mainly for religious purposes. Reading continued to be an important component of the elementary school curriculum throughout the history of the nation, and remains so today. Indeed, at the early levels, more time is spent on the teaching of reading than on anything else, and some critics say that even today elementary schools are essentially reading schools.

The concern for literacy, of course, goes beyond the teaching of reading. In recent years there has been a national outcry for schools to place a greater emphasis on "the basics." Used in this context, "the basics" refer to fundamental literacy skills—

---

[1] *A Nation at Risk: The Imperative for Educational Reform.* Report of the National Commission on Excellence in Education (Washington, D. C.: U.S. Department of Education, 1983), p. 1.
[2] Ibid.

reading, writing, and mathematical operations, in other words, the 3Rs. These learnings are judged to be *basic* in the sense that without them the individual would be handicapped in being able to learn other things. These are the *tools* one uses in learning, and without them the individual is stymied in learning how to learn. Without having command of these basic skills, an adult would also be handicapped in ordinary living in a society that relies so heavily on written communication and quantitative operations.

Although the 3Rs are basic, education for literacy must include some additional knowledge and skills. We assume that when people have attended school, they have gained a general background of knowledge about the world and its people, that they are familiar with basic scientific information, and that they have a modicum of cultural awareness. Important beginnings in these fields must be made in the early years. Basic education that is provided by the elementary school must include elements of the common culture that are presumed to be a part of the intellectual background of everyone.

CITIZENSHIP EDUCATION

A second purpose of elementary education, also having a long tradition in American schools, is citizenship education. Education for intelligent and loyal citizenship was introduced in the school curriculum early in the nation's history to ensure self-government at an enlightened level. Citizenship education was to take place through the formal study of such subjects as history, government (civics), and geography, and through the indoctrination of such values as freedom, human dignity, responsibility, independence, individualism, democracy, respect for others, love of country, and so on. Informally, citizenship education was promoted through an educational setting that included learners from a broad social and economic spectrum of the white society. Unlike its European counterparts, the American dream of the "common" school was to provide an institution that would serve all the children of all the people. Although that ideal has not been reached completely, it comes close to being realized in the elementary school. With the advent of court-ordered desegregation of schools in recent years, the mix of schoolchildren includes those of many racial and ethnic groups.

Citizenship education in the elementary school should include the development of affective attachments to this nation and its democratic heritage. The pageants, plays, creative stories, poems, and creative dramatics, under the direction of an imaginative and stimulating teacher, can make the struggle for freedom and the history of this nation's development an unforgettable experience for young children. These are powerful tools in building appreciations, ideals, and values. The folklore and legends associated with the development of this nation are important and valuable vehicles for teaching citizenship when they are sensibly used. A certain amount of symbolism, such as saluting the flag and reciting the Pledge of Allegiance, is a necessary part of citizenship education, and if kept within reasonable limits, has some value in engendering feelings of fidelity. Teachers should not overuse such activities and should not substitute them for more thoughtful approaches to citizenship education.

PERSONAL DEVELOPMENT

Personal development did not take on major significance as a goal of elementary education until the present century. Today the personal growth of individual children, concern for each individual's potential for development, and the broadening of school goals to include emotional, social, and physical growth as well as intellectual development are seen as major purposes of elementary education. The nation expects its elementary schools to be concerned about *individual* children, to help them develop a sense of self-identity, to help them get to feel good about themselves, to help them know what their individual talents are, and to help them set realistic goals for themselves. Out of necessity, schools must teach aggregates of children in what we call classes; but the teacher's concern is and must always be the individual human beings within those groups.

The dimension of personal development that *has* had a long tradition in elementary education is something that might be called character education or moral education. Elementary schools are not simply information supermarkets, they are shapers of human beings. The earliest schools in this country recognized this reality—schools for young children were to extend and reinforce moral and character education begun in the home and in the religious life of the family. As schools became public, secular institutions, moral and character education became separated from their religious orientation. Schools, nonetheless, were

(Courtesy of Terri Malinowski.)

What does this photograph suggest about the breadth of the elementary school curriculum?

expected to continue to concern themselves with principles of right and wrong under the assumption that such knowledge would be used to serve the betterment of society. Teachers continue to develop classroom settings that encourage children to develop a sense of fair play, do what is right, live up to verbal commitments, show consideration for others, be trustworthy, and so on. The fact is that society cannot survive unless a high percentage of its people internalize common values and live their lives in accordance with them. Character education and moral education in some form will doubtless always be important concerns of elementary education.

Organizational Structures of Elementary Schools

State compulsory school attendance laws require children to attend from about age six to age sixteen. These ages vary slightly from place to place—the beginning age may be as late as seven of eight for *required* attendance, and in some states the terminal age is eighteen. The kindergarten, typically a one-half day experience for five-year-old children, is not considered one of the required years of school attendance. Nonetheless, kindergartens are a well-established part of the educational enterprise, especially in urban areas, and few persons question their value as a bridge between home and school. Thus, the elementary school usually enrolls children between the ages of five and eleven, converting these ages to grades, we get K–6. In some places the elementary school grade ranges are K–8. The K–6 elementary schools are usually followed by a three-year junior high school, or a middle school, followed by a three-year senior high school (K–6–3–3). The K–8 elementary schools ordinarily are followed by a four-year high school (K–8–4). A K–6 elementary school with a two-year middle school and a four-year high school is also used in some places.

Schools in colonial America and those of the early national period did not use an age-sorting system we call "grades." Children of varying ages were assigned to a single teacher who tutored the youngsters on an individual basis, or who taught them in small cross-age groups. It was not until the middle of the nineteenth century that the practice of grouping children according to age, i.e. age-grading, became widespread. This practice was developed in Germany in the eight-year *Volkschule*. It appealed to American educators as an efficient way of managing the teaching of a large number of children. Following the Civil War, there was rapid acceptance of the practice of grouping children who were of a similar age, and keeping those groups intact from one year to the next as children progressed through school. Schools were therefore "graded" by age, and communities and states used that term in curriculum documents, school regulations, and in naming their schools. Even today it is possible to find etched into the stonework of some of the remaining old school buildings such names as Frederic Graded School. The expression "grade school" is commonly used in ordinary parlance in speaking of the elementary school.

The graded concept has some genuine strengths, and that is why it is so well established in school systems around the world: (1) it does reduce *some* variability within instructional groups by keeping the age constant; (2) it attempts to equalize educational opportunity by exposing all children to the *same* curriculum; (3) textbooks, instructional materials, and achievement tests can be constructed on the basis of age-grade norms; (4) children's social development to some extent relates to age, therefore, age groups tend to be natural social groups; (5) it is an efficient way to accommodate a large number of children who are required to attend school; (6) it allows teachers to specialize their teaching skills in terms of the age of children with whom they work best; (7) it is possible to require set standards of achievement for the various grades.

There are also a number of limitations associated with the graded idea, and its critics have been numerous. They say that (1) it is a lock-step program that encourages teachers to disregard individual differences in children and in their individual developmental pattern; (2) it sets unrealistic standards for children and treats low achievers unfairly; (3) it encourages mechanical teaching, analogous to assembly-line production in industry; (4) it encourages traditional recitation-response teaching practices; (5) the curriculum becomes rigid and undifferentiated; (6) the competitive and comparative system of determining grades (marks of achievement) and promotion are often educationally and psychologically unsound; (7) it encourages an authoritarian classroom atmosphere.

There has been no shortage of suggested alternatives to the graded system. The proposed reforms, which have enjoyed only limited success, deal with some combination of the following variables:

1. cross-age grouping—use of nongraded classrooms; homogeneous ability grouping of children of varying ages for specific subjects, such as reading, mathematics, or spelling.
2. differentiated staffing—team teaching; use of specialists; use of teacher aides, parents, and paraprofessionals; departmentalized arrangements.
3. flexibility—open classrooms; individually prescribed instruction; continuous progress education.
4. individualized instruction—individually guided instruction; pupil contracts; programmed instruction; individually prescribed instruction; computer-assisted instructions.
5. child-centeredness—combines several of those listed above.
6. societal needs—middle schools; magnet schools; year-around schools; storefront alternative schools.

The tendency of schools to experiment with innovative organizational structures has slowed in the decades of the 1980s. The flurry of activity that characterized the decades of the 1960s and the 1970s is not apparent today. In elementary schools today we find the self-contained classroom—that is, one teacher with a single group of similar-age children—to be the prevailing mode. Within this organizational pattern, we see incorporated many of the concepts generated through the efforts of innovators of the past: a concern for the individual child; flexible classroom arrangements; some use of specialists and teaming; use of teacher aides; some cross-age grouping; and so on. Most large school districts do offer some options to parents in the way of alternative classrooms or schools.

The Social World of Childhood

In any historical period, there are social conditions, trends, or movements that have an impact on the work of the school. The broad goals of elementary education discussed in a preceding section are greatly influenced and conditioned by social realities external to the school. In this section, we examine a few trends and social realities that have direct relevance for teaching and learning in the elementary school.

A PLURALISTIC SOCIETY

In recent years, Americans have developed an increased awareness of the pluralistic nature of their nation. There are clear signs that minority group membership no longer carries the stigma it once did.

But the interest in ethnic identity has also moved beyond the generally recognized ethnic minority groups. There is a strong interest in ethnic heritage being expressed by many groups. Descendants of European immigrants, who have by now been assimilated by white America, are identifying themselves with the culture of the homeland of their forebears. There is widespread recognition that this nation truly does represent a confluence of world cultures. It is apparent that a part of this nation's greatness comes from the contributions of many and diverse peoples of the world who brought a part of their homeland with them when they came to these shores.

It is doubtful that immigration to this nation will ever again approach the 8,895,000 figure reached in the decade of 1901 to 1910. Nonetheless, the flow of immigrants has accelerated in recent years to a point that has caused some Americans to be concerned about its impact on American society. Barring restrictive federal legislation, however, the influx of immigrants to this country will doubtless continue at a high level for years to come.

Today's immigrants are most likely to come from the Middle East, Asia, Mexico, and Central and South America. Many are refugees fleeing the oppressive governments of their homelands; others come because of the increased economic opportunities provided here. Some enter the country illegally. A large number bring with them languages and customs that are unfamiliar to mainstream America. The children of these new immigrants have cultural and physical characteristics that make them easy targets for discrimination and unfair treatment.

Ethnic diversity of schoolchildren and pluralism in our culture present the teacher with particularly important responsibilities. Teachers are obligated to recognize and respect the diversity of American life that has resulted from our cultural origins. At the same time, they also have the responsibility to help all groups and all individuals, regardless of background, to become attached to those core values that hold us together as a nation, especially freedom, equality, and human dignity. Should pluralism be stressed to the extent that it destroys a sense of common identity that we share as a people, the effect could be civil strife and conflict just as has happened in every place in the world where pluralism, rather than unity, has been emphasized.

One of the implications of the greater acceptance of multiethnicity and pluralism is that teachers need to know more about the cultural characteristics of ethnic groups, many of which are unfamiliar to Americans. Each ethnic group has its own unique history, problems, and concerns. Teachers need to have a great deal of information about the kinds of specific learning problems that children from particular ethnic environments are likely to have. What does a child's ethnic background really have to do with how he or she learns, adapts to school, and makes life choices? This is the relevant *educational* question that relates to ethnic identity.

LIFE STYLES—OLD AND NEW

Prior to the time children have formal contact with school, they have, of course, been receiving early education from their families. There can be little doubt that these early experiences in the family are among the most powerful and pervasive influences on the development of the human being. A family that is doing its child-rearing job properly will help the child learn some of the most important and fundamental things he or she needs to know in life. It is in the home that language is learned and linguistic skills developed. Here, too, the child learns to give and receive emotional support. The family should provide security and reassurance, thereby supplying the psychological support needed to face life and to function confidently and competently. In the process, the child develops feelings of personal worth and a positive self-concept. It is in the family that the child first learns what is right and wrong, what things are prized and valued, and what standards of conduct are expected. Lifetime ambitions and aspirations are planted and germinate in one's early family life. The extent to which the family has handled these responsibilities well, or poorly, will reflect itself in the child's life in school.

In terms of the upbringing of children within the expectations of a family, there are obvious advantages to an extended-family arrangement. The young child has more contact with closely related adults and consequently has a greater range of adult role models available. Similarly, child behavior can be more closely and constantly monitored by concerned and caring adults. There is also likely to be a more elaborate family culture or set of rituals that provide emotional stability and roots for the growing child, as for example, the gathering of the entire family for holidays, anniversaries, birthdays, and other special events. In structures of this type, the child is hardly ever out of range of the supervision of some member of the immediate family.

A variety of factors has contributed to changing the traditional extended-family pattern. People tend to move in the direction of increased economic opportunity. Thus, a young couple may locate hundreds of miles away from any of their relatives. Children growing up in such nuclear families today may hardly know relatives other than their parents. Babysitters replace grandparents in part-time care of children. Neighbors and friends may assist with the supervision of children in the neighborhood.

In recent years there has been an increase in innovative marriage and family arrangements. The conventional sharp delineation of adult male-female roles within the family is changing to the extent that many couples share all responsibilities associated with maintaining the family. The wife and mother may be employed outside the household, along with the husband and father. Conversely, both may share in the care of the children, housekeeping chores, food preparation, and other household tasks. In some instances the wife and mother is the sole wage earner and the husband and father becomes the homemaker, known as the "house-husband."

Undoubtedly, the most common exception to the conventional family arrangement is the one-parent family. Death, separation, and, most commonly, divorce not only dissolve the marriage but leave one or the other of the partners with the responsibility of carrying on as a family. Because custody of children is usually given the mother in the case of divorce, the one-parent family for the most part means a mother and her children. Divorce rates in this country have continued to rise for the past century, peaking during the years immediately following World War II, receding during the 1950s and early 1960s, and rising sharply again in the 1970s and remaining high in the 1980s.

Through the years, teachers have found it convenient to blame home conditions for the poor achievement of children in school. The behavior problems or low achievement of children from one-parent families is explained away on the basis of their being products of "broken homes." This, of course, ignores the fact that many children from one-parent families achieve at high levels and present no behavior problems in school, although many from so-called intact families are low achievers and do present behavior problems. It also ignores the psychological and emotional damage to a young child that results from growing up in a family filled with conflict and hostility.

Whether we consider one-parent families, innovative family structures, or conventional intact marriages, great changes are occurring in the life styles of families. People move about a great deal. Approximately one fourth to one third of all Americans change their places of residence each year. With increasing numbers of parents employed outside the home, greater numbers of children are enrolled in day-care centers, are placed in the care of persons other than parents for several hours each day, or are "latch-key kids" who are on their own before and after school. Although child abuse has always existed, the frustrations of contemporary life may contribute to its continued high incidence. Teachers of elementary school-age children find themselves enmeshed in these complex life styles of modern families as they work with the children who are products of those homes.

Social-Class Influences On Teaching and Learning

Social stratification occurs because individuals are ranked by others as being higher or lower on some standard of preference. When a segment of the society is set apart as having characteristics different from the others, we have the beginning of a social class. In time, a hierarchy of groups develops in accordance with societal preferences, and a social-class structure emerges.

If a group of individuals has particular characteristics that are valued by a society, the group so identified will enjoy high status. The reverse is also true. Thus, when speaking of upper or lower classes, we are referring to groups of individuals who either have or do not have qualities in common that are prized by the larger society. In America, upper classes are those groups that have wealth, advanced education, professional occupations, and relative freedom from worry concerning material needs.

Conversely, lower classes are those groups that live in or on the edge of poverty, have poor educations, are irregularly employed or employed in jobs requiring little or no training, often require assistance from government welfare agencies, and are constantly concerned with meeting their basic needs of life.

There can be no question that one variable that separates the "haves" from the "have nots" in this or any other society is level of education. The people who are the decision makers, the people who have good jobs, those who contribute in significant ways to the health and welfare of their fellow citizens, those who have power and wealth, are almost always educated people. It is patently clear from research, as well as from the personal experiences of countless thousands of individuals, that limited education forecloses many social and economic options for the individual and thereby severely restricts opportunity for upward social mobility. It does not follow, of course, that improved education will alleviate all of the problems surrounding the poverty life styles of lower social classes. Restricted or foreshortened education, for whatever reason, simply means limited opportunities to exercise alternatives and options for self-development.

Evidence that the largest number of educational casualties come from the lower social classes is overwhelming. These children come from environments that are educationally impoverished, and this conditions nearly every aspect of their lives. Most significantly it contributes to the perpetuation of educational deprivation. The traditional school program simply has not been able to deal successfully with the educational needs of these children. We are likely to have large numbers of miseducated children until we commit ourselves to the idea that the teachers and schools must accommodate learners, rather than the other way around.

Equality of Educational Opportunity

Equality of educational opportunity traditionally has been interpreted to mean *access* to education, and the nation has made a substantial effort to make schooling available to all of its children. No area of the country is so remote as to preclude the opportunity for children who live there to go to school. Children of all racial and ethnic groups; children of migrants; children of the poor; children who are physically or mentally disabled—all of these are not only encouraged, but required, to attend school. But does school attendance in itself ensure equality of educational opportunity? Many think not, because there are social, psychological, and economic inequities that condition both the quality of schooling provided from place to place and that affect the ability of the individual to take full advantage of what is offered.

It is apparent that tremendous inequities in educational opportunity exist in this country. Educational inequity is usually thought of in terms of differences in dollar amounts spent on education from one place to another. Because communities differ in their *ability* to support education and in their *willingness* to support it, the average amount of money spent per pupil to educate children varies significantly from one district to another even within the same state.

The amount of money spent on education does not, however, fully explain prevailing inequities in educational opportunity. The quality of education tends to follow the pattern of power and wealth in a community. Those parents who are reasonably well educated themselves, and who have average or above average incomes, select residences in areas that provide well for the education of their children. The poorly educated, low-income families tend to live in areas that provide less well for the education of children. It is not so much a matter of actual dollars spent on education in the more favored areas, but a combination of complex forces coalescing to produce better quality education.

Education, and most especially early education, must be concerned with the way it either opens or forecloses subsequent opportunities for learning. If a child does not learn to read, it should be a matter of great concern to the teacher and the school because this deficiency severely limits the options open to the child later on. Similarly, if a child grows to dislike school or to dislike particular subjects studied in school, this also imposes limiting conditions on continued educational achievement. *Any* experience that a child has that discourages or terminates continued ability or motivation for further learning imposes a restriction on the equality of educational opportunity.

The Teacher and the Classroom As Self-Fulfilling Prophets

The self-fulfilling prophecy, in one form or another, has been a part of folk wisdom for countless generations. Basically, this phenomenon has to do with the notion that one's mind-set, that is, what one believes to be true, whether consistent with reality or not, has a great deal to do with influencing contingencies that flow from such beliefs. Golfers and bridge players report that they invariably play better games when their competitors are skillful, because they are then expected to perform at a higher level of proficiency. In recent years, considerable attention has been given to the implications of the self-fulfilling prophecy for the education of children.

Most authors and researchers in education agree that the self-fulfilling prophecy needs additional study and further analysis. The literature on this subject, which is considerable, suggests strongly that the authors assume that predictions influence achievement levels, especially in the education of ethnic minorities and so-called disadvantaged youngsters. In most cases these assumptions stem from the application of professional judgment to observed relationships or from inferences based on what appear to be co-related conditions. The research to substantiate the hypothesis that teacher attitude and expectation influence the performance of pupils tends to support such a relationship.

How do teachers communicate these increased expectations to children, which thereby encourage them to expect more of themselves? Little is known about these processes. It may be that teachers treat pupils in more pleasant and enthusiastic ways when they expect them to perform at a high level. Teachers provide recognition for certain pupils by calling on them to respond more frequently than others. Undoubtedly there are a variety of nonverbal signals that subtly communicate feelings and attitudes of the teacher to the child. These might be facial expressions, gestures, physical contacts, or particular looks. The tone of voice and choice of words in verbal communication might also be significant.

There are clear implications in this, not only for teachers who work with children of ethnic minorities, gifted children, lower-social-class children, or exceptional children, but for all teachers. Many school practices need to be examined critically in light of what is coming to be known about the impact of the teacher's attitude and influence on children's learning. What is important is that procedures, such as those following, not be misused. Any practice that tends to stereotype or label a child must be suspected of influencing the child's expected performance. A few of the more common ones include:

1. *Cumulative Records.* The school history of a child can be of value in planning a program of instruction. It can also condition the teacher's perception, resulting in the setting of inappropriate levels of expectation for the youngster. A single comment by a previous teacher may be damaging to subsequent teachers' assessment of a pupil's learning capacity.

2. *Achievement Examinations.* Poor scores on achievement tests may indicate not only the present level of performance but also set future levels of expectation.

3. *Homogeneous Ability Grouping.* Efforts to disguise ability groups have been unsuccessful in preventing children and parents from knowing which groups are the high-, medium-, and low-level achievers. Once placed in a group so labeled, the learner is likely to perform in accordance with expectations set for that group. The infrequent movement of children from one ability group to another confirms this fact, teachers' claims of flexibility of such groups notwithstanding.

4. *Report Cards.* Through report cards children are labeled as A or B or C or D students; these labels in turn provide an obvious level of expectation for the child, the parents, and the teachers, thereby affecting the child's level of performance.

5. *Nonpromotion Policies.* Nonpromotion from one grade to the next is perhaps the most devastating of all experiences in terms of lowering expectations for oneself. However such policies are rationalized, their long-term effects on the individuals involved are usually detrimental.

It is important to stress that teachers who engage in the practices described are usually well-meaning, humane individuals. They often deal with children in kind and loving ways. Nonetheless, the *effects* of these procedures are so subtle that teachers may not be—and in most cases probably are not—aware of the power such practices have on their attitudes toward, and expectations of, individual children.

HOW DID YOU GET THAT WAY?

Are you what your teachers, parents, and fellow students call an A student? B student? C student? What kind of a student do you perceive yourself to be? Are your perceptions of yourself the same as those of your teachers, parents, and friends? When did you first discover that you were an A, B, or C student? How did you get classified that way? Must you forever remain in the category in which you are now perceived?

Does this tell you anything about the self-fulfilling prophecy?

Race and Racism

It is perfectly obvious that human beings differ in their physical characteristics. Some are fair skinned; others are dark. Some have curly hair and others have straight hair, which may be light or dark. Through the centuries, groups of people who have occupied certain geographical areas of the world and who have, more or less, physical traits in common, have been identified as subspecies of homo sapiens and have been called *races.* These physical traits are inherited qualities and are, therefore, innate and immutable. But because the differences *within* these groups are as great as they are, it is sometimes impossible to assign an individual human being to any such group on the basis of unique characteristics. Consequently, anthropologists have not found the use of geographical races to be an altogether satisfactory way of grouping human beings. Be that as it may, the fact that groups of human beings have differing physical characteristics, and that we designate these groups as races, does not in itself give rise to social and educational problems.

There is nothing inherently wrong in defining human groups on the basis of innate and immutable physical characteristics. Problems of race arise when nonphysical, social, or cultural qualities are assigned to individuals simply and only because they are members of those groups. When this happens, race becomes defined socially, rather than on the basis of objective physical qualities. Racism inevitably follows the practice of associating significant cultural abilities and/or characteristics with groups that are defined socially as races. Racism becomes institutionalized when these associations, whether overt or subtle, are given legitimacy and social approval.

Racism, particularly institutionalized racism, is difficult to deal with because of the tendency to associate it with overt and conscious acts of prejudice. It has been referred to as the "disease of hate." Thus, individuals who generally have humanitarian attitudes toward others may be shocked and outraged to be accused of racist behavior. The practices may have become so thoroughly institutionalized that awareness of their racist dimensions has been hidden.

Institutionalized racism consists of practices that have been *legitimatized* by the society and that result in the *systematic* discrimination against members of *specific* groups. Practices that have been legitimatized are accepted. Few question them. Until recently, even those against whom the discrimination was directed have accepted these practices. The word *systematic* in this definition is also important. This means that the discrimination is not a random occurrence; the discrimination is practiced with consistency and regularity, thus making it systematic rather than whimsical or capricious. It is directed against specific groups (perhaps not even by design), because members of those groups have certain characteristics or qualities.

What are examples of practices that would qualify as institutionalized racism? Here are a few:

1. Unnecessary and irrelevant references, especially in social studies and current events, to an individual's or group's racial or ethnic identity, such as "The black mayor of . . . ," "The black candidate from . . . ," "Asian parents gathered . . . ," "A group of predominantly Chicano citizens . . . ," or "The driver, an Indian from Forks, was charged with drunken driving." (Such references are almost never used when the individual or group is white.)

2. Use a duel norms. (This implies that ethnic minorities are not able to achieve as well as whites.)

3. Optional, "free choice" educational programs that require a

certain level of affluence in order to participate in them as, for example, not being able to afford bus fare to attend a particular magnet school or not being able to participate in enrichment opportunities (music, dance, sports, art, clubs) because of costs associated with them. (This affects low-income groups, many of whom are ethnic minorities.)

4. Homogeneous grouping. (This discriminates against ethnic minorities because it often results in their being placed in low-achieving groups.)

5. Higher expectation that children of color will misbehave, combined with more harsh and more frequent punishment for those children, especially black males. (This form of discrimination is so subtle that it often goes undetected.)

6. Curriculum content unrelated to the life of certain groups. (This discriminates against those who are not represented in the subject matter of the school, usually ethnic minorities.)

7. Social acceptance of the high incidence of failure and dropout rate among minorities, especially blacks. (This is usually explained on the basis of a presumed disinclination of minorities for academic and scholarly work.)

8. Bias against the use of a language other than English. (This may result in hidden discrimination against the child who speaks English with a non-English dialect.)

Sex Equity Education

Just as racism is the practice of ascribing certain abilities and characteristics to individuals on the basis of their identification with groups socially defined as races, sexism does the same thing on the basis of one's sex.[3] Historically, female roles have tended

---

[3] We use the term *sex* because it is popularly associated with this type of discrimination. It is important, however, to distinguish between *sex* and *gender*. Sex has to do with differences attributed to genetics; that is, one is born either male or female. Gender, on the other hand, has to do with the differences attributed to the roles males and females play in a society. A society defines the idealized role behavior of males and females—what is masculine and what is feminine—and these differences are correctly called *gender* differences.

to be stereotyped along the lines of domestic and child-rearing responsibilities, whereas male roles have been stereotyped in the world of work outside the home. Also, women have been portrayed frequently in roles subservient to men, for example, ones in which they serve, wait on, and pick up after men.

There can be little doubt that such stereotyping has worked to the disadvantage of women by restricting the range of significant opportunities for self-development. Additionally, this has led to discrimination against women that has been manifestly unfair. Changing attitudes, the growing independence of women, and legislative reforms have aided in combating the invidious distinctions between males and females that are the result of sex-role stereotyping.

Educational programs, and particularly the part teachers play in them, are vitally important in shaping the young child's image of sex roles. If children always see males rather than females in preferred, prestigious occupational and social roles, they are bound to conclude that the male is superior; because these positions are obviously not available to women, therefore women must not be sufficiently capable of holding them. It hardly seems necessary to add that when sex roles are presented this way, boys *and* girls come to believe in the superiority of the male.

Some of the more common teacher behaviors that do violence to the concept of sex equity are these:

1. Consistently using generic terms such as *man, mankind, early man,* and *common man* when the reference is to humanity. Terms such as *people, human beings, ordinary people, humankind,* and *early people* can be substituted.

2. Exaggerating the emphasis on the socialization of children into traditional sex roles—neatness, conformity, docility, and fastidiousness for females; competitiveness, aggressiveness, and physical activity and strength for males. A balance in emphasis should be maintained.

3. Segregating children on the basis of sex, such as in the seating arrangement in the classroom, in playground games, and in classroom learning activities.

4. Establishing a classroom environment dominated by traditional female norms such as orderliness, politeness, obedience, and submissiveness.

5. Neglecting or ignoring the contributions of women in social studies and science classes.

6. Accepting implicitly the assumption that females are less capable than males in such fields as mathematics, science, and sports; conversely, that males have less aptitude for art, literature, music, and dance.

7. Expressing a preference for teaching either males or females.

8. Displaying charts and graphs that compare the achievement of males and females.

9. Identifying certain leadership positions or specific activities in the classroom as being solely for males or females.

10. Making light of, ignoring, or even ridiculing the social movement or the individuals associated with the movement to secure greater feminine equity.

11. Administering more harsh punishment to males than to females for the same misbehavior.

12. Interacting more with males than with females in class discussions, even when there are more females than males in the class.

If sex equity is to be achieved as a social goal, a broad range of role models needs to be presented to young children as a part of their formal education. Children must learn that it is just as appropriate for a woman to be a business executive, a judge, a mayor, a senator, an astronaut, a bus driver, a carpenter, or any of a variety of occupations as it is for a man. They must also learn that there is nothing wrong with a man's taking care of and feeding his young children, doing household duties, secretarial work, nursing in a hospital, or being engaged in any of several tasks and occupations that have traditionally been associated with women.

What is important is that sex-role models must be presented in ways that provide the individual with a maximum opportunity for choice. Perhaps many men and women will want to conduct their lives along more or less traditional sex-role patterns. Some may wish to exercise other choices, and they should not be prevented from doing so or be handicapped in doing so because of prejudicial attitudes and ridicule. The opportunity for choice should be almost unlimited if sex-role barriers are removed.

Current Issues and Trends in Elementary Education

MINIMUM COMPETENCY TESTING

Minimum competency testing means that certain minimum standards of proficiency are required for promotion from one grade to the next and/or for graduation from elementary or secondary schools. All states have passed legislation requiring such testing, have legislation pending, or have state board studies underway that would authorize it. Many states now require minimum competency tests before grade seven, and some use the results in grade promotion decisions. A great deal of controversy surrounds this issue, with the major question being whether or not minimum competency testing contributes to the improvement of elementary and secondary education.

Minimum competency testing has come about in part because the public is not confident that the schools are doing an adequate job of teaching basic skills and basic school subjects. This lack of confidence seems to be the result of (1) general observation of academic skills of school graduates, (2) the poor showing of achievement on the National Assessment of Educational Progress, and (3) the declining scores of students on standardized tests. A number of surveys and studies in the early 1980s reporting inadequacies in American education provided additional support for the practice of competency testing not only for students but also for teachers.

Those who support minimum competency testing see it as a way of improving basic education, and as a way of making the educational enterprise accountable to its constituents. They claim that under minimum competency testing, educational objectives are more sharply defined, thus making teaching more precise. They also suggest that such testing will call attention to children who have difficulty and, therefore, will be given the additional help they need in order to master the material. They also see competency testing as a safeguard against social promotion of children from one grade to the next. This policy, i.e., the elimination of social promotion, will presumably restore meaning to the high school diploma. Advocates indicate that the requirement of mastery level learning will ensure that every high school grad-

(Courtesy of Patricia A. Conrard.)

Most schools consider physical education to be an essential part of the curriculum. How does physical education contribute to the overall goals of the school?

uate possesses certain skills at the required minimum level of proficiency.

These views, of course, are not shared by the opponents of minimum competency testing. They insist that such tests freeze the curriculum around the test content. Moreover, because teachers are evaluated on the basis of how well their children score on the tests, it is inevitable that teachers will "teach for the test." This means that other important areas of the school curriculum will be neglected or omitted altogether. Opponents say that in order to be workable, the minimum levels required must be low enough to be achievable by the slowest learning children. When this happens, the standard becomes meaningless for average and above average achievers. There is the possibility, too, that minimum levels will be perceived as maximums, causing a plateau effect on the distribution of achievement test scores.

There is currently great variation in the implementation of minimum competency testing. Teachers will need to familiarize themselves with local policy. Some difficult decisions confront the teacher in those areas where social promotion is not permitted, where teacher accountability is based on pupil test scores, and where minimum levels of attainment are required for graduation. At this writing, many issues surrounding minimum competency testing are unresolved.

EDUCATING THE DISABLED

The traditional approach to the education of disabled children was to segregate them into what was, and still is called, "special education." Public schools, state departments of education, and colleges and universities typically have departments or divisions of special education that concern themselves with educational programs for handicapped persons. But in recent years there has been a strong movement away from the segregation of the handicapped from the main stream of social life, whether this be in school or in the larger society. Increasingly, public accommodations are taking into account the need for "barrier free" environments that make it easier for orthopedically handicapped and/or blind persons to negotiate them. In schools this movement has taken the form of placing children in what is for them a "least restrictive environment," also called, although not altogether correctly, mainstreaming.

In 1975, Congress passed, and the President signed into law, the Education for All Handicapped Children Act, otherwise referred to as P.L. 94-142. This law stipulates the rights that must be extended to all disabled children, including the right to a free and appropriate public education. It also details procedures that must be followed in implementing programs for the handicapped. But most important for the classroom teacher is the requirement that an Individualized Education Program be developed for each child and that each child with a handicapping condition be provided instruction in the least restrictive environment. The process of preparing the IEP must include (1) the teacher; (2) a representative of the school such as the principal or school counselor; and (3) the child's parent(s) or guardian(s). The IEP must indicate the child's present level of performance; a statement of annual goals as well as shorter-term objectives; the specific educational services to be provided; a statement of the extent to which the child will be able to participate in the regular curriculum of the school (mainstreamed); and objective assessment criteria and evaluation procedures and schedules.

Federal legislation requires that states establish procedures that will assure that, *to the maximum extent appropriate,* handicapped children are educated with children who are not handicapped. It stipulates additionally that separate schooling or the removal of handicapped children from the regular educational environment should occur only when the educational service cannot be provided in the regular classroom. The qualification, "to the maximum extent appropriate," is an important one. This means that disabled children cannot simply be deposited on a massive scale in regular classrooms. Such children are to be placed in the most beneficial environment for learning. In some cases this may mean special instruction, perhaps even tutoring on a one-to-one basis. In other cases, the most beneficial environment might be the regular classroom. In any case, the clear intent of the legislation, as well as public attitudes generally, is calling for the integration of disabled children into the regular classroom, wherever possible.

The education of all handicapped children has become a reality during the decade of the 1980s because it is the law of the land. This development places new demands on regular classroom teachers in the area of diagnostic and prescriptive teaching. As the philosophy of *inclusion* (as opposed to *segregation*) becomes fully operational, most elementary school classrooms will have, for all or part of the day, one or more children who are in some degree disabled. This means that elementary school teachers will need to know a great deal about the nature of handicapping conditions and the technical and legal aspects of working with handicapped children, as well as the specific teaching strategies that are uniquely suitable to the education of them.

ENGLISH AS A SECOND LANGUAGE (ESL) AND BILINGUAL EDUCATION

From early Colonial America to the present, the people of this nation have been multilingual. People from every ethnic and cultural group of the world came to these shores and, of course, brought their language with them. Often they settled in communities inhabited by immigrants from the same part of the world. Consequently, throughout America there were, and still are, areas in which people speak a language other than English on a more or less regular basis. Immigrant groups in large cities such as New York, Chicago, Cleveland, and Milwaukee organized and maintained foreign language schools where their languages and cultures could be maintained.

The use of languages other than English was so widespread

that in some cases those languages were used for instructional purposes in public schools. All of this was changed, however, in the period during and after World War I, when adverse feelings toward immigrant groups in general, and German-speaking people in particular, were so great that several states passed legislation prohibiting instruction in languages other than English in public schools. At the federal level legislation was enacted to severely restrict immigration from southern and eastern Europe, and from Asia. The xenophobia that spawned suppressive legislation at the state and federal levels was destructive of foreign-language learning in America. The attitude was so widespread that to speak in a language other than English was considered to be un-American.

There have been some changes in these attitudes and practices, probably as a result of growing ethnic awareness and identity, and the increased militancy of certain ethnic minority groups, particularly those who are Spanish speaking. The movement to legitimatize bilingual education as a part of the curriculum of the public schools has been partially successful. The enactment by Congress in 1965 of the Bilingual Education Act and Title VII of the Elementary and Secondary Education Act, along with the Educational Amendment Act of 1974, gave substantial support to the concept of bilingual education. In 1974, the United States Supreme Court, in a now famous case known as *Lau* v. *Nichols,* ruled that the San Francisco schools had to provide bilingual education to non-English-speaking children. Several states have passed laws requiring schools to provide special instruction for children who do not speak English, and have allocated additional funds for this purpose.

One of the central issues concerning bilingual education is whether these programs are to be transitional or maintenance oriented. That is, should the bilingual effort be undertaken for a relatively short period of time, such as three years, until the child learns English, at which time English becomes the language of instruction? Such programs are *transitional* and are the most common. English as a Second Language (ESL) programs are of this type. The child who speaks Samoan, for example, is taught English, but until English is learned, regular school instruction may be in Samoan. Bilingual *maintenance* programs are those in which the bilingual instruction continues for several years in an effort to maintain a fluent command of both languages. Militant advocates of bilingual education, who represent non-English-speaking ethnics, often support maintenance rather than transitional programs. They argue that it makes no sense to allow the knowledge of an alternate language, already mastered, to deteriorate.

Many other controversies surround bilingual education. For example, should it also be bicultural? Often the two are linked as bilingual-bicultural, and advocates claim that language and culture cannot really be separated. Additionally, there is the question of the status to be accorded the non-English language. It may be true that one language can convey ideas as well as any other language, and, therefore, value judgments should not be made about language worthiness. The problem here is that ours is an English-speaking society, claims to the contrary by advocates of bilingualism notwithstanding. This country has *one* and only one language in which the affairs of business and government are conducted, and that language is English. An individual who is not fluent in English is likely to be handicapped in conducting the affairs of ordinary living in this society. This suggests that schools should be cautious in entertaining alternates to the accepted use of the English language.

DAWNING OF THE COMPUTER AGE

Just as controlled fire and the use of electrical energy wrought thoroughgoing changes to existing lifeways, the computer seems destined to have a profound effect on life in modern cultures. The influence of the computer is pervasive in contemporary life, and research now in progress in this country and abroad will result in computers many times more sophisticated than the ones in use today. Most college students now in teacher certification programs will doubtless see an enormous transformation in the way education is conducted as a result of the application of computer technology to the educational process.

It is impossible to secure accurate data on the extent of the use of computers in public schools. It is, however, safe to say that the number of schools that have computers available for student use is growing rapidly, and by the end of the 1980s they will be found in all schools. At the present time, schools— and even colleges of education—are playing "catch-up" with the students with regard to computers. Because of the number of home computers and the popularity of video games, children have a greater familiarity with these "high-tech" devices than

The computer has become commonplace in today's elementary schools. What implications are there in this reality for the preparation of the elementary school teacher?

(Courtesy of Terri Malinowski.)

do many of their teachers. This situation, however, is rapidly changing.

The elementary school teachers need to be equipped technically and psychologically to deal with the computer in at least three ways. First, teachers can expect to be asked to assume some responsibility to teach the technical skills needed to operate computers. These skills are referred to as "computer literacy." Teacher education programs at both the preservice and inservice levels are now including special courses and workshops to acquaint teachers with computers and to help them develop computer literacy.

Second, teachers need to know how to integrate computer-assisted instruction (CAI) in teaching conventional school subjects—mathematics, science, social studies, language arts. Additionally, they need to know the capability of the computer in diagnosing learning difficulties, providing remedial instruction, independent study, and other potential uses as an instructional tool.

Third, teachers need to have some sense of the social consequences that flow from the widespread application of computer technology. For instance, if robots managed by computers displace large numbers of workers, what will those people do to earn a living? What ethical issues are involved in the storage of personal, confidential information in computer banks? Should "high-tech" demands be allowed to determine priorities in the school curriculum? Will society place a greater value on interacting with machines than with people? What needs to be done to assure adequate attention to the humanities and social studies in a society dominated by computer technology?

The field of education has been particularly susceptible to faddism; ideas and practices that are touted as developments that are supposed to transform the educational process too often fizzle and burn out in a short while. It is fair to ask, therefore, whether the use of the computer is simply another short-lived comet streaking across the educational sky. No one knows for certain. Although we can expect to hear exaggerated claims for what computers can accomplish, and we can expect to see some abuse of these devices, the fact is that computers are already institutionalized as information storage, retrieval, and processing devices in the larger society. Thus, the school cannot escape from their influence.

BRAIN RESEARCH AND SCHOOL LEARNING

Research in the fields of medicine, psychology, and education is providing information of potentially significant importance to the intellectual development of human beings and how they learn. Much of this information is in the form of theories and hypothetical concepts, but does, nonetheless, provide some interesting insights into the nature of that complex mass of nerve tissue we call the brain. Researchers are suggesting that learning styles, particular aptitudes and/or limitations, and differences in rates of learning may be accounted for, in part, by developmental differences in brain growth.

Perhaps the most widely publicized concepts relating to brain development have to do with hemispheric specialization. Researchers pursuing this line of inquiry suggest that the left hemisphere of the brain controls such functions as speech, writing, mathematics, logical sequencing of ideas, rules, time orientation, and analytical-symbolic skills. The right hemisphere of the brain has more to do with visual-spatial stimuli—creativity, pattern recognition, arts and music, holistic relationships (as opposed to sequential relationships), and intuition. The behavior and aptitudes of an individual would, therefore, reflect his or her lateral specialization. Presumably individuals would be more efficacious in their learning if the presentation mode were consistent with their lateral orientation. That is, "left-brain" people presumably prefer logically organized, sequential, structured presentations whereas "right-brain" individuals do better with presentation modes that are more loosely structured, humanistically oriented, and holistic in their scope.

Another avenue of research has produced the concept of the "triune brain." It is based on the idea that the human brain is actually three brains, each of which was appropriate to earlier evolutionary stages, but continues to control certain aspects of the behavior of contemporary human beings. This theory helps explain why the behavior of individual human beings is often contradictory, why a human being can be logical, rational, as well as impulsive and emotional.

A third area of current brain research deals with the stage theory of brain growth. This research suggests that brain growth occurs at an irregular rate. The brain grows rapidly for awhile, but then slows its growth, then resumes rapid growth. This irregular brain development of spurts and plateaus continues into the late adolescent years. Those who are attempting to apply these findings to school learning suggest that new ideas and concepts should be presented at those times when the learner's brain is in the rapid growth stage. The plateau periods should be used to consolidate and integrate learnings already presented.

The research on brain growth does not at the present time provide uncontestable guidelines for teaching and learning of children. These developments, however, appear to be promising sources of information to give direction to school practices in the future. The beginning teacher will want to stay close to the educational literature in order to remain informed of breakthroughs in this field.

Study Questions and Activities

1. What reasons can you give for the national concern over excellence in education at this particular time?

2. The text explains that literacy, citizenship, and moral education have been important goals of the elementary school since its beginnings in Colonial America. Speculate on how the teaching methods used to achieve these goals have changed through the years.

3. What are your most vivid pleasant memories of your elementary

school experience? Do you think such experiences or activities are still enjoyed by children today? Why or why not?

4. Provide examples to illustrate that how parents rear their children has a great deal to do with their children's success in school.

5. Some believe that intergroup conflict in America today is more a result of social class differences than racial or ethnic differences. What are your views on this matter?

6. Provide specific examples of teacher behavior in the classroom that would illustrate how the "self-fulfilling prophecy" might work to the disadvantage of a child.

7. Is a disabled child necessarily handicapped? Explain.

8. Do the concepts "least restrictive environment" and "mainstreaming" mean the same thing? Explain.

9. Critics have taken school leaders to task for investing in computers at a time when schools are under fire for not adequately teaching conventional literacy skills. What do you think? Should schools procure computers when children are not showing satisfactory progress in basic skills?

10. What behavioral characteristics might suggest to the teacher that a child has a left-brain or a right-brain orientation to learning?

11. What are the main advantages claimed for a self-contained classroom organization? Is it possible to have a self-contained classroom that also has cross-age grouping of children? Explain.

For Further Professional Study

Banks, James A. *Teaching Strategies for Ethnic Studies.* Newton, Mass.: Allyn and Bacon, Inc., 1984.

Best, Raphaela. *We've All Got Scars: What Boys and Girls Learn in Elementary School.* Bloomington, Ind.: Indiana University Press, 1983.

Escobedo, Theresa H., ed. *Early Childhood Bilingual Education: A Hispanic Perspective.* New York: Teachers College Press, 1983.

Gonzales, Phillip C. "How to Begin Language Instruction for Non-English-Speaking Students." *Language Arts,* **58** (Feb. 1981), 175–180.

Goodlad, John I. *A Place Called School: Prospects for the Future.* New York: McGraw-Hill, 1983.

Hart, Leslie A. "The Three-Brain Concept and the Classroom." *Phi Delta Kappan,* **62** (March 1981), 504–506.

Jarolimek, John. *The Schools in Contemporary Society: An Analysis of Social Currents, Issues, and Forces.* New York: Macmillan Publishing Co., Inc., 1981.

McQueen, Richard. "Spurts and Plateaus in Brain Growth: A Critique of the Claims of Herman Epstein." *Educational Leadership,* **41** (February 1984), 66–71.

Parker, Franklin. "Ideas That Shaped American Schools." *Phi Delta Kappan,* **62** (Jan. 1981), 314–319.

Phi Delta Kappan (Jan. 1982; Oct. 1983). These two issues contain a total of twenty articles dealing with the use of computers in education.

Shepherd, Gene D., and William B. Ragan. *Modern Elementary School Curriculum.* 6th ed. New York: Holt, Rinehart and Winston, 1982. Part I.

Sylwester, Robert. "A Child's Brain." *Instructor* (Part I September 1982; Part II October 1982; Part III November-December 1982).

The Qualified and Competent Teacher

The recurring question, "What makes a school a good school?" has been asked with increasing frequency during recent years. Many things have contributed to the widespread interest in this question. Declining test scores of graduating high school seniors and data showing that teacher education students do not represent the academically strong segments of the population on the college and university campuses have contributed to the concern. The rising cost of education and the negative view of the public toward increasing taxes to meet these expenditures also have been strong indicators of discontent. As a result there has been a flurry of proposals for improving schooling. Interest in the question has been kept at a high level by an unprecedented amount of attention by the news media at the national, state, and local levels.

Thus, the decade of the 1980s has featured a reexamination of what constitutes effective schooling. Both old and new concepts related to this matter are receiving attention. As a result of this development, attention to factors that are associated with the qualified and competent teacher has increased greatly. Prior to this time, the prevailing belief was that the success or failure of schools depended largely on the quality of classroom teachers. This point of view held that teachers made the difference as to whether children learn or fail. Other factors, such as adequate funding, were considered important, but essentially the teacher was held responsible. A challenge to this point of view was made by the research of James Coleman and Christopher Jencks and their associates. These researchers, who were concerned with the effect of schools on education, concluded as a result of their research, that socioeconomic variables, such as home background, are the chief factors in determining the level of pupil achievement.[1] Thus, the end result of the Coleman and Jencks studies was contradictory to the notion that "teachers make the difference." Instead, these researchers believed that the effects of schooling were dependent upon the kind of socioeconomic backgrounds represented by the children within the school.

These two contradictory beliefs have been tempered somewhat by the emergence of a contemporary approach to the improvement of education in America—one that focuses on the importance of effective schools. This approach is based on the belief that several factors within the school itself largely condition the effects of teaching insofar as learner achievement is concerned. In this model, the qualified and competent teacher operates within a combination of several environmental variables that function within the school. Although these characteristics vary across the literature, Ralph and Fennessey state that they generally involve the presence of a combination of (1) strong leadership by administrators, (2) a school climate that is safe and orderly, (3) an emphasis on basic academic skills, (4) a high level of teacher expectation for all learners, and (5) a system for monitoring and assessing pupil performance.[2] Given these

---

[1] For references on the effects of schools research see James S. Coleman, E. Campbell, C. J. Hobson, A. Mood, J. McPartland, F. Weinfeld, and R. York, *Equality of Educational Opportunity* (Washington, D. C.: U.S. Government Printing Office, 1966), and Christopher Jencks, Marshall Smith, Henry Acland, Mary Jo Bane, David Cohen, Herbert Gintis, Barbara Heyns, and Stephan Michelson, *Inequality: A Reassessment of the Effect of Family and Schooling in America* (New York: Basic Books, 1972).

[2] John H. Ralph and James Fennessey, "Science or Reform: Some Questions About the Effective Schools Model," *Phi Delta Kappan*, 64 (June 1983), 694. For a presentation on the effective schools model, also see Ronald R. Edmonds, "Programs of School Improvement: An Overview," *Educational Leadership*, 40 (December 1982), 4–11.

variables, the impact of teaching on pupil achievement appears to be dependent on certain powerful conditions within the school that lie beyond the control of the classroom teacher.

The report of the National Commission on Excellence in Education appeared in April 1983. Entitled, *A Nation at Risk: The Imperative for Educational Reform,*[3] the report cast a somber reflection on the state of education in this nation. Very few aspects of education escaped attention in the report. Among these aspects was the need for qualified and competent teachers.

The authors concur that much needs to be done in order to provide the knowledge necessary for an intelligent reform of education. Each of the beliefs about schooling described in the preceding paragraphs purports to have the correct answer. Only time will tell, however, which belief has the most merit. Each requires continuing thought and testing. We believe that, in the meantime, qualified and competent teachers are necessary for effective schools to exist and for the effects of schooling to be productive for citizens of this nation.

The knowledge base on effective teaching has increased continuously as a result of research on the effective classroom and on teacher effectiveness.[4] This research focuses primarily on the effects of teacher behavior on pupil achievement. As a consequence, educators have been provided with data that serve to depict characteristics of teachers whose learners show gains in achievement.

Personal Qualifications for Teaching in the Elementary School

Those who aspire to teach in the elementary school should be aware of its critical role in the development of citizens. Elementary school teachers have a unique opportunity to influence learners because pupils learn early to respect knowledge or to scorn it. They learn "how to learn" or to become "teacher depen-

[3] *A Nation at Risk: The Imperative for Educational Reform.* Report of the National Commission on Excellence in Education (Washington, D. C.: U.S. Department of Education, 1983).
[4] For a review of several significant studies on teacher behavior see Allan C. Ornstein and Daniel U. Levine, "Teacher Behavior Research: Overview and Outlook," *Phi Delta Kappan,* 62 (April 1981), 592–596.

dent." At the elementary school level children must master the rudiments of the basic skills in order to avoid an ever increasing complexity of learning difficulties as they proceed through school. They also develop respect for themselves and for others, or they learn to reinforce existing prejudices. Too, the development of habits consistent with democratic processes must begin at this level. All of these are critical outcomes and are considered basic to effective citizenship.

The concept of a common school for the nation's children has been a foremost guiding factor in the development of education for over a century. This ideal has been realized most completely at the elementary school level. The elementary school, free and open to all, is uniquely fitted to the democratic ideal. This status makes it extremely important that basic citizenship education, as discussed in Chapter 1, occurs at this level. Efforts to provide citizenship education along with an emphasis on academic skills, however, have resulted in an overcrowded curriculum.

As a result of so many expectancies, the elementary school has become a "cognitive pressure cooker" for both teachers and children. Learning in such an atmosphere produces many questionable side effects. There are some children who learn to read but who, in the process, learn to dislike reading. There are others who learn basic mathematical concepts and skills but develop a fear of the subject. The overstressing of cognitive learning has been at the expense of pupil development in the affective and psychomotor areas. This is not to suggest that cognitive learning is unimportant—rather, it is to express a concern for the neglect of affective learning in citizenship education.

Psychologists have known for a long time that children's attitudes affect how they perceive learning tasks. A high-pressure learning environment does little to promote positive attitudes toward learning. The teacher who plans carefully can reduce the pressure to a degree, but more must be done to lighten the burden imposed by an overloaded program.

Elementary school teachers often find it very difficult to provide instruction in the large number of subjects found in the elementary school curriculum. The problem is becoming increasingly complicated as a result of new programs such as the introduction of computer education. During the past decade, elementary school teachers have attempted to keep pace with such new curriculum developments by attending late afternoon classes offered by colleges and universities, and through participation in

(Courtesy of Patricia A. Conrard.)

This teacher is making a positive comment on the child's creative work. Why is it especially important to provide encouragement for the self-expression of children?

staff development activities. These obligations, added to an already crowded agenda for teachers, are very demanding of their time and energy. Teachers have little time left to plan a variety of learning experiences for children. The thrust to improve teaching in the cognitive area and its related skills has produced much that is good, but at the same time, it has created a curriculum with a heavy cognitive bias. The recent emphasis on competency testing also has reinforced attention being given to cognitive learning. Thus, balance needs to be restored in the curriculum if the elementary school is to familiarize children with the full range of educational experiences. In any event, the elementary school teacher must confront these realities as part of the everyday business of teaching.

Nevertheless, teaching in the elementary school offers many rewards for those who are qualified. For those who lack the necessary qualifications, frustrations and failures take the place of rewards. The elementary school teacher must be many things to many people. At no other educational level is there a greater demand on the time and energy of the teacher to provide both personal and educational services for children.

In most instances, the same children are with the teacher all day, beginning with the opening exercises, continuing through the lunch period, until the ending of the school day. In this setting, the teacher has many opportunities to provide learning experiences that support the needs and interests of the individual. But superimposed on these personal relationships is the necessity to provide learning experiences in a broad area of subject fields. In addition, the teacher must be a record keeper of the child's progress, and also is responsible for disseminating this information to parents.

This setting requires a teacher who likes children. One who does not would lack the patience to work and live, day in and day out, with children in such a confined and highly personal setting. The psychological support roles that the teacher performs are very important in setting the stage for motivating children to learn. We must emphasize that the personal interactions between the teacher and children in the elementary school are greater in number and extent than at any other level. Excellent possibilities for learning occur when children exhibit such behaviors as fear, hostility, or alienation related to the teacher, other learners, or learning itself. These situations should be used as learning experiences because in many instances they are as important as the knowledge and skills that are taught. But this requires a teacher who likes children and one who is endowed with an infinite capacity for patience.

The teacher must be a good student. Demands to know a wide range of subject matter assume that the teacher is interested in knowledge and learning. Teachers who possess this quality are openminded. They are curious about the world around them and are able to reach out beyond a single field of knowledge to inquire about matters that span a continuum from simple to complex. The child's world is one of wide-ranging interests, a curiosity that needs only to be directed toward positive ends. The qualified teacher is able to capture this interest and to make the most of it. Elementary school children should have teachers whose zest and interest in learning are contagious to those around them. The successful teacher is able to create a situation where children like and respect learning for learning's sake, and this requires that the teacher have this quality, too.

The ability to organize and to plan is an important qualification. Without it the teacher would be unable to navigate successfully through a normal school day, one which contains numerous transitions from one activity to another. Organization presumes skill in planning. This skill is one not possessed by many people, but it is one that can be learned. Those who fail to learn it, or who do not respect it, frequently find teaching frustrating. A positive classroom atmosphere is dependent on these skills; the necessity to enforce control occurs infrequently among teachers who are good organizers and planners.

Knowledge of the major teaching modes is a basic qualification. The typical teacher education program devotes much time to this aspect. The assumption is that this can be learned by the prospective teacher during the preparation program. Perhaps too much time is devoted to teaching modes, and not enough spent on the psychological support roles in teaching.

In any case, an understanding of teaching modes is necessary to enable the teacher to select a mode that best serves a particular need or interest of the group. Knowledge of modes should provide the teacher with a selection that ranges from highly teacher directed to highly child centered approaches. The teacher who is inflexible usually relies on the teaching mode that best suits his or her needs, as opposed to serving the needs of the group. Such a practice is unproductive and generally is associated with unsuccessful teachers.

The teacher must be able to adapt teaching modes to the variables that influence the lesson. The variables take many shapes and forms: the nature of the subject matter, the characteristics of the learners, the learner outcomes sought, as well as numerous other considerations. Thus, the qualified teacher has a repertoire of approaches from which to select the one that best fits the occasion.

Communication skills are essential. Contacts with parents are productive and pleasant experiences for teachers who possess these skills. Parent conferences require skills in communicating on a one-to-one basis, for the conference may be critical to a child's future. The teacher frequently must reassure a parent, assist in resolving conflicts that are essentially centered in the home, offer suggestions to enable the parent to provide support and guidance to the child in school subjects, and so forth. Many parents are at least as well educated as the teacher. It is no longer true that the teacher is among a relatively few college-educated persons in the community. This reality places a greater burden of responsibility on the teacher to be professionally competent. The teacher also must be proficient in group communication skills. These skills are obviously important in everyday teaching, and they are becoming increasingly important in adult groups in which school-related topics are discussed. Parent Teacher Student Association (PTSA) and "open house" type meetings frequently require presentations by the teacher relative to objectives and curriculum processes.

A healthy self-concept promotes good mental health in the classroom. Teachers who possess it are positive, confident, accepting of others, intellectually curious, and usually have a sense of humor. Evidence suggests that the teacher is a powerful model of behavior. Children are very sensitive to the teacher's behavior as it relates to what the teacher values and rewards. The teacher who has a healthy self-concept is likely to reward children's behavior that is consistent with it. Some teachers seem to need the constant assurance that others are dependent on them; such a feeling does little to encourage independence in children. Teachers who are pessimistic do little to encourage optimism and self-confidence in others. Those teachers who are impatient with failures do little to reassure children with learning problems. And those who are deadly serious miss countless opportunities to experience the laughter and joy of the child's world.

There is a growing recognition of the fact that "good teaching" does not just happen. It is based on many qualifications. The selection and preparation of elementary school teachers who possess these qualifications deserve the full support of the profession and public.

**THE NEWER TEACHER EDUCATION PROGRAMS
ARE EMPHASIZING THE QUESTION**

"Are you really sure you want to be a teacher?"

The time, expense, and effort required to complete certification requirements are very substantial in the newer programs. Many students underestimate this investment because an initial teaching certificate can be obtained along with a bachelor's degree. These same students would take a second look before entering law or medicine, because certification in those fields requires an extended preparatory program beyond the bachelor's degree before the individual can practice the specialty. Teaching is one of the few professions that certifies practitioners after only four years of preparation. This may well be a mistake; some students enter teacher education programs because they can get a degree and a teaching certificate at the same time.

But teacher education is becoming more rigorous every year. The newer programs require a full-time involvement during the last two years. Some programs require a decision during the freshman year. They no longer make it possible for the student to get a degree and a teaching certificate "on the side." Professional groups are beginning to talk about controlling the number of students who enter teacher education. Thus, selection and admission procedures also are becoming more rigorous.

1. With the possibility that fewer students will be selected for teacher education programs in the future, what criteria would you suggest for screening applicants in order to get the best?

2. When did you decide you wanted to become a teacher? On what evidence did you base your decision?

What Is Teaching?

The question, "What is teaching?" has yet to be answered to everyone's satisfaction. There are numerous definitions of the term, some of which have been generated from the way people actually teach. Other definitions are based on philosophical assumptions; still others are based on anthropological, psychological, or sociological premises. Even within the ranks of these disciplines, there are profound differences in the way teaching is defined. As a consequence, teachers and those who evaluate them do not always have a common frame of reference with which to approach their tasks.

The failure to achieve a consensus on a definition of teaching creates problems for educators who attempt to evaluate it. It is equally difficult for a teacher to practice self-evaluation when there is no conceptual frame of reference. Even though many teachers are aware of the "why and how" of teaching, some are not. When asked how they developed their particular, generalized teaching styles, some respond that they imitate former teachers whom they admired. Others reply that they have no consistent style, that they teach by intuition—whatever their "hunches" suggest is considered appropriate for the situation.

Imitation is a low-level method of learning how to teach. It works very well for the learning of simple skills and tasks, but few would agree that teaching is a simple task. Teaching is extremely complex, and for one to base his or her pattern of teaching behavior on imitating someone else is inadequate. For one thing, it is difficult for a second person to imitate successfully the behavior of another, human nature being far too complicated to be reduced to such a simple process. Also imitation does not permit flexibility because the teacher would be unable to provide options for meeting the changing conditions of classrooms or for the wide variance found in the abilities, needs, and interests of children. The teacher who is an imitator is limited in the capacity to grow beyond the pattern of teaching behavior that has been copied from someone else. Yet a surprising number of teachers teach as they do as a result of imitation.

Teachers who say they teach according to their intuition have a highly unpredictable style. Even though intuition is a valuable resource in some instances, it falls short of serving as a dependable guide for teaching. Intuition can serve the teacher well in making ad hoc modifications while a lesson is in progress. It may provide a useful resource in diagnosing children's interests and needs. By itself, however, intuition is little more than a hunch or a guess. Competent teachers recognize the importance of collecting data before making a decision about a child's needs or problems. Intuition is mainly an extension of the perception of the person who employs it. Thus, it is subject to all of the weaknesses, as well as the strengths, of that person. Something more definitive is needed in order to provide the teaching process with a framework that lends itself to analysis. There are many ways to teach, but the process must have recognizable characteristics, and these must be basic to the point that they are discernible to an observer, regardless of time or situation.

TEACHING DEFINED

We believe that *teaching* as practiced by teachers in a school setting is a process wherein the teacher engages in behavior and establishes mediating conditions that are intended to achieve desired learner outcomes. *Learning* occurs when the child's behavior is changed in the direction of the desired learner outcomes. The mediating conditions that are established by the teacher take many forms, such as the development of a positive classroom atmosphere, the employment of modes of teaching that reflect the needs and interests of learners, and the establishment of a classroom management system that provides children with a maximum opportunity to learn.

Teaching to Promote Learner Achievement

During the last decade, research on the teaching of basic skills has provided data that have promising implications for enhancing learner achievement. This research has focused on effective classrooms and teacher effectiveness. Much of the research has been conducted in elementary school classrooms that are located in inner-city schools. We believe, however, that the results of these studies have implications for teaching in a variety of school settings in which achievement in the basic skills represents the desired learner outcomes.

The point to be stressed is that the implications for teaching derived from this research pertain essentially to teaching that is designed to produce learner gains in scores on basic skills tests. These implications do not refer to teaching that is based on process goals such as the improvement of social skills or creative expression, a type of achievement that is usually found in the social studies and arts curricula.

Research studies of effective classrooms have confirmed that teachers do make a difference in whether or not children achieve in the basic skills area. The teachers in those classrooms where there was a high level of achievement were found to differ systematically from those teachers in classrooms where the achievement level was low.

The qualified and competent teacher realizes that principles and techniques of teaching that have been found to be effective in one classroom are not always equally effective in a different classroom. Thus, the teacher must use judgment in deciding when and how to apply these principles and practices. The differential results achieved by applying recommended procedures are the result of the variability in schools and classrooms. The school and the classroom *context* affect the extent to which certain procedures produce desired results. One school may be located in a low socioeconomic neighborhood whereas another may be situated in an affluent area. Within each type of school, classrooms differ from one another. Differences in pupils, classroom atmosphere, and parental expectations are examples of *context variables* that affect teaching and learning.

The following observations are presented as guidelines for effective teaching. The teacher must determine the efficacy of these guidelines based on the teaching and learning context of his or her particular school and classroom.[5]

1. *Effective teachers take their jobs seriously.* They have high expectations for their learners. The children are expected to learn and when they fail to do so, the teachers try again, using a different approach if necessary. These teachers have confidence in themselves and they do not write off any child as unteachable.

2. *Effective teachers provide children with an opportunity to learn.* They organize their time in order to ensure that most of it is spent in instruction. Therefore, the pupils of effective teachers spend many more hours on learning tasks than do those of ineffective teachers who are unable to organize the school day efficiently.

Recent research on effective teachers also has underscored the importance of "time on task." The implications of this research

---

[5] These guidelines on effective teaching are based on reviews of research contained in the following sources: Jere Brophy, "Successful Teaching Strategies for the Inner-City Child," *Phi Delta Kappan*, 63 (April 1982), 527–530. Also Thomas L. Good, *Classroom Research: What We Know and What We Need to Know.* The University of Texas at Austin: Research and Development Center for Teacher Education. Report No. 9018. Austin, Texas 78712. February 1982. 92 pp.

stress the importance of time variables in the instructional process. One such study was sponsored by the California Commission for Teacher Preparation and Licensing.[6]

This study identified Academic Learning Time as an important factor in good teaching. Academic Learning Time is defined as the amount of time that is allocated to pupils for a learning task, how much of that time children are engaged actively in working on the task (engaged learning time), and the resulting success rate of the pupil in achieving the task.

Studies show clearly that the amount of time that the teacher provides children for academic learning tasks must be accompanied by task assignments that are meaningful to pupils and that provide them a high rate of success. Also, it is important that learners receive immediate feedback on their efforts to complete the assigned tasks. Thus, "time on task" must be considered within a context that includes these considerations rather than on the assumption that simply providing more time to perform academic tasks will result necessarily in improved achievement. Effective teachers understand the complexity of the "time on task" variable and ensure that children are not only given ample task time but that they are also engaged actively in activities that provide them with a high level of success as determined by immediate evaluation and pupil feedback.

3. *Effective teachers manage their classrooms efficiently.* They plan their classroom organization early in the school year and employ effective group management techniques for teaching and learning. Their children are instructed in classroom procedures that will be employed during the school year. They review these procedures until they are realized by learners. In the primary grades, children are instructed in making smooth transitions from one learning task to another and are taught how to use classroom equipment. Older learners are included in the teacher's classroom management plan. Children at all levels learn that they will be held accountable for following established classroom procedures. These teachers are skillful also in using group management techniques that provide for both large and small group instruction.

---

[6] See Charles Fisher, Richard Marliave, and Nikola N. Filby, "Improving Teaching by Increasing Learning Time," *Educational Leadership,* 37 (October 1979), 52–54. For additional information on the allocation of academic learning time, see Jane Stallings, "Allocated Learning Time Revisited, or Beyond Time on Task," *Educational Researcher,* 9 (December 1980), 11–16.

(Courtesy of Terri Malinowski.)

Should a teacher "call" on all children to respond to questions or only those volunteers who raise their hands? What advantages and disadvantages can you name for each procedure?

4. *Effective teachers pace the curriculum to ensure that learners are involved in meaningful tasks.* They provide a good match between the pupils' achievement level and what is to be learned. Children proceed in small steps from one level of learning to the next higher level. These teachers know that children present behavior problems when they consistently are given learning tasks that are too difficult for them. Effective teachers realize that children must experience a high success rate. Learners engaged in seatwork require a higher success rate than those engaged in group instruction. Children of effective teachers are given more material to learn than pupils of ineffective teachers, but it is paced in small steps.

5. *Effective teachers are active teachers.* They teach learners in large and small groups and are careful to demonstrate skills, explain new words or concepts, and provide practice sessions before expecting children to work on their own. Effective teachers realize that most children are not capable of learning strictly on their own or from one another. Thus, they take the responsibility of actively directing the instruction through a high level of teacher-pupil interaction.

6. *Effective teachers have learners master desired outcomes.* They teach new knowledge and skills to the point of overlearning. A complex skill or new information is taught step by step, with the child progressing to the next step only after the previous level is mastered. Children are given opportunities to apply the skills or knowledge in new situations under teacher supervision. Learning objectives are written on a low level, and these are realized by children before proceeding to higher level objectives.

7. *Effective teachers recognize grade-level differences that require different teacher behavior.* Primary-grade-level teachers realize the importance of one-to-one interaction with learners in providing them with practice and direct feedback. These teachers follow an ordered method in calling on children to read or to recite. They do so to equalize the extent of participation of children and to permit them to be involved on a regular basis.

Effective teachers of older children employ large group instruction and use small group activities for remedial instruction. This is because older children do not require one-to-one attention to the extent needed by primary age children. These teachers realize, however, that individual learners must receive close monitoring of their independent work and also need to receive assistance and feedback.

8. *Effective teachers provide a supportive learning environment.* A positive classroom atmosphere supports a strong academic focus in the classrooms of effective teachers. These teachers require high standards but they are not punitive or hypercritical in their pupil relationships. Thus, they are supportive of learners, especially those children who are experiencing learning difficulties. They get the most from such children by providing them with positive reinforcements and recognition of evidence of achievement. Effective teachers provide the support that children need with the expectation they will require less attention as they become independent learners.

These implications of the research on effective teaching to enhance learning are reassuring because they demonstrate the fact that the dedicated, well-organized, and hard-working teacher can make the difference between success and failure for children. This assurance will continue to grow as scientific research continues to yield new indicators of effective teaching.

Teaching to Provide Psychological Support for Children

The teacher should be aware that the effective performance of psychological support roles contributes to the well-being of children and to a positive classroom atmosphere. A psychological support role is teacher behavior that occurs in response to a given classroom situation. The qualified and competent teacher has mastered the knowledge and skills necessary for the performance of these support roles.

PSYCHOLOGICAL SUPPORT ROLES

A Social Model

Traditionally, the teacher was expected to be a social model for the values that the community held dear. In performing this role, the teacher served as a model for the children. In the multicultural atmosphere of the present time, the teacher must recognize that values differ from one subculture to another, and that a group of children probably represents several sets of values, some of which may be contradictory. Thinking recently has shifted away from the importance of the teacher's modeling a value to that of providing instruction in value setting as a process. Nevertheless, the teacher must be aware that certain communities still expect the teacher to be a model for the social values found therein. Thus the teacher is expected, through the use of precept and example, to inculcate those moral values, life styles, and career goals that have high priority in the community.

An Evaluator

The way the teacher performs the role of an evaluator frequently can determine how children view themselves. On countless occasions the elementary school teacher is evaluating something about the child. Sometimes it concerns the way the child behaves in the hallway or lunchroom; at other times it pertains to the manner in which classroom work is performed. But at other times it is even more critical—when report cards or parent-conference time comes. Because children are sensitive about all matters concerning success or failure, the way in which the teacher performs the evaluator role is often more critical than the evaluation itself. Children should be made to feel good about themselves and to have confidence in themselves; in short, to possess a strong, positive self-image. The elementary school teacher who approaches the tasks that go along with the evaluator role in a positive, helpful manner is contributing to the healthy development of the child's personal and psychological makeup.

A Walking Encyclopedia

From the earliest elementary schools until well into the twentieth century the teacher was expected to perform the role of a walking encyclopedia. Even today the role is an important one, but its meaning has changed substantially from that of former times. The competent teacher recognizes that it is impossible to be an unfailing source of information for the vast number of questions children are prone to ask. It is more important to help children learn how to locate the information they are seeking.

To be sure, the elementary school teacher of today must be knowledgeable in a wide range of subjects. Some teacher education programs require elementary school teachers to study a field of knowledge in some depth. But more important than what the teacher actually knows is the teacher's respect for knowledge and the power it offers. The elementary school teacher who is curious, always searching for answers to challenging questions— one who provides a positive model for acquiring and applying the tools that produce knowledge—is one who is performing the role in an exemplary manner.

A Moderator

The elementary school teacher portrays the moderator role on many occasions. Especially in the area of personal conflicts, the role must be performed with objectivity. Children are sensitive to the fairness of the teacher's judgment when settling disputes. The pupil who is a perennial troublemaker presents a challenge if the teacher is to handle the child in a consistently objective manner. The role of moderator affords the teacher a powerful opportunity for modeling behavior. In reconciling disputes, the fair, calm teacher can set examples for others to follow. The teacher who performs the role well is assured of the abiding respect of pupils.

A Morale Builder

The role of morale builder requires a teacher to be a good listener. Children sometimes develop anxiety in the process of learning to control their impulses; this is part of growing up. But the process must be understood by teachers. The role of a morale builder is one too often overlooked by teachers who are preoccupied with teaching children to succeed in their school subjects.

Some children are afraid that, if they are given too much freedom, they are certain to do something wrong. Some children worry about falling victim to imaginary dangers or threats; others worry about turning out to be like someone who is bad, or ill. The majority of children have these thoughts and feelings, and they look to the teacher as a source of reassurance. As such, the teacher who responds by listening to these needs of children in an understanding way is providing important psychological support for them. Children will usually confide in those teachers who exude a confident and competent air, who set limits for permissible behavior and who are consistent in enforcing them, who deal intelligently with negative behavior, and who understand that children worry about many things.

A Group Leader

The teacher who is a good group leader understands that certain children behave differently in a group situation than when encountered on a one-to-one basis. Many teachers are effective with children in a one-to-one relationship but have difficulty interacting with pupils in a group. To be sure, dealing with twenty-five or thirty children in a group presents a situation quite different from dealing with pupils singly. The phenomenon of a group personality and of group mentality can sometimes be frightening to teachers. Effective teachers consciously work to help children to develop the ability to work well in group settings.

A Substitute Parent

Teachers act as parents for many children. With little children, the role becomes one of serving as a parent during school hours.

IDENTIFYING PSYCHOLOGICAL SUPPORT ROLES OF TEACHERS

Situation no. 1 Tommy comes from a "different" neighborhood.

Remark: "I'm sorry Tommy, but you should use correct English even though you say your parents and neighbors don't."

Situation no. 2 Mary just failed a reading test.

Remark: "That's all right, Mary. You'll do better next time. All of us fail now and then."

Situation no. 3 Mr. Wise explains that he isn't the fount of all knowledge.

Remark: "Yes, I can see that you are surprised that I couldn't answer your question. But I know where we can find the answer."

Situation no. 4 Jane Todd decided to teach fifth grade instead of kindergarten.

Remark: "I thought I wanted to teach kindergarten until I observed in a class for several weeks. You couldn't pay me enough to babysit 25 kids all day."

Situation no. 5 Ms. Hunter introduces herself to her student-teaching class of sixth graders.

Remark: "My name is Miss Hunter, but my friends call me Skippy. I want to be your friend, so why don't you call me Skippy, too?"

Situation no. 6 Andrew, a fourth grader, confides in his teacher that he worries frequently about being kidnapped.

Remark: "Andy, you're too big to worry about imaginary things. Now go back to your desk and don't fret anymore."

1. Identify the psychological support role in each of these examples.
2. What do the teachers' remarks, in each instance, tell you about how well the teacher performed the support role?

With very young children, the teacher frequently must assist the child with personal attire, as well as help to perform a number of other essentially psychomotor tasks. With older children, the teacher performs the role on a more subtle level, by shifting from physical to psychological support. The role may represent the teacher as a confidante, for those who have no parent or who come from one-parent families. The courts have ruled that in a limited, legal sense, the teacher may perform in *loco parentis,* that is, in the place of a parent during the time the child is in school.

A Friend

Children sometimes expect teachers to be their friend. This role, when carried too far, can have unproductive consequences. Probably too many beginning teachers are so overly concerned with "winning over" their children that they attempt to become close friends with them. This is not necessary. A friendly atmosphere can be established without becoming a friend to each child. It must be remembered that teaching is a professional endeavor, one that is, to be sure, deeply human, but should be based upon objectivity.

Professional Status of Elementary School Teachers

Teaching in the elementary school has come into its own in relatively recent times. The professional status of elementary school teachers has been slow to develop in the 375 years since elementary school education took roots in this land. The history of elementary school education had its inception during the colonial period, even though the present system of state-supported schools did not begin until the latter half of the nineteenth century. The public, from the beginning, has viewed teaching in the elementary school as a woman's job—a notion that is equally unflattering to both sexes. For many years elementary school teachers were paid substantially less than secondary school teachers. During the 1980–81 school year, the average salary of elementary school teachers was $17,204, whereas the average for secondary school teachers was $18,082.[7] These data show that this salary gap has been almost closed. Certification requirements for teaching at the elementary school level have been lower than those required for teaching in secondary schools.

---

[7] National Center for Educational Statistics. *Digest of Educational Statistics, 1982* (Washington, D. C.: U.S. Government Printing Office, 1983), p. 56.

This discrepancy also has been erased for the most part throughout the nation's schools.

The expanding economy of the 1940–1970 era provided the public funding necessary to develop and support the growing demands for elementary education. Funding support for public education began to wane toward the close of the decade of the 1970s. An economic recession accompanied by a public reaction against taxation at the local, state, and national levels were the major contributors to the declining support for education.

Today, however, elementary school education continues to be a major enterprise in this nation. During the 1980–81 school year, about $110 billion was spent on public and private education at the elementary and secondary school levels.[8] During this same year, the total amount spent on education in the United States was $181 billion, or roughly 6.5 per cent of the gross national product.[9] Viewed from an economic perspective, this expenditure represents a significant investment in education. As a result, the public sector has increased its pressure for accountability in education.

In this atmosphere, teaching competence is becoming increasingly important. Attention to the qualifications of the elementary school teacher has reached its highest level in the history of the enterprise, and there are signs that it will continue to be important.

Coupled with the emphasis on accountability, a decrease in the demand for teachers during recent years has created additional problems for elementary school teachers. In the face of a decreasing school enrollment, an inflationary economy, and strong demands from taxpayers to economize, school districts have reduced the number of elementary school teachers. At the same time, the rate of teacher turnover has decreased. Hence, the market for beginning teachers has shown an overall drop during the past few years. Elementary school enrollment peaked in the fall of 1969 and continued to decrease throughout the 1970s, thereby decreasing the need for teachers.[10]

The future for teacher demand has begun to brighten as a result of an increased birthrate that has been occurring over

---

[8] Bureau of the Census, U.S. Department of Commerce, *Statistical Abstracts of the United States, 1982–83* (Washington, D. C.: U.S. Government Printing Office, December 1982), p. 135.

[9] Ibid.

[10] National Center for Education Statistics. *Digest of Education Statistics, 1982* (Washington, D. C.: U. S. Government Printing Office, 1982), p. 37.

(Courtesy of Terri Malinowski.)

The qualified and competent teacher needs to have a broad range of professional skills. What particular skill do you think the teacher in this photograph is using?

the past few years. As a result of the change in this demographic factor, the demand for teachers has been predicted to reflect an increase during the latter half of the 1980s. One source states that it is reasonable to assume the teacher supply and demand situation during 1986–1990 will be similar to what was experienced in the 1965–69 period, when the demand for teachers averaged 224,000 per year.[11]

An increased need for teachers also may develop as a result of the public demand for quality education. This could mean a greater diversity in the kinds of teachers that are needed for a quality elementary school. It could also mean an actual increase in the number of teachers required to perform the tasks necessary to prepare citizens who will spend most of their lives in the

---

[11] National Center for Education Statistics. *Projections of Education Statistics to 1990–91, Vol. 1, Analytical Report* (Washington, D. C.: U.S. Government Printing Office, 1983), p. 76.

twenty-first century. Greater attention to special education, parent education, preschool education, community education, and computer education are other examples of dimensions that could contribute to the need for additional teachers.

In short, there is always a demand for qualified and competent teachers. Competition for positions is becoming very keen, and prospective teachers should explore the qualifications required for elementary school teaching before investing in it as a career.

Study Questions and Activities

1. Select a teacher whom you admired when you were an elementary school pupil. What characteristics did this person possess?
2. Prepare a statement of your own definition of teaching. Explain how you decided on your definition.
3. The text provides a review of selected research on effective teaching. Arrange to observe two elementary school teachers and describe their teaching behavior in terms of this research.
4. Some believe that too much emphasis is placed on pupil achievement in the basic skills. What is your position on this issue? Explain why you believe the way you do.
5. Various psychological support roles are presented in the text. Which of these roles do you believe will be easy for you to perform? Are there any that may be difficult for you? If so, why?
6. What do you believe is the most important change that needs to be made to improve the professional status of elementary school teachers?

For Further Professional Study

Anderson, Linda M. "Short-Term Student Responses to Classroom Instruction." *The Elementary School Journal,* **82** (Nov. 1981), 97–108.

Bickel, William E., guest ed. "Effective Schools." *Educational Researcher,* **12** (April 1983), 3–31.

Cuban, Larry. "Effective Schools: A Friendly but Cautionary Note." *Phi Delta Kappan,* **64** (June 1983), 695–696.

Denham, Carolyn and Ann Lieberman, co-eds. *Time to Learn.* Commission for Teacher Preparation and Licensing. Sacramento, Ca., 1980, 1–246.

Goldberg, Milton, and James Harvey. "A Nation at Risk: The Report of the National Commission on Excellence in Education." *Phi Delta Kappan,* **65** (Sept. 1983), 14–18.

Goodlad, John I. *A Place Called School: Prospects for the Future.* New York: McGraw-Hill Book Company, 1984, Chap. 1.

Orlich, Donald C., Robert J. Harder, Richard C. Callahan, Constance H. Kravas, Donald P. Kauchak, R. A. Pendergrass, Andrew J. Keogh, and Dorothy I. Hellene. *Teaching Strategies: A Guide to Better Instruction.* Lexington, Mass.: D. C. Heath and Company, 1980, Chap. 1.

Orlosky, Donald E., ed. *Introduction to Education.* Columbus, Ohio: Charles E. Merrill Publishing Company, 1982, Chap. 1.

Purkey, Stewart C., and Marshall S. Smith. "Too Soon to Cheer? Synthesis of Research on Effective Schools." *Educational Leadership,* **40** (December 1982), 64–69.

The Elementary School Journal. A Special Issue. "Research on Teaching," **83** (March 1983), 261–500.

Tonelson, Stephen W. "The Importance of Teacher Self-Concept to Create a Healthy Psychological Environment for Learning." *Education,* **102** (Fall 1981), 96–100.

Planning for Teaching and Learning

THE QUALIFIED AND COMPETENT TEACHER . . .

1. Understands the planning process.
2. Appreciates the importance of getting acquainted with a new school.
3. Understands the nature of critical planning times.
4. Understands the importance of parent-teacher communication.

Performance Criteria

As a result of the serious study of this chapter, the student should be able to . . .

1. Organize the first few days of instruction.
2. Plan a good learning atmosphere.
3. Select goals for the year in the various curriculum areas.
4. Plan for getting instruction underway.
5. Develop a sketch plan for several days of learning and instruction.
6. Develop a daily lesson plan.
7. Prepare a pupil-progress report.

Teaching, like any other complex process, requires careful planning for its success. Teachers who realize the importance of planning for effective instruction and classroom management assign planning a high priority as a teaching skill. Planning in any walk of life requires the individual to make choices and to select alternatives that are consistent with one's goals. When planning is done in a sequential and orderly manner, the end result is more likely to be realistic in terms of the goals desired. To achieve such results, decisions need to be made at several points in the process. Each point of decision making requires sorting out and establishing priorities for the variables at hand. The process, when applied intelligently, is problem solving at its best. But decision making becomes difficult when there is no provision for processing the data that bear on the situation. The teacher who plans effectively follows a sequence that flows through a number of planning phases. Each phase provides an opportunity to sort out data in order to make realistic decisions before moving on to the next step. Experience has shown that many good teachers employ a planning procedure that follows a continuum of several phases. These phases occur in a cyclical progression that, when completed, repeats itself.

The Planning Process

Beginning teachers sometimes have the mistaken idea that planning for instruction ends when the lesson begins. But the competent teacher realizes that pupil attainment of expected objectives is dependent on careful planning throughout the instructional process. The planning process is depicted in the following diagram.

THE PLANNING CYCLE

Once the objectives are determined, the planning cycle begins with the teacher's *assessment of pupil characteristics.* This procedure enables the teacher to examine *what* the children are supposed to learn in terms of *how ready* they are to learn it. The data needed for the assessment are obtained from a variety of sources, such as (1) cumulative files containing test data, anecdotal rec-

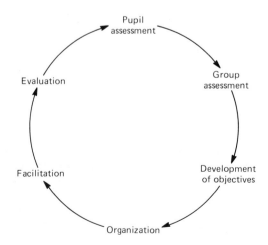

ords, pupil-progress reports, samples of schoolwork; (2) observations; (3) interviews; and (4) pretests. Next, and equally important, is the *assessment of the group.* The teacher is able to ascertain the extent of the group's cohesiveness, the readiness of the group to participate in activities that require cooperative behavior, and the children who are leaders and those who seem to have difficulty with task-oriented activities. These data enable the teacher to make an assessment of the characteristics of the children and to plan instruction on the basis of where the children are in terms of their needs and interests. The information acquired by the teacher is basic to good instruction and classroom management.

Once the teacher has carefully analyzed the abilities, needs, and interests of children and has assessed carefully the available resources, *instructional objectives* can be stated in the form of expected learner outcomes. This is a critical decision-making point in the planning process that initiates the phase of the planning cycle where the teacher makes decisions on *organizing for instruction.* The lesson plan, developed by the teacher, ultimately contains the organizing elements that will be included in the lesson. But, first, alternatives for reaching certain objectives may have to be considered. In a situation in which the textbook is the major learning resource, the teacher may have to center instruction on it. But other modes of teaching should also be provided. Sometimes this task may be difficult. If the teacher believes that the integrated curriculum mode would be valuable for the development of certain skills needed by the group, but finds that the school principal discourages noise and movement in the classroom, an alternative may have to be found. This phase in the planning process also provides the teacher with information needed to make plans consistent with the human and material resources at hand. Beginning teachers sometimes fail to give adequate attention to this consideration and discover, too late, that their teaching strategies cannot be used because of the absence of needed resources.

The *facilitation* phase provides numerous opportunities for evaluation. The elementary school teacher soon learns to develop the capacity for being "all eyes and ears." In the event the lesson is not proceeding smoothly, modifications are made at that point, not later on. For instance, a teacher may plan to have the class work in small groups to accomplish a learning task, but finds that the children are not able to use the time well. The teacher should assess the situation with the children at that point, and perhaps make a decision to change over to large group instruction to accomplish the task.

The *evaluation* phase is the appropriate time to conduct a comprehensive assessment. An examination is made of the objectives in order to determine whether they were realized as a result of the instruction. In other words, the teacher must determine whether the children learned what they were expected to learn. The teacher also can employ the evaluation phase to assess what actually occurred during the lesson to promote or to prevent the attainment of the objectives. Questions such as the following are useful to the teacher in the assessment of the lesson.

Did the children respond with interest when I introduced the lesson?

Did the pupils seem to understand what was expected of them?

Did I organize the learning environment sufficiently to reduce distractions and interruptions?

Did I provide sufficient learning resources for the lesson?

Was there a high level of verbal and nonverbal interaction among the children and between them and me?

Did I pace the learning activities to permit children adequate time for the various activities in the lesson?

Did I provide pupils with an opportunity to evaluate what occurred and to make suggestions for the next lesson?

Were the objectives for the lesson appropriate to the needs and interests of the children?

Was my planning successful in anticipating the mediating conditions?

Were the expected learner outcomes realistic?

Did I select a teaching mode that was appropriate for the accomplishment of the desired learner outcomes?

Do I need to follow up immediately with learning activities that will produce a greater degree of achievement of the desired learner outcomes, or should I go on with extended learning?

The responses to the foregoing questions provide the teacher with information about the effectiveness of the lesson. Teachers may find that pupils did not achieve an objective because they did not possess the knowledge or skills required for its achievement. These children may require follow-up instruction on learning *how* to attain the expected outcome. In any case, the teacher is able to evaluate the lesson with respect to what needs to be done next, such as reteaching it or moving on to a different focus. Thus, the planning cycle begins anew.

Planning for Critical Instructional Episodes

This chapter is based on an application of the planning process to selected instructional episodes that occur during the school year:

1. Getting acquainted with a new school.
2. Organizing the first few days of instruction.
3. Selecting goals for the school year.
4. Planning for getting instruction underway.
5. Planning for the first pupil-progress report.

These critical instructional episodes will be presented as vignettes based on examples selected from a primary-and an intermediate-grade classroom taught by Ellen Baxter and Jim Bond, respectively, who are fictitious teachers. The narratives are presented as lifelike situations that teachers actually face. Ellen Baxter and Jim Bond are prototypes of numerous beginning teachers throughout the nation. They are faced with situations that, when modified to fit a specific locality, are typical of those found in many school districts today. The vignettes should be read for the purpose of analyzing the ideas and principles embodied in them.

Ellen Baxter and Jim Bond respond to their teaching situations with approaches we believe are appropriate to the philosophy of the schools where each of the two beginning teachers were assigned. You will find that Miss Baxter was free to plan in a relatively open situation while Mr. Bond was restricted to a situation somewhat more structured. This is not to suggest, however, that the specifics of either approach are those the reader may choose to follow as a beginning teacher. Rather, each approach exemplifies a general procedure that includes elements of the planning process presented at the beginning of this chap-

(Courtesy of Patricia A. Conrard.)

The children in this photograph are participating in a traditional fall harvest activity by gathering, sorting, and drying filberts. What does this tell about the teacher's philosophy regarding planning?

ter. The successful teacher selects specific techniques appropriate to the given situation. The successful application of specific teaching techniques, however, is dependent on the teacher's having selected and followed an appropriate planning approach in the first place.

GETTING ACQUAINTED WITH A NEW SCHOOL

Miss Baxter was hired to teach at the primary-grade level in East Elementary School located in a city of fifty thousand people. Most of the children were from lower-middle-class homes, with a few from well-to-do families. There was also a mix of ethnic minorities in the school. She looked foward eagerly to reporting to her first assignment.

Mr. Bond was delighted to accept a teaching position in an intermediate-grade-level classroom. West Elementary School was located in a section of a city similar to the one in which Miss Baxter had secured a teaching position. Similar socioeconomic conditions prevailed in both East and West Schools. Mr. Bond, too, eagerly awaited his first day on the job.

Miss Baxter and Mr. Bond were aware of the challenge teachers face in organizing for a new school year. Their challenge was even greater because they were beginning teachers, facing a new school year in a new school assignment.

What Miss Baxter Found

Miss Baxter drove through the school neighborhood noting several possibilities for supplementing learning activities. The traffic flow was light and the school was located away from heavily traveled streets and approaches to the freeway. This discovery pleased her because it meant she could take the children on walks to various community agencies, businesses, and industries. She noted that there was apparently a community effort to keep the environment clean. Many houses and businesses had been painted recently, and several were being renovated. She noted also that there was still room for improvement, especially in the care of vacant lots and unoccupied buildings. All in all she was pleased with what she saw during the reality assessment of the school neighborhood.

Miss Baxter's first impression of her assignment was a positive one. She felt good when she saw the school building. Roomy and attractive, with an open court, the one-story structure had a warm atmosphere. She immediately thought, "What a nice place to work." When she saw her classroom, her initial impression was reinforced. The room was large and the furniture consisted of small tables and chairs that could be arranged flexibly. There were ample work spaces, a sink, and much wall space that could be used for displays. She immediately realized that she could arrange the room in whatever way would best suit the children's needs as well as her own. She noticed, too, that the wall adjoining the next room was constructed to be opened, permitting the two rooms to become one large open space. There was also a door opening out to a patio in the court.

Shortly after receiving her teaching contract, Miss Baxter had received a letter of welcome from Mrs. Ginsburg, the school principal. She congratulated her on her appointment and assured her that she would be warmly welcomed at East School. Mrs. Ginsburg had closed the letter by suggesting that Miss Baxter come in for a conference with her when she arrived in town.

The visit with Mrs. Ginsburg had been a rewarding one. Miss

Baxter was welcomed enthusiastically and was introduced to Miss Johnson, the school secretary. Miss Baxter was impressed with the secretary's offer to assist her in any way she could. She was pleased to learn that the principal was well acquainted with her background and teacher-preparation experiences. Mrs. Ginsburg made several references to the fact that Miss Baxter's teacher education program was a good one, especially so because of the substantial amount of actual experience in the classroom it had provided.

The principal explained that she liked to see classes in which children went about their schoolwork with a sense of purpose and a feeling of happiness and belonging. Miss Baxter noted that Mrs. Ginsburg emphasized the importance of good planning and the relationship it seemed to have to effective classroom management. She concluded that the principal would look for a high level of participation by the children in the planning of learning activities.

What Mr. Bond Found

On driving to West School, Mr. Bond found it to be located in a rather congested area that was slowly being rezoned for business and light industry. He assumed that some of the children had to ride a bus to school because the residential area had receded some distance from it. He concluded that opportunities for informal excursions with the children probably would be limited.

West School was traditional in appearance—a large, two-story brick building, built several decades ago. It was durable, to be sure, and had been maintained with care. It was clean and well furnished insofar as conventional equipment was concerned. Mr. Bond's classroom was located on the second floor. The room had a bank of windows overlooking a narrow front lawn. There were storage cabinets under the windows, with a countertop that extended along the length of the windows. A chalkboard was located along the length of the opposite wall, and there were bulletin board spaces on the wall behind the teacher's desk at the front of the room. A map rack was suspended from the wall. The rear wall provided coat hooks and storage spaces for the children's coats. Mr. Bond was struck by the fact that the pupils' desks were in rows facing the teacher's desk. He suddenly became aware of the humming sound of a large clock on the front wall. Mr. Bond was impressed with the solidness of the atmosphere. It suggested strength and durability, if nothing else, and he reflected on the fact that teaching and learning had been occurring in this room for many years. As he stood behind the teacher's desk, idly spinning the world globe in its cradle, he felt that if he had the freedom to do so, he could provide the children with learning experiences that would interest and challenge them.

During the meeting with Mr. Park, the school principal, Mr. Bond concluded early that there would be a few constraints on his selection of learning experiences. Mr. Park stressed his

---

WHAT'S ALL THIS FUSS ABOUT ACCOUNTABILITY?

Mr. Park actually stressed only one aspect of accountability with Mr. Bond. He talked about the parents wanting assurance that their children were learning. That is rather basic to the concept, but there is more to it than just that. The idea of accountability is highly controversial in the professional and private sectors. It is being applied across the board to public servants at the local, state, and national levels.

The concept of accountability is no stranger to business and industry, where success has always been measured by the product—it is a different matter in education, where the product is people rather than things. Few would argue that a teacher should be held responsible for what he or she does, but they do question whether the teacher can be held responsible for what the child does or fails to do. Some say the teacher can no more be held responsible for a pupil's unwillingness to do schoolwork than a physician can be held responsible for the health of a patient who refuses to follow orders.

The present concern for accountability in education stresses pupil achievement in the basic skills. Mr. Park is right—this is usually recognized as achievement or nonachievement. The public is demanding a return on its tax dollar. As a prospective teacher, you are going to hear a lot more about accountability in the future, particularly as it relates to merit pay.

1. Do you think that teachers should be held accountable for whether or not their children learn?
2. Should the responsibility for accountability be left to the integrity of the teacher, rather than imposed from the outside?

---

concern about "accountability," a notion, he said, that was receiving overwhelming support in the community. He explained that it really meant only one thing—that the school provide evidence the children were learning the basic skills. He explained to Mr. Bond that, so long as the children learned according to their potential, he did not expect to receive any criticism from their parents. Mr. Bond saw immediately that the principal believed firmly in having children follow a structured scope of learning.

ORGANIZING THE FIRST FEW DAYS OF INSTRUCTION

The opening of school is a critical planning time. The psychological impact of the first day on children is tremendous, as it is on a beginning teacher. A good first day, like a good opening night in the theater, goes a long way toward promoting a successful engagement. Experienced teachers have learned that they can anticipate many characteristics of a new group of children prior to their first encounter with them. By perusing the children's cumulative folders, they discover many important facts. By doing this, much can be learned about the children's abilities, needs, and interests. If the group has the same children as the former year, the previous teacher's anecdotal notes concerning group traits and behavioral patterns are very helpful. The teacher's prior knowledge of goals and objectives for the instructional program also is important in planning meaningful learning activities. In the same way, the teacher's knowledge of available human and material resources is necessary for effective planning.

HOW MISS BAXTER WENT ABOUT IT

She Establishes Priorities for Her Primary-Grade-Level Classroom

Miss Baxter decided to divide her efforts three ways: (1) to get acquainted with her children as quickly as possible; (2) to prepare a room environment that would be attractive and interesting; (3) to develop tentative plans for the first few days of instruction.

Miss Baxter jotted down the following priorities for the first week of school:

1. Observe the children as they work independently and as they relate to others in the group.
2. Establish classroom management procedures by introducing routines and expected behaviors.
3. Provide a stimulating and provocative learning atmosphere.
4. Provide incentives for pupils to practice responsibility and industry in a group setting.
5. Help the children develop a sense of purpose for the school year.

She Plans a Daily Schedule

With her priorities for the first few days in mind, Miss Baxter decided to establish a tentative daily schedule. She knew that, as the children became more efficient in helping to plan the day, modifications could easily be made. She decided to stress this point with them from the start. During her student teaching experiences, she had made notes of daily schedules in various classrooms, and she had also examined the schedule left in the previous teacher's notebook. With these resources at hand, she planned her schedule to allow as much flexibility as possible, permitting her to unify learning from various school subjects. She decided on the following schedule and printed it on a large chart for the children:

Our Daily Schedule

Opening Activities
Planning the Day
Reading (to include Language Arts)
Social Studies
Lunch
Mathematics
Science
Creative Experiences (Art, Music, Drama)
Health and Physical Education (alternate days)
Closing Activities

Miss Baxter decided that the length of each period should be left flexible.[1] Later, teacher-pupil planning would determine the actual length, but she decided that probably a thirty to ninety minute range would provide a reasonable beginning frame of reference.

She Plans a Good Learning Atmosphere

Miss Baxter's classroom provided numerous possibilities for organizing the physical aspects of it in a cheerful, positive manner. A door opened onto a patio in the courtyard; the movable furniture enabled flexibility in room arrangement. She decided to organize the room according to various learning centers. With the subject areas in mind, she decided to establish a science center that would be built around a large aquarium (a terrarium could be added later). On the wall behind the aquarium were various pictures of marine life, with captions such as, "What is my name?" For social studies, she used a community map with the caption, "Can you find East School?" Photographs of occupations and industries were arranged around the map. Books on community life were also placed on the study table at this center. A third center contained puzzles and other manipulative materials designed to illustrate mathematics. There was a center for reading and language arts as well, complete with an attractive display of poetry, fiction, and factual books. She also prepared an attractive bulletin board display. On it were scenes of the local community, with the caption, "How many of these places have you visited?"

Because the children would be grouped for various purposes during the year, Miss Baxter prepared name tags and made a tentative seating chart, based on a more or less random selection of children. She knew that quite early in the week the children themselves would demonstrate the feasibility of her choices. Her basic concern was to work toward a positive group feeling. Groupings for specific learning would follow soon.

She Plans Learner Activities for the First Few Days

Miss Baxter organized the first few days of school with the following activities in mind: (1) introduce the various school

---

[1] Generally, state education codes stipulate minimum requirements of time to be spent on the various school subjects. Miss Baxter was not unmindful of the fact that she would need to adhere to those requirements.

subjects; (2) diagnose the needs, abilities, and interests of children; (3) determine the pupils' readiness for independent, small and large group activities; (4) diagnose their level of responsibility; and (5) determine the amount of teaching necessary to establish study, work, and social skills. Her planning for the first week resulted in the following arrangements.

READING AND LANGUAGE ARTS

Use informal discussion activities to establish rules for speaking and listening. Use the social studies "Our Community" theme to provide children with writing activities to produce samples of their handwriting, spelling, and composition skills. Read to the children on a daily basis to further determine listening skills, and also to ascertain critical thinking skills. From the children's cumulative folders, use reading-test scores to determine tentative assignments of textbooks as well as tentative groupings for reading instruction. Regrouping will be done later on the basis of specific needs or interests, and on results of the fall testing program. Plan to correlate the spelling program with reading by extending word-attack skills into the study of spelling. Make maximum use of sharing and planning activities to establish guidelines for effective speaking habits.

SOCIAL STUDIES

Planning for this subject is presented later in the chapter.

MATHEMATICS

Identify skill levels of children from the cumulative folders. Administer tests to determine their present level of reasoning and computational skills. Provide reinforcement activities for those who have regressed since last spring. Anticipate opportunities to correlate mathematics with the social studies unit.

SCIENCE

Have discussions based on the aquarium. Record children's questions. Summarize discussions by sorting out children's questions, and determining relevant sources of data to provide information on questions. Correlate science, when possible, with study of marine life as it relates to the social studies unit on community life.

(Courtesy of Patricia A. Conrard.)

The teacher plans the room environment to provide children with appropriate aids to learning. What other provisions might a teacher make in the room environment to accommodate learner needs?

CREATIVE EXPERIENCES

Encourage children to suggest songs they like to sing. Have children discuss their interest and involvement in music. Provide listening experiences based on records that highlight both instrumental and vocal selections.

Keep art activities uncomplicated until more is known about the group's ability to work with various media. Provide opportunities for self-selection of the form of expression. Help the children develop good work habits and a concern for the proper care and use of materials.

HEALTH AND PHYSICAL EDUCATION

Review good health habits learned in prior years. Use the warm fall weather to take short walks around the neighborhood. Provide opportunities for group play and make use of them to observe children's behavior. Note the leaders, the subgroups, the very active, and the retiring children. Introduce a simple group game. Relate health to the study of the community in the social studies program.

ROOM CITIZENSHIP

Plan the day's program with the children each morning. Begin immediately to determine with them a few simple rules for good citizenship as an individual and as a group member. Record these on a chart or on the chalkboard and have the children write them in their own notebook. Refer to these from time to time to evaluate behavior and to reinforce their importance. During the first few days, teach for the mastery of routines pertaining to the playground, cafeteria, lavatories, and the like. Conduct discussions with the children on "How well we did today" in observing good playground habits, and so forth. Use every occasion to comment on good behavior by citing examples that prompted it.

Take time during the beginning and ending of the class period to discuss the work habits necessary for effective learning. Close each day with a brief discussion of the day's activities, and solicit suggestions from the children about "What I really liked today."

With these notes in mind, Miss Baxter felt more confident. She had developed a plan of action. Now she could plan more specifically for the learning needs of her children.

HOW MR. BOND WENT ABOUT IT

He Establishes Priorities for His Intermediate-Grade-Level Classroom

Mr. Bond followed procedures very similar to Miss Baxter's. Even though he was concerned about the principal's emphasis on "accountability," Mr. Bond knew that very little would be accomplished if he failed to get the children interested in what they were supposed to do. He decided that he should give priority to the basic skills, but in doing so he wanted to teach them in a meaningful context. He also gave priority to the need to:

1. Observe the children to determine study habits and ability to work within a group.
2. Establish classroom management procedures through teacher-pupil planning.
3. Develop a positive learning atmosphere through the display of stimulating media.
4. Reinforce positive and task-oriented pupil behavior.
5. Assist children in developing a sense of purpose for the school year.

He Plans a Daily Schedule

Mr. Bond developed a tentative daily schedule and wrote it on the chalkboard. He selected the basic skills for the beginning period as this would permit him to use the skills instruction to prepare the children for learning tasks in the following periods.

Daily Schedule

Opening Activities

Planning the Day

Basic Skills Block (Math, Reading, Language Arts)

Break

Basic Skills Block (continued)

Lunch

Social Studies and Literature

Science

Creative Experiences on alternate days with Health and Physical Education

Closing Activities

He Plans a Good Learning Atmosphere

Mr. Bond's classroom presented limitations on what he could do. He did the best he could, however, and was able to equip one corner of the room as a reading center, with supplementary books on science, literature, and social studies, which he displayed on a table. He arranged an attractive map and picture display on the bulletin board. It was designed to generate discussion on the social studies topic, "American People and Lands." He also located a table that he arranged as a science center, with materials and equipment that would be used in the study of "Electricity and Magnetism."

He Plans Learner Activities for the First Few Days

Mr. Bond consulted several sources to help him determine possible learner activities for the first week of school. The teachers' guides to the various children's textbooks had numerous suggestions for introducing the subjects. His planning for the first week resulted in the following ideas.

BASIC SKILLS BLOCK (MATHEMATICS, READING, LANGUAGE ARTS)

(Mathematics) Use the basal series math textbook to have children demonstrate level of computation skills in addition, subtraction, multiplication, and division. Also ascertain level of skill in working with fractions. Knowledge of measurement needs to be determined also.

(Reading) Use the basal reading text materials to obtain information on pupils' vocabulary development and their ability to employ word-attack skills. Oral and silent reading related to social studies activities will provide information about the children's ability to use such comprehension skills as selecting the main idea and recalling details.

(Language Arts) Provide children with writing experiences in order to determine their skill in using correct word forms, capitalization and punctuation, and sentence structure. Check handwriting skills with special attention to letter formation, legibility, and neatness. Also give spelling tests that contain words taught the previous year.

SOCIAL STUDIES AND LITERATURE

Plan the social studies activities around the room bulletin board, "American People and Lands." Assign reading based on the social studies topic to ascertain how well children can read in a content field.

SCIENCE, CREATIVE EXPERIENCES, HEALTH AND PHYSICAL
EDUCATION

Delay the beginning of formal learning activities in these curriculum areas until the children's basic skills levels have been
ascertained. The basic skills and social studies focus will con-
sume most of the instructional time during the first week.
A school library visit to obtain reading materials, group discussion on beginning a room weather station, and the discussion
time necessary to establish room citizenship will take up the
remaining time.

SELECTING GOALS AND OBJECTIVES

The teacher who plans on a weekly or daily basis, with knowledge of major goals for the school year, has a clear sense of
purpose and direction. The following days and weeks of instruction then can be planned within this general framework. In many
curriculum areas, the major goals to be achieved are already
stated—sometimes in the teacher's manual accompanying the
children's textbook, or in a "curriculum guide." In any event,
the beginning teacher should take the time necessary to preview
the various curriculum areas to ascertain major goals.[2]

NOTE TO READER

Now that you have seen how Miss Baxter and Mr. Bond went
about the task of organizing for the first few days of instruction,
you should make an effort to . . .

1. Talk with an experienced teacher about how to organize for
   the first few days.

2. Begin collecting ideas about the kinds of room environment—
   bulletin boards, learning centers, charts, displays—that would
   be useful in orienting children to the first few days of school.

---

[2] The goals, objectives, and learning activities included in the following sections have
been adapted from the Macmillan Basic Elementary-School Social Studies Series: Teacher's Annotated Edition, *Communities: Today and Yesterday,* Grade 3; and Teacher's Annotated
Edition, *The United States and the Other Americas,* Grade 5 (New York: Macmillan Publishing
Co., Inc., 1983).

Miss Baxter Identifies Objectives for the Social Studies

Miss Baxter selected the social studies area for a major unit of study with which to begin the school year. She selected this area because it offered so many possibilities for unifying learning from the various school subjects. She had considered the possibility of scheduling the social studies first thing in the morning, but decided against it. Her decision was based mainly on the fact that, on the primary-grade level, the language arts usually are scheduled first. She recalled a conversation with one of her professors during the past year, about the justification for scheduling language arts at the beginning of the school day. She had explained that it was largely because of tradition—a very powerful influence in education—and also because of the assumption that children are rested and fresh at the beginning of the day, and are better prepared to learn the complex skills included in reading and language instruction. Miss Baxter concluded that she could still relate learning from the social studies with the other subjects by scheduling it immediately after recess.

The social studies goals for the year were based on a study of "Communities." Miss Baxter discovered that Unit One in the social studies textbook was a good starting point for the children as it offered numerous possibilities for informational learning and skill building that could draw from a variety of curriculum areas. Miss Baxter selected the following objectives.

OBJECTIVES FOR A UNIT OF STUDY ON "MOVING TO A NEW COMMUNITY"

As a result of the study of this unit learners will

- understand that people, no matter where they live, need water, food, clothing, and some kind of shelter.
- know that a community is a place where people live and work together.
- develop reading skills such as skimming to locate specific information, reading for detail, and reading for main ideas.
- use beginning skills in reading maps, globes, and charts.
- gain information from pictures.
- organize and begin to carry out effective group work.
- appreciate the community as an organization for providing basic needs.

Mr. Bond Identifies Objectives for the Social Studies

Recalling the principal's emphasis on having the children follow the scope of learning contained in their textbooks, Mr. Bond decided to become thoroughly acquainted with what lay ahead. Because the first several days of school would be devoted to testing and review exercises in the basic skills, he decided to preview the social studies textbook to become acquainted with the goals for the year.

Mr. Bond found that he could easily adapt the textbook goals to the conditions that Mr. Park had stressed, at the same time permitting himself adequate leeway for improvisation. He selected the following objectives for the first unit of study.

OBJECTIVES FOR A UNIT OF STUDY ON "AMERICAN PEOPLE AND LANDS"

As a result of the study of this unit learners will

- know that the Americas have a great variety of climates, land surfaces, and natural resources.
- know that the American Indians probably came to the Americas from Asia; they developed varied civilizations in the Americas long ago.
- know how to use different parts of the book—table of contents, index, word lists, and so on.
- be able to work together in groups.
- appreciate contributions of the first Americans to our lives today.

PLANNING FOR INSTRUCTION BASED ON OBJECTIVES

Determination of objectives is a major accomplishment for the classroom teacher. It is only one step, however, in the continuous planning process. Once the objectives have been determined, the teacher must select learning activities that promote them. Many experienced classroom teachers have found it very useful to identify, in the form of a *sketch plan,* a variety of learning activities that can be developed over a period of several days. By doing this, the teacher also is able to anticipate the needed instructional materials. Beginning teachers, especially, should be prepared to engage in this type of planning, because school principals frequently ask them to do so. But experienced teachers also do "daily lesson planning," designed to implement the learning activities contained in the sketch plan. Skill in this form of planning provides a margin of confidence that goes a long way toward ensuring a good lesson. The teacher who begins a lesson by having anticipated a probable course of action for it has made progress toward removing barriers to learning. Skill in preparing sketch plans for a period of several days, and skill in developing a daily lesson plan, are prerequisites for the competent and qualified teacher.

Sketch Plan

The sketch plan provides an outline of suggestions for the teacher to draw on over the course of several days. It provides flexibility for teacher-pupil planning, because it is not locked into a day-by-day prescription of what is to be done. A complete realization of each objective is unrealistic for many children; thus, the teacher must evaluate carefully the extent to which individual children are succeeding. The plan should provide activities designed to implement the evaluation process.

NOTE TO READER

Ellen Baxter's sketch plan and daily lesson plan are included in the following sections to serve as examples of format and activities that are appropriate to each type of plan. The authors believe that the format for both types of plans is appropriate for any curriculum area.

Even though complete examples of Mr. Bond's sketch and daily lesson plans are not provided, references to their content will be made in the following chapter.

Miss Baxter's Sketch Plan

Miss Baxter decided to select several learning activities that would initiate instruction based on the objectives that she had selected earlier for the following unit of study.

A SKETCH PLAN FOR THE FIRST TEN TO TWELVE DAYS OF INSTRUCTION ON UNIT OF STUDY, "MOVING TO A NEW COMMUNITY"

Introductory Activities

1. Before beginning the unit of study have the children leaf through the book to become aware of pictures, maps, charts.

2. Discuss general organization of the book as outlined in the Contents.

3. Have learners examine the title page and ask questions about the title, "Moving to a New Community."

4. Introduce new words and terms presented in the unit.

5. Relate new words to pupils' own experiences, current events, and topics previously studied.

6. Discuss photographs of the two communities.

7. Discuss the importance of the globe and the map of the United States as a learning resource for the children in their study of communities.

8. To reinforce map and globe skills, it may be necessary to:
   • teach (or review) directions north, south, east, and west on maps
   • teach intermediate directions, e.g. "southwest" on maps
   • teach location of United States on classroom globe
   • teach locational skills and cardinal and intermediate directions on globe

9. During daily silent and oral reading assignments in textbook, include tasks that will prepare children to:
   • skim to locate specific information
   • read for detail
   • read pictures

10. Plan activities that extend the children's learning through working with others in small groups or on an individual basis to:
    • relate their own travel experiences along the route discussed in the textbook
    • interview others about their experiences
    • prepare a bulletin board on current events along the route traveled by the textbook family
    • begin a list of questions they would like to explore about their own community.

Possible Concluding Activities

1. Presentation of a bulletin board display entitled "Our Community."

2. Discussion of pupils' oral and written reports on trips they have made.

3. Presentation of art activities designed by the children to depict activities that provide for "basic needs" in a community.

4. Evaluation of pupils' understanding of "What is a community?" "What basic needs must be provided by a community?" "How communities differ in the way they satisfy basic needs," and "Why families sometimes move to other communities."

Daily Lesson Plan

The daily lesson plan contains specific provisions for teaching and learning. The sketch plan can serve as the source of the content for the daily lesson plan. These provisions make possible the successful interaction of instruction and management.

Every lesson should have a purpose that is understood by the children. In the daily lesson plan, the purpose is usually stated in the form of objectives that explain *what* pupils are to learn. The pupils also should understand the *why*. Lessons that do not provide sufficient clarity of purpose tend, more often than not, to fail. The daily lesson plan also should include the instructional materials necessary for the conduct of the lesson. The competent teacher appreciates the necessity of having identified, located, and made available the materials needed for the lesson. When this provision is missing the lesson often degenerates as a result of management problems. The sequence of the daily lesson plan provides for building readiness for what is to be done, delineates the learning activities, and provides for a summary and evaluation of the lesson.

There is no one best form for a lesson plan, nor is there a consensus on the level of specificity that should be included. As a general rule, teachers use brief, directional statements rather than detailed sentences that include what the teacher will actually say. A lesson plan should *not* be a narrative of what the teacher hopes to do. The importance of the daily lesson plan is based on the teacher's having planned for the components, as identified in the following format.

COMPONENTS OF A DAILY LESSON PLAN

1. Purpose

   Contains a statement of instructional objectives that include the specific learner outcomes that should result from the lesson.

2. Instructional Materials

   Provides a list of the materials or media needed to teach the lesson.

3. Procedure

   Describes the work-study activities that will occur during the lesson.

4. Summary and Assessment of Lesson

   Describes the closing activities designed for the lesson and evaluation in terms of the purposes stated in number 1.

Experienced teachers do not always write out in detail the specifics for each and every lesson during the day. This would be an awesome task. They rely on the sketch plan to provide direction for many ongoing activities. They do appreciate the need, however, to plan specifically for those lessons that introduce new skills, as well as those that require children to participate in a variety of activities. They realize lessons that do not require careful planning are those restricting children to a single learning activity—usually an assign-read-recite procedure. To reduce learning to this level would deprive children of acquiring the work-study and social skills they need in order to become productive citizens. The qualified and competent teacher accepts the fact that good teaching is hard work, and the habit of daily lesson planning can make it more enjoyable. The following is an example of a daily lesson plan Miss Baxter developed from her earlier sketch plan.

DAILY LESSON PLAN FOR BEGINNING THE UNIT OF STUDY "MOVING TO A NEW COMMUNITY"

1. Purpose of Lesson

   As a result of this lesson the children will

   - demonstrate their readiness to use the textbook and wall map.
   - be able to respond orally to questions about the likenesses and differences between two communities.
   - practice silent reading skills including skimming and identifying the main idea.

- participate in making suggestions for additional study about their own community.

2. Instructional Materials
   - Pupils' textbooks
   - Wall map of the United States

3. Procedure
   - Show children photographs of communities that differ from one another. Have them guess the type, location, and time period for each community. Discuss differences between the two communities.
   - Explain that they will be learning about new communities in their next few lessons.
   - Have them open their textbook to pages containing photographs of the family who is moving from one community to another. Ask questions about the pictures.
   - Ask children to read pages silently in order to answer questions about the family. (skimming skill)
   - Have designated children locate on the wall map the community where the family lives. Also locate the community where the family will be moving.
   - Have children do silent reading to identify the main idea that "communities provide four basic needs for people." List these on the chalkboard.

4. Summary and Assessment of Lesson
   - Close the lesson by asking children to be thinking of ways to learn more about their own community.
   - Explain that tomorrow they will learn more about the family and its plan to move to a new community.
   - Decide how much review will be needed for the lesson tomorrow, based on pupil participation in today's lesson.

COMPLETING THE FIRST WEEK OF SCHOOL

With their planning for the first few days of instruction completed, Miss Baxter and Mr. Bond were ready to begin formal group instruction. They now were faced with the challenge of managing children in groups. Both of these beginning teachers appreciated the importance of providing children with learning experiences in differentiated groups.

(Courtesy of Patricia A. Conrard.)

The teacher of the child in this photograph has planned to use the library resources to supplement classroom work. What provisions in the teacher's planning are necessary to make this experience successful?

Planning for the First Pupil-Progress Report

Barely having gotten the school year underway, Miss Baxter and Mr. Bond were confronted with the task of preparing pupil-progress reports. They were aware that elementary school teachers across the nation also were involved in a process that has become almost a ritual during the early part of November. Because a considerable amount of emphasis had been placed on its importance in their teacher education programs, they were fully aware of its major purposes:

1. To inform the child of his or her progress.
2. To provide parents with an assessment of the child's strengths and weaknesses.
3. To serve as a two-way mode of communication between home and school.

They also were aware that there are several basic types of pupil-progress reports used in elementary schools. The most common are (1) numerical or alphabetical ratings, (2) written narratives, (3) checklists, and (4) parent conferences. In actual practice, some schools use a combination of all of these.

MISS BAXTER PREPARES HER FIRST PARENT CONFERENCE

The parent conference is more prevalent at the primary-grade level than in the intermediate grades. This is partly because progress in beginning reading is easier to interpret in a conference setting than on a report card. The teacher can do a better job in explaining to the parent what the child is actually doing, what the needs are, and what the home can do to assist. The conference also enables the teacher to become aware of the parent's attitudes about the child, the home, and the school. This information is very useful to the teacher in establishing the best possible learning climate for the child, and in selecting appropriate materials for an individual.

Many primary-grade teachers conduct parent conferences during the first pupil-progress reporting period and write narrative reports during the remainder of the school year. Some teachers alternate parent conferences and written reports. Frequently, the first parent conference follows an "Open House," when parents are invited to attend school, meet the teacher, and listen to an explanation of the school program. This was the procedure at East Elementary School where Miss Baxter taught. The school principal began planning with the teachers early in September for the November "Open House" and the parent conferences. She stressed the following points:

1. Prepare a folder with samples of the child's schoolwork. Include for each subject representative products that show progress or the lack of it over a period of time.
2. Write anecdotes that reflect an objective description of the child's behavior.
3. Interpret the child's performance on readiness and achievement tests. Be sure to specify the level of performance in terms of his or her potential.

The principal also gave some helpful hints on conducting a good parent conference:

1. Begin on a positive note.
2. Accept the parent's feelings.
3. Emphasize the child's strengths.
4. Be specific about the pupil's learning difficulties.
5. Provide constructive suggestions.
6. Be receptive to the parent's suggestions.
7. Close on a positive note, and with a plan of action.

Miss Baxter discovered that the parent conferences were very rewarding. The conferences were scheduled over a period of two weeks, during which the children were dismissed an hour early. The "Open House" had tested her ability to describe for parents the type of work the children would be doing that year. She began to appreciate the time she had spent in determining goals for the school year and in getting acquainted with the textbooks and other instructional resources. These early planning activities had provided her with a frame of reference that made the pupil-reporting tasks much easier.

MR. BOND PREPARES HIS FIRST PUPIL-PROGRESS REPORT

Mr. Bond received pupil-progress report forms early in September. The school principal emphasized that teachers should keep a work folder for every child. He also suggested that in certain instances the teacher might find it useful to schedule a parent conference in order to inform the parents of the child's progress. The work samples would be very worthwhile to have in such instances.

Mr. Bond was disappointed that the form did not provide for pupil self-evaluation. He made the decision to improvise his own system for this purpose. He developed a simple report form that would allow children to evaluate their "School Habits." He began discussing it with the children as soon as the class had demonstrated that it could work together as a group. He told the class that he would discuss the form with each of them personally, at which time they would be asked to complete it. He prepared a large-scale version of the form for a wall chart. All pupils were given a copy for their notebooks.

When he began to confer with the children about their self-evaluations, he learned that some of them were realistic in their ratings, others were not. In each instance Mr. Bond was able to have a candid discussion with the child about behavior that is important to personal, social, and academic development. He felt much closer to each child following the discussion. He also spent a few minutes each day discussing the pupil-progress report form with them. He wanted them to know ahead of time what they were being evaluated on.

My School Habits

	Always	Usually	Seldom	Never
I assume responsibility				
I contribute to the group				
I work well with others				
I play well with others				
I do my best in my studies				
I take care of materials				
I follow school rules				

Mr. Bond found the planning he had done at the beginning of the year had been of great value to him in completing the pupil-progress reports. He followed the advice of a colleague in beginning the task of writing the reports a couple of weeks before they were due. He was very glad he had listened to the advice instead of waiting until the last minute to complete them.

Mr. Bond sent the pupil-progress reports home on schedule, and was pleasantly surprised to learn that many parents were pleased with their child's performance. He formed this conclusion on the basis of their written remarks when the forms were returned. Two parents requested follow-up conferences; Mr. Bond scheduled them during after-school hours. He found these personal contacts to be very useful in establishing a closer rapport with the parents.

Study Questions and Activities

1. List the things that a teacher should learn about when getting acquainted with a new school. Briefly describe how you would go about getting acquainted with the items on your list.

2. The text presents planning as a systematic, cyclical process. Some contend, however, that many teachers do "mental" planning on an impromptu basis rather than always following a systematic procedure. Are there occasions when the latter approach would be appropriate? If so, provide examples.

3. Miss Baxter and Mr. Bond were placed in elementary schools in which the school principals had different ideas about the purposes of education. Briefly describe each of these. Given a grade level of your choice, in which school would you feel more comfortable? Why?

4. What are the characteristics of a good learning atmosphere for children?

5. Interview three teachers and find out how they plan for learning activities:
   (a) Over a period of several days.
   (b) On a daily basis.

   Identify the similarities and differences in the types of planning done by these teachers. Is there any one of the three types you prefer? If so, why?

6. What are the essentials of a good parent conference?

7. Examine several examples of pupil-progress report forms to ascertain the emphasis that is placed on the child acquiring

    (a) Informational outcomes.

    (b) Skills outcomes.

    (c) Affective outcomes.

    Did you find a balance of informational, skills, and affective outcomes? If not, what did you find?

8. During a parent conference, how would you respond to a parent who is critical of a teacher colleague, or to a parent who is critical of the school, or to one who is critical of other children in your class?

    (a) Interview two experienced elementary school teachers to obtain examples of difficult questions they have received from parents and how they responded.

    (b) Role play a parent conference with one of your classmates. Include parent questions that challenge the teacher to provide a thoughtful, discreet response.

For Further Professional Study

Eisner, Elliot W. "The Kinds of Schools We Need." *Educational Leadership*, 4 (Oct. 1983), 48–55.

Forbes, Eileen, Kathy Thornburg, Barbara Birnie, Eva Schmidler, Linda Halas, Lana and Perry McWilliams, and William C. Millet. "Working with Parents." *Instructor*, 89 (March 1980), 51–58.

Goodlad, John I. *A Place Called School: Prospects for the Future*. New York: McGraw-Hill Book Company, 1984, Chaps. 5, 6, 7, 8.

Hunter, Madeline. "Knowing, Teaching, and Supervising." Chap. 2 in *Using What We Know About Teaching*. Philip L. Hosford, ed. Alexandria, Virginia: Association for Supervision and Curriculum Development, 1984, 169–192.

Kracht, James B., and James Patrick McGuire. "Developing Social Studies and Language Skills Using Community Resources." *Social Education*, 47 (Nov./Dec. 1983), 536–540.

Orlich, Donald C., Robert J. Harder, Richard C. Callahan, Constance

H. Kravas, Donald P. Kauchak, R. A. Pendergrass, Andrew J. Keogh, and Dorothy I. Hellene. *Teaching Strategies: A Guide to Better Instruction.* Lexington, Mass.: D. C. Heath and Company, 1980, Chap. 5.

Shepherd, Gene D., and William B. Ragan. *Modern Elemetary Curriculum,* 6th ed. New York: Holt, Rinehart and Winston, 1982, Chaps. 4, 5.

Yinger, Robert J. "A Study of Teacher Planning." *The Elementary School Journal,* (Jan. 1980), 107–127.

Instructional Objectives

THE QUALIFIED AND COMPETENT TEACHER . . .

1. Understands the role of educational goals and instructional objectives in the teaching and learning process.
2. Is familiar with the major types of instructional objectives and their purposes.
3. Is able to write nonbehavioral and behavioral objectives.
4. Understands the nature and interdependence of informational, skills, and affective outcomes.
5. Recognizes the importance of sequencing instructional objectives according to sound educational principles.
6. Is sensitive to the need to select instructional objectives that are relevant to the needs, abilities, and interests of children.

Performance Criteria

As a result of the serious study of this chapter, the student should be able to . . .

1. Distinguish between educational goals and instructional objectives.
2. Cite examples of the major types of instructional objectives.
3. Recognize the three elements of a behavioral objective.
4. Write nonbehavioral and behavioral objectives.
5. Identify and prepare examples of instructional objectives in the informational, skills, and affective areas.
6. Prepare a sequence of instructional objectives based on sound educational principles.

Schools are expected to serve the purposes that society has established for them. As noted in Chapter 1, schools in this nation traditionally have been expected to develop *basic literacy,* provide *citizenship education,* and to contribute to the *personal development* of children. Over the years, these purposes have found expression through *educational goals* that contain statements of desired outcomes of schooling. Statements such as "to develop literacy in oral and written English," "to develop an understanding and appreciation of our cultural heritage," and "to develop a healthy self-concept" are examples of educational goals that reflect the three traditional purposes of schooling as established by society.

Each of these statements identifies a desired outcome of schooling.

Educational goals are achieved over an extended period of instruction. The three examples cited previously normally would require several school years for their accomplishment, perhaps even an entire school career for some pupils. Nevertheless, educational goals provide a sense of direction for American education. One finds educational goals that reflect the basic purposes of education stated in a variety of sources that includes news releases in communications media, documents prepared by local schoolboards, state departments of education, and policy statements of agencies and commissions at the national level. Teachers frequently encounter educational goals in curriculum documents and in teachers' manuals that accompany pupil textbooks.

Most professional associations express their purpose through statements of educational goals that they seek to achieve. Several of these sources are described in Chapter 12. Experienced teachers are acquainted with such sources and rely on them for guidance in curriculum planning.

At the classroom level, teachers focus their attention on attaining learner outcomes that will result from the effective teaching of a lesson or unit of study. Desired learner outcomes at this level are stated as *instructional objectives.* These statements have an immediate intent. They also specify the learning outcome more sharply than do educational goals. Thus, the educational goal, "to develop literacy in oral and written English," when translated into an instructional objective for children, might be stated, "As a result of this lesson, pupils will increase their awareness of sentence structure by using the subject, verb, and object correctly in oral and written expression."

Even though the terms *goals* and *objectives* sometimes are used interchangeably in educational literature, this practice fails to acknowledge the proper relationship between educational goals and instructional objectives. Educational goals ordinarily reflect a synthesis of the expressed ideas or values of a given society or cultural group. They usually are normative in this respect, in that they reflect the prevailing ideas and values considered to be the most desirable by the society or cultural group. As such, they do not account for the variability that teachers encounter in specific classroom situations. To be made operational, these broad general statements must be translated into instructional objectives that are relevant to the specific situation. Both types of statements serve the critical purpose of providing the means for teachers to conceptualize the direction and shape of learning activities.

Using Instructional Objectives

It is important that the teacher prepare instructional objectives that reflect the related educational goal. For example, at the present time, schools are stressing the goal, "to prepare citizens who are competent in the basic skills." Such a goal requires teachers to use objectives that enable them to measure the extent to which it has been achieved. This approach is a reflection of the thrust for accountability in education. It is based in part on the assumption that the best criterion for evaluating the teacher's performance is to determine whether or not pupils are learning. Some who favor *merit pay* for teachers use this assumption as the basis for the determination of teacher merit. Educational literature frequently contains references to the "evaluation of the product," another way of emphasizing the use of objectives that can be measured. As a result, this type of objective has been given high visibility in educational circles. However, experienced teachers realize the importance of providing children with a variety of learning experiences. If instructional objectives are limited to those that restrict learning to "what can be measured," the richness that a variety of learning activities brings to children would be lost. Further, if teachers develop the habit of selecting instructional objectives from a ready-made list, composed in another setting, the spontaneity and the capacity to meet the needs, abilities, and interests of a particular group of children would be greatly reduced.

We believe that instructional objectives should be selected or prepared by the classroom teacher for a particular group of learners. Referring to other sources containing examples of instructional objectives may well be desirable when it is done to provide variety and enrichment. But when a ready-made list is followed exclusively, teaching and learning might become a "cookbook" activity. Hence, a good instructional objective states clearly what pupils are supposed to learn. It provides a good match between the expected learner outcome and the capacity of the children to achieve it. This requires that the objective be based on the realities of the actual classroom wherein the learners are located.

PURPOSES OF OBJECTIVES

Teachers prepare objectives to serve a variety of purposes in education. They are essential to:

1. The development of unit plans and daily lesson plans.
2. The individualization of instruction.
3. The development of effective study habits.
4. The development of group socialization skills.
5. Evaluation of pupil growth and development.
6. Self-evaluation by the teacher.

Each of these purposes contributes to the development of a program of instruction that emphasizes significant rather than trivial learner outcomes. The preparation, implementation, and evaluation of objectives constitute a sorting out process that results in the continual improvement of the quality of teaching and learning.

TYPES OF INSTRUCTIONAL OBJECTIVES

There are several ways to classify instructional objectives. One way is to refer to them as "general" or "specific" statements of expected learner outcomes. This particular dualism has prompted the recent emphasis on so-called behavioral objectives. Proponents of specificity contend that statements of specific, concrete, and measurable outcomes are necessary to provide quality learning and instruction. Advocates of generality insist that such specific statements restrict learning opportunities to those that require measurement. They conclude that objectives based on higher-order learning are likely to be eliminated because they frequently do not lend themselves to precise measurement. Thus, these teachers feel uncomfortable with instructional objectives that tend to quantify learning to such an extent.

Advocates of specificity for instructional objectives believe equally strongly that learner outcomes must be observable immediately or that they must lend themselves to measurement in order to determine whether or not learning has occurred. Teachers who subscribe to this point of view prepare instructional objectives that comply with the elements of a *behavioral* objective. This type of instructional objective frequently describes the mediating conditions through which the expected learning is to be achieved. Also, it describes the means for determining whether or not the level of attainment set forth in the objective has been achieved. An example of each type of instructional objective follows.

EXAMPLE 1. A BEHAVIORAL OBJECTIVE

Given a worksheet following a lesson on subtraction, pupils will be able to rename and subtract numbers named by three-place numerals at the rate of two problems a minute with 80 per cent accuracy.

EXAMPLE 2. A NONBEHAVIORAL OBJECTIVE

Following a lesson on subtraction, the pupil will know how to rename and subtract numbers named by three-place numerals.

The use of the term *behavioral* is confusing to many beginners because they tend to view any statement of an expected learner outcome to be based on one form of behavior or another. The behavior may be somewhat vague, as in the case of the objective designed to enable the pupil to "know how to rename and subtract numbers named by three-place numerals." Nevertheless, the infinitive "to know" certainty implies a behavior. The essence of the distinction between a nonbehavioral and a behavioral objective seems to require a more careful examination in order to determine the difference.

Many teachers strongly oppose the use of behavioral objectives because they believe these objectives are an expression of behaviorism. They insist that there is much learning that does not result in overt pupil behavior. These are the more subtle forms of learning that stem from feelings and appreciations, and are referred to as *affective* learning. At a philosophical level, a conceptual dualism has resulted from the attention to behavioral objectives. This may be described as a behavioristic-humanistic dualism. Some educators argue that the more important learning behaviors—those on the higher informational levels, and especially those that reside in the area of feelings and attitudes—cannot be stated behaviorally.

On the other side of the debate are those educators who subscribe to E. L. Thorndike's statement, made over sixty years ago, to the effect that:

> Whatever exists at all exists in some amount. To know it thoroughly involves knowing its quantity as well as its quality. Education is concerned with changes in human beings; a change is a difference between two conditions; each of these conditions is known to us only by the products produced by it—things made, words spoken, acts performed, and the like. To measure any of these products means to define its amount in some way so that competent persons will know how large it is, better than they would without measurement.[1]

Thorndike, a pioneer in educational psychology, insisted that objectives must be validated through the measurement of learner outcomes. His views were based on a theory of learning that regarded the learning process as the forming of bonds between specific stimuli and observable responses. This theory has been refined and readapted since Thorndike's time. The most recent adaptation has resulted from a combination of several forces: instructional technology and programmed instruction; the accountability movement; and the operant conditioning theory supported by B. F. Skinner's assumptions about learning. Skinner defines teaching "as an arrangement of contingencies of reinforcement under which behavior changes."[2] Learning, then, becomes divided into a sufficient number of very small steps, in which reinforcement is dependent upon the accomplishment of each step. Skinner has a wide following. There are educators who believe that his theory is highly appropriate in the field of special education devoted to children who have problems or disabilities which impede learning. There are other educators who insist that his theory is inappropriate for the instruction of all children. They argue that many pupils are capable of learning without the need for reinforcement at every step of the way.

---

[1] E. L. Thorndike, "The Nature, Purposes, and General Methods of Measurements of Educational Products." The Seventeenth Yearbook of the National Society for the Study of Education, Part II, *The Measurement of Educational Products* (Bloomington, Ill.: Public School Publishing Company, 1918), Chap. 2, p. 16.
[2] B. F. Skinner, *The Technology of Teaching* (New York: Appleton-Century-Crofts, 1968), p. 113.

Still other educators criticize Skinner's assumptions about learning on the grounds that they are based on a mechanical interpretation of human nature.

It seems unfortunate that this movement, which could result in a sharpening of the educational process through more precise attention to its outcomes, finds authorities polarized in their views concerning it. We believe there is a place for both perspectives on instructional objectives. It can be argued that learning has taken place when there is, on the part of the learner, a change in personal meaning. This change in personal meaning may or may not be reflected in a change in observable behavior. Whenever practicable, of course, an observable change in behavior should be sought. Circumstances may dictate the particular approach best suited to enhance learning. Because instructional objectives provide the directional statements necessary to facilitate and to assess learning, it follows that they must reflect variety and balance. This is best accomplished by giving priority to the nature of the expected learning prior to making a decision as to which type of instructional objective would be most appropriate.

Writing Instructional Objectives

NONBEHAVIORAL OBJECTIVES

Experienced teachers are cognizant of the fact that all instructional objectives should be stated with sufficient precision to make clear what pupils are supposed to learn. Consequently, teachers sometimes prepare nonbehavioral objectives that express in broad general terms what the children are supposed to learn. This type of objective does not include the precision contained in behavioral objectives. It does, however, state clearly what the child is expected to learn. The following statements are provided as illustrations of nonbehavioral objectives.

As a result of instruction the learner will

- learn to interpret the symbols on a map of the community.
- learn that a community is a place where people live and work together.

- gain a knowledge of how animals prepare for winter.
- learn to write the cursive form of the letter *b*.
- learn that verbs are action verbs.
- develop the ability to do short division of numbers.
- gain an appreciation of the importance of cooperation in the lunchroom.

The preceding examples of nonbehavioral objectives provide clear statements of what children are expected to learn. Many teachers prefer to prepare instructional objectives in this manner and to specify the details at the time the lesson is taught. These teachers like the flexibility allowed by nonbehavioral objectives. They would feel uncomfortable with the precision that behavioral objectives require.

BEHAVIORAL OBJECTIVES

A behavioral objective does not necessarily possess an inherent quality that makes it better than a nonbehavioral objective. What actually makes the difference is the purpose each is supposed to serve. Because this may be determined by the nature of the desired learner outcome, the argument about which type of objective is superior is, at best, an unproductive exercise.

Behavioral objectives do more than simply state an immediately observable learner outcome—they also describe how it is to be achieved and at what level of attainment. These characteristics make a behavioral objective ideally suited to simple lessons that can be taught in a short period of time and evaluated immediately.

With the current societal expectations for basic skill learning, the beginning teacher should be competent in writing behavioral objectives. These objectives provide an excellent format for instructional objectives that are designed to teach factual information and low-level skills. Behavioral objectives enable the teacher to determine quickly whether to:

1. reteach the lesson, or to
2. extend the learning from the lesson through additional practice activities, or to
3. progress to more difficult learning tasks.

(Courtesy of Herb Williams.)

Experiences such as the one in this photograph can serve multiple objectives. Name three objectives that might be appropriate for this situation.

The three elements of behavioral objectives are (1) the expected learner behavior; (2) the condition within which the behavior is to occur; and (3) the acceptable level or standard for the expected behavior.

The following is an example of a behavioral objective containing these three elements:

> On a science quiz containing twenty examples, pupils will differentiate between descriptions of physical and chemical changes, with 80 per cent accuracy.

In this example, the *expected learner outcome* is that "pupils will differentiate between descriptions of physical and chemical changes;" the *condition* is that the learner will provide evidence of success "on a science quiz containing twenty examples," and the *acceptable level of attainment* is "with 80 per cent accuracy."

The following examples illustrate other observable criteria for determining whether or not the acceptable level of attainment has been achieved.

1. After reading the story, "The Tallest Tree," children will write the story in their own words, including a minimum of five events.
2. During class discussion, children will ask permission before speaking by raising their hands.
3. In response to a lesson on creative writing, children will produce a written product of their own choosing and design.
4. Given a spelling list of twenty words, children will write the words with 80 per cent accuracy.

ACTION WORDS

A verb is a verb, or is it? A good verb to use in a behavioral objective is one that denotes an observable behavior. Which of the words in the following list meet this criterion?

To understand	To solve	To cite
To locate	To read	To define
To appreciate	To feel	To write
To compare	To name	To listen
To believe	To realize	To recall
To list	To comprehend	To know

Instructional Objectives in the Curriculum

The best known effort to classify instructional objectives according to the nature of expected learner outcomes is that of Bloom, Krathwohl, and their associates who have provided educators with two taxonomies of educational objectives.[3] The taxonomies have given educators a system that provides a frame of reference for communicating about learner outcomes. Bloom, Krathwohl, and their colleagues originally classified instructional objectives according to three basic domains: (1) the cognitive domain, based on the recall or recognition of knowledge and the development of intellectual skills; (2) the affective domain, based on a hierarchy of interests, attitudes, appreciations, and values; and (3) the psychomotor domain, based on a variety of learning activities that are dependent on the acquisition of attendant manipulative or motor skills.

The cognitive and affective taxonomies have been widely used. A third taxonomy for the psychomotor domain was authored by Harrow at a later date.[4] Bloom, Krathwohl, and associates discovered in their early research that the preponderance of instructional objectives reflected in the literature was based on cognitive and affective behaviors, but only a few dealt with psychomotor learner outcomes. Priority was placed on the development of the first two—the cognitive and the affective domains.

The developers of the taxonomies acknowledged that it is difficult to separate cognitive and affective behaviors. Their decision to classify the behaviors according to two separate domains was based on the assumption that educators do make distinctions between the two in developing instructional objectives. They assumed, therefore, that the applicability of the taxonomies would be greater by separating them.

In using the taxonomies to develop objectives, the teacher should be careful to avoid isolating cognitive, affective, and psychomotor behaviors from each other. It is perhaps unfortunate that the term *domain* is used, because it implies a separation of spheres of activity. But these separate classifications are useful for the development of a broad range of learner behaviors. As such, the taxonomies are excellent tools for curriculum development and evaluation.

At the classroom level, the teacher must remember that planning for learning and instruction should be based on the recogni-

---

[3] Benjamin S. Bloom, ed., *Taxonomy of Educational Objectives, Handbook I: Cognitive Domain* (New York: David McKay Co., Inc., 1956). Also David R. Krathwohl, Benjamin S. Bloom, and Bertram B. Masia, *Taxonomy of Educational Objectives, Handbook II: Affective Domain* (New York: David McKay Co., Inc. 1964).
[4] Anita J, Harrow, *A Taxonomy of the Psychomotor Domain* (New York: David McKay Co., Inc., 1972).

tion that these domains are interdependent in terms of the learner's needs, abilities, and interests. The child who is asked to reproduce a picture or a map is performing a psychomotor task; however, the quality of performance is dependent on cognitive and affective behaviors as well—knowledge of maps and the extent of interest. Children who have poor muscular coordination may learn a particular psychomotor activity, but their attitude toward it may remain forever negative unless they have a teacher who understands the interdependence of these areas of learning. Many adults seem to have a fear of mathematics, which originated early in their school life. Evidently their teachers did not understand the importance of the interdependence of the domains to build their confidence and self-esteem in learning mathematics. There are many examples that could be cited to illustrate the interdependence of the three so-called domains. Suffice it to say that instructional objectives should reflect a balance of the three.

We believe that instructional objectives in the curriculum can be developed for teaching purposes according to those that provide for (1) informational, (2) skills, and (3) affective outcomes. Examples of each of these are presented in the following sections.

DEVELOPING OBJECTIVES FOR INFORMATIONAL OUTCOMES

In the broad area of informational learning, the most important thing for the beginning teacher to remember in developing objectives is to provide children with opportunities to acquire intellectual abilities that extend beyond the acquisition of knowledge. One of the perennial criticisms of teaching is based on the assertion that children are bored with spending their time in memorizing and recalling facts. This is unfortunate, because the teacher has countless opportunities to provide children with learning activities that are intellectually challenging and interesting to them. The careful development and sequencing of questions, and the use of the inquiry and the integrated curriculum modes of teaching, are suited to the development of these higher-order levels of informational learning. The interdependence of the informational, skills, and affective areas of learning is actualized by the teacher who, during the course of the school year, prepares instructional objectives that include a sampling of various dimensions of informational learning. Not all children will be capable of acquiring informational learning on the higher levels at the same time. A few children in the typical classroom may not be able to get beyond the literal level of comprehension during the year. But certainly the majority of children are capable of doing so when the teacher is skilled in varying instruction to accommodate pupil differences.

The following examples of nonbehavioral and behavioral objectives illustrate a range of informational outcomes in the science and social studies areas of the curriculum.

NONBEHAVIORAL OBJECTIVES

Following the study of units in the social studies and science, children will understand that

- communities were developed to serve different purposes.
- communities depend on one another for many necessities of life.
- communities consist of many kinds of workers.
- air transportation has changed the way we live.
- balloons are lighter-than-air types of air transportation.
- airplanes are heavier-than-air types of air transportation.
- animals require oxygen for survival.

BEHAVIORAL OBJECTIVES

- After reading a chapter on why European settlers came to the English colonies, children will recall four of the five major reasons given.
- The child can apply rules developed by the class for good citizenship by following them on the playground during free-time activities.
- On a science quiz containing twenty examples, children will differentiate between descriptions of physical and chemical changes, with 80 per cent accuracy.
- Following a science lesson, the child will demonstrate that a current-carrying wire acts as a magnet.

DEVELOPING OBJECTIVES FOR SKILLS OUTCOMES

The elementary school curriculum provides for skills outcomes in the areas of the basic skills, study skills, intellectual skills, and socialization skills. Each of these four skill areas includes a number of skills and subskills that require careful teaching in order for successful pupil learning to occur. The teaching of these major skill areas is dealt with in Chapter 9.

The emphasis in this section is on those skills that have a psychomotor basis. The current societal emphasis on the basic skills requires the teacher to give careful attention to the psychomotor development of the child as a necessary prerequisite for the learning of the basic skills.

Objectives for skills outcomes that are based on the child's psychomotor development emphasize learning activities that involve movement. Frequently the objectives include the manipulation of objects or materials that require psychomotor coordination. At other times they focus on various movements of the child in an effort to develop such skills as eye-hand coordination and the like.

Skills outcomes are stressed in those areas of the curriculum that place emphasis on desirable movement behavior such as in the areas of the arts, physical education, special education, and early childhood education. The qualified and competent teacher, however, recognizes the importance of psychomotor development as the prerequisite for achieving various learner outcomes in *all* areas of the curriculum. The following instructional objective illustrates this point.

> After a demonstration of manuscript writing, pupils will write the letter *a* in conformity with the specifications presented by the teacher.

In this example, the child's eye-hand coordination, small muscle control, and skill in forming circles and curved lines are prerequisites for the achievement of the objective. The experienced teacher ascertains the status of each child's development before setting such an objective.

The psychomotor domain, as developed by Anita J. Harrow, contains six classification levels of psychomotor development, beginning with simple movements and proceeding along a continuum of increasing complexity to movements that are highly complex. These classification levels include, in order of difficulty, reflex movements, basic fundamental movements, perceptual abilities, physical abilities, skilled movements, and nondiscursive communication.[5]

The following examples illustrate instructional objectives that emphasize skills outcomes in the language arts, physical education, and math areas.

NONBEHAVIORAL OBJECTIVES

As a result of instruction, children will

- be able to perform long division of numbers.
- demonstrate the ability to jump rope.
- discriminate between circles, squares, and rectangles.
- be able to distinguish between the consonant and vowel sounds.

BEHAVIORAL OBJECTIVES

- Following a demonstration by the teacher, the child will be able to draw vertical and horizontal straight lines according to the teacher's specifications.
- Given four coins of different denominations, the child will be able to identify each coin by touch, with 100 per cent accuracy.
- The child will be able to identify consonant and vowel sounds presented audibly by the teacher, with 100 per cent accuracy.
- As a result of the lesson, the learner will be able to find the least common multiple of ten numbers with 80 per cent accuracy.
- Following a demonstration by the teacher, the child will be able to hop and skip correctly.

DEVELOPING OBJECTIVES FOR AFFECTIVE OUTCOMES

The recent emphasis on informational and basic skills learning has occurred at the expense of other kinds of learning, such as affective outcomes. Affective education contributes to the total

[5] See Anita J. Harrow, *A Taxonomy of the Psychomotor Domain* for a description of the six classification levels of the psychomotor domain.

(Courtesy of Patricia A. Conrard.)

What instructional objectives might the teacher have in mind for involving children in an activity such as the one shown here?

development of children, who need to develop an appreciation of various aspects of their cultural and physical environments. At the same time, children need to be able to discriminate between those aspects of their daily lives that have aesthetic value and those that do not. They should be able to discern behavior that is constructive rather than destructive. Hence, they must be skillful in the process of valuing in order to appreciate aspects of their existence that are aesthetic and constructive.

Affective education is not intended to indoctrinate children with a single point of view or the "correct belief." Rather, it is intended to produce enlightened citizens who have an open mind and who are capable of perceiving the affective aspects of living. Instructional objectives that promote affective outcomes are necessary to provide learning activities that promote the affective growth of children.

The following examples of instructional objectives in the art, music, and school citizenship areas emphasize affective outcomes.

NONBEHAVIORAL OBJECTIVES

As a result of instruction, children will

• enjoy rhythms and pantomimes.
• appreciate art depicting pioneer life.
• understand the importance of folk music in the development of the nation.
• accept the importance of classroom rules and routines.

BEHAVIORAL OBJECTIVES

• Following the lesson, the child will be able to repeat a simple melody with accuracy.
• Following a demonstration, the learner will be able to move in rhythm to music.
• During free-choice time, children will choose music and art activities that were presented in previous lessons.
• Following the teacher's discussion about the need for assistance in caring for classroom materials and equipment, children will volunteer.

Sequencing Instructional Objectives

So far we have emphasized that teachers should (1) be able to distinguish between educational goals and instructional objectives, (2) know the major types of instructional objectives, (3) be able to write nonbehavioral and behavioral objectives, and (4) understand the nature and interdependence of informational, skills, and affective outcomes. An equally important competence consists of effectively sequencing instructional objectives.

As noted at the beginning of this chapter, there are two ways of stating objectives. One is to provide an educational goal to identify a learner outcome that requires an extended period of time to accomplish. The second is to state an instructional objective that specifies a behavior to be achieved on a short-time basis—at the end of a single lesson or the conclusion of a unit of work. Sequencing requires that there be a relationship between these two types of statements, one that provides direction and continuity leading to long-range achievement.

The most commonly used way to order instructional objectives is to sequence them according to a given curricular area such as math, language arts, or science. Objectives also may be ordered within a particular curricular area according to the informational, skills, and affective outcomes desired. The teacher should examine instructional objectives to ascertain the most effective way to sequence them for instruction. Given the proper relationship between the objectives and the underlying educational goal, many teachers prefer to sequence objectives according to levels of difficulty. Thus, objectives are sequenced on a simple-to-complex continuum. This approach provides a sound psychological basis for teaching and learning. It permits children to move from one objective to the next only after having acquired the knowledge or skill prerequisite to the mastery of the following objective.

The following example illustrates the sequencing of instructional objectives on a simple-to-complex continuum.

As a result of instruction, children will

- develop an awareness of the importance of the sentence by telling a story using complete sentences.
- demonstrate awareness of sentence structure by writing a complete sentence.
- identify the subject, verb, and object in sentence form.
- use subject, verb, and object correctly in written sentence form.
- identify simple adjectives, adverbs, and prepositional phrases in sentence form.
- use simple adjectives, adverbs, and prepositional phrases in sentence form.

- independently use correct sentence structure in daily oral and written work.

The fact that children learn at differing rates sometimes necessitates that the teacher provide differentiated instruction. Small group and individualized instruction frequently is used to accommodate the different learning rates among pupils. Clearly written instructional objectives that are sequenced effectively enable teachers to meet the individual needs and interests of children. When these conditions are present, teaching and learning can proceed with a reasonable assurance of success.

Study Questions and Activities

1. Select a children's textbook in a subject area and grade level of your choice. Consult the teacher's manual that accompanies the textbook for the *instructional objectives* that are included. Examine the objectives in order to determine whether they would provide children with a variety of learning experiences.

2. The text presents six purposes that are served by instructional objectives. Refer to the teacher's manual that you selected for Study Activity number 1 and determine which of the six purposes are met by the objectives in this source.

3. What kinds of learning activities are served best by nonbehavioral objectives? By behavioral objectives? Give specific examples.

4. Refer to the teacher's manual that you selected for Study Activity number 1. Select three nonbehavioral instructional objectives and rewrite these as behavioral objectives.

5. Use the subject area and grade level of your choice and prepare three original instructional objectives for:
   (a) Informational outcomes.
   (b) Skills outcomes.
   (c) Affective outcomes.

6. Most educators would agree that it is difficult to prepare behavioral objectives for affective outcomes. Why do you think this is so?

7. Why is it important that instructional objectives be sequenced carefully?

For Further Professional Study

Brophy, Jere E. "How Teachers Influence What Is Taught and Learned in Classrooms." *The Elementary School Journal,* **83** (Sept. 1982), 1–13.

Davis, O. L., Jr. "Liberating Learning." *Educational Leadership,* **41** (Oct. 1983), 58–60.

Goodlad, John I. *A PLace Called School: Prospects for the Future.* New York: McGraw-Hill Book Company, 1984, Chap. 2.

Melton, Reginald F. "Resolution of Conflicting Claims Concerning the Effect of Behavioral Objectives on Student Learning." *Review of Educational Research,* **48** (Spring 1978), 291–302.

Orlich, Donald C., Robert J. Harder, Richard C. Callahan, Constance H. Kravas, Donald P. Kauchak, R. A. Pendergrass, Andrew J. Keogh, and Dorothy I. Hellene. *Teaching Strategies: A Guide to Better Instruction.* Lexington, Mass.: D.C. Heath and Company, 1980, Chaps. 2, 3, 4.

Orlosky, Donald E., ed. *Introduction to Education.* Columbus, Ohio: Charles E. Merrill Publishing Company, 1982, Chaps. 5, 10.

Shepherd, Gene D., and William B. Ragan. *Modern Elementary Curriculum,* 6th ed. New York: Holt, Rinehart and Winston, 1982, Chaps. 6, 7, 8, 9, 10, 11.

Thornell, John G. "Reconciling Humanistic and Basic Education." *The Clearing House,* **53** (Sept. 1979), 23–24.

Modes
of Teaching

5

THE QUALIFIED AND COMPETENT TEACHER . . .

1. Is familiar with the assumptions, major purposes, role of the teacher, role of the learner, role of instructional resources, and methods of evaluation for each of the four modes of teaching.
2. Knows when and how best to use various modes of teaching.
3. Is skillful in using specific teaching methods associated with each of the four modes.

Performance Criteria

As a result of the serious study of this chapter, the student should be able to . . .

1. Describe, behaviorally, the role of the teacher and the role of the learner in the expository, inquiry, demonstration, and integrated curriculum modes.
2. Provide a specific example of applications of different modes of teaching from at least two areas of the school curriculum.
3. Demonstrate his or her ability to use the expository, inquiry, and demonstration modes by teaching a group of children or a peer group.
4. Provide a detailed description of how he or she would organize a classroom in the integrated curriculum mode, or, where circumstances will allow, actually demonstrate the ability to use the integrated curriculum mode by teaching a class.

Human beings have been teaching other human beings for a long, long time; even from the beginning of their tenure on earth many millions of years ago. Having been doing it for such a long time, one might assume that a great deal is known about the teaching process. One might think that there may have evolved, over these countless generations, at least some principles of teaching on which there is general agreement. Regrettably, this is not the case. There is a great deal of disagreement, even among well-informed persons, about what constitutes good teaching and how teaching should take place. Perhaps this will always be so, because teaching involves not only the conduct of instruction; it reflects one's social philosophy regarding how children should be treated, what the ultimate values of education are, how the results of learning are to be demonstrated, how teachers and children should interact, and a host of similar issues. Outside of the teaching profession, much of what we think we know about teaching and learning is a distillation of folk wisdom that has come down through the ages, and that is unacceptable today in terms of present social values. Examples are "Spare the rod and spoil the child"; "Children should be seen but not heard." In this century the profession of teaching has made some progress in moving away from a reliance on folk wisdom and has sought to base more of its decision making on the findings from research. Needless to say, in the research on teaching, the surface has hardly been scratched.

It is undoubtedly true that much of good teaching is the application of common-sense principles. For example, when one is interested in something, one is more likely to want to learn than if one is not interested in it. Consequently, anything the teacher can do to create interest would be beneficial to learning. Young children have difficulty sitting quietly for long periods of time; therefore, on a common-sense basis, the teacher would provide a balance among activities calling for quiet time and those requiring movement. Children learn at differing rates, and it therefore follows that slower learners need more time and teacher assistance than faster learners. There is nothing wrong with the application of common sense to teaching. Indeed, the problem is quite the contrary. As has been noted by many observers, it is unfortunate that common sense is such an uncommon commodity.

The act of teaching is so complex that it is nearly impossible to demonstrate that a specific way of teaching is superior to other ways for all purposes, with all teachers, with all children, for all times, and in all circumstances. Time and again, those who supervise the work of teachers report remarkable exceptions to standard practice. Certain procedures, teaching styles, and techniques that are generally not recommended seem to work well for a specific teacher. We are forced to conclude that there are many good ways to teach. Although there are sound guidelines now available from research, individual teachers need to adapt what they do to their own personality styles and to the idiosyncrasies of the situations in which they find themselves. The dynamics and flow of day to day work with children call for teacher behavior that is flexible and fluid, accommodating and adjusting to the constant unfolding of classroom circumstances. This means that the teacher is continually making decisions—when to negotiate, when to hold firm, when to intervene, when to let events play themselves out. The decision-making ability and the judgment that goes with it undoubtedly have much to do with the success of the teacher.

It is important for the teacher to be mindful of the relationship between management of the classroom and conducting instruction. Some modes of teaching make learner behavior more manageable because children are not placed in situations where it is easy for them to become disruptive. Other teaching modes are an invitation to management challenges because of the permissive environment in which children work. Beginning teachers may find it advisable to defer the use of loosely structured modes of teaching until they have developed a sense of confidence in their classroom management capability.

Contrasting the Teaching Modes

Each of the four modes of teaching to be discussed here has value in achieving specific purposes. The teacher may develop a preference for one or another of these modes but the competent teacher must be skillful in using more than a single mode appropriately. In order to do so, the teacher will have to understand the basic theory that underlies each and must also be able to use specific teaching skills associated with each. It is important to note that some methods, such as discussion, can be used effectively with any mode. We now turn to an examination of the four modes of teaching in terms of (1) the assumptions underlying each, (2) the purposes to be served, (3) the role of the teacher, (4) the role of the learner, (5) the use of instructional materials, and (6) the methods of evaluation to be used by each.

The Expository Mode

The term *expository mode* is derived from the concept *exposition*, which means, most simply, to provide an explanation. In the context of teaching, exposition has to do with the teacher's providing facts, ideas, and other essential information to the learners. Expository strategies are *telling* or *explaining* strategies. Suppose, for example, that a teacher was about to present the concept *boundary line* in a social studies lesson, using an expository strategy. Displayed about the room might be maps of the local community or city, a home-state map showing counties, a map of the United States showing the states, and one of North America showing the countries. There might also be photographs showing stateline markers, border crossings between countries, and a photograph of the sign at the entrance to the city. Perhaps the teacher would begin the explanation by citing an analogous situation familiar to the children, such as the areas assigned to different groups on the playground. Visual devices would be used to explain the meaning of the concept *boundary line*. Children would be provided not one but many examples of the concept in a variety of settings. After this explanation, there would be some discussion, along with follow-up work calling for the application of the concept to new situations. The reader will recognize this as a familiar mode of teaching.

In the example cited, it was the teacher who was doing the explaining; but other sources of information and data are often used in expository teaching. The most frequently used resource other than the teacher is the textbook. Any of the standard learning resources such as films, filmstrips, pictures, encyclopedias, the library, and community resources can be, and frequently are, used in expository teaching.

Expository teaching is the primary object of criticism by those who favor inquiry strategies. Often it is claimed that exposition concerns itself with the *"mere* transmission of information." We do not share this point of view. Exposition, if well done, can be an effective teaching strategy, even with children in the primary grades. Some of the most interesting and long-remembered experiences of elementary school children are short and exciting explanations provided by an animated teacher. The problem is that teachers often do *too much* expository teaching; *too much* talking and explaining, with a corresponding reduction in the use of other, more learner-involving strategies. It is doubtless true that schools have relied too heavily on expository teaching. This does not mean that it should be eliminated; rather, it should be appropriately balanced with other strategies.

Because of the overuse of expository strategies, serious efforts have been made to redress the balance in favor of inquiry. In this process, the contrast between the two modes of teaching is often overdrawn. Exposition is associated with the worst practices in teaching—unimaginative use of textbooks, rigidity, emphasis on factual learning and memorization, misuse of lecture methods, and so on. In contrast, inquiry is associated with all that is good in teaching—a warm and friendly teacher, flexibility, concern for higher-level thought processes, and highly motivated learners searching out data to test hypotheses they themselves have proposed. Such exaggerated criticisms of exposition and acclaim for inquiry actually misrepresent both modes of teaching. The expository mode often is not as bad as is suggested. Similarly, the inquiry mode is not necessarily as productive in terms of learning as its most enthusiastic supporters would have us believe.

Research studies that compare the effects of inquiry and expository teaching do not suggest consistent superiority of one method over the other. In spite of the great values attributed to inquiry teaching, the research data leave an objective observer unconvinced of its demonstrable advantage in terms of achievement. It might be argued that inquiry makes its contribution in the development of specific problem-solving, reflective-intellectual skills, rather than in measurable pupil achievement. This can be accepted as a hypothesis, but the evidence to support the idea has yet to be gathered.

Assumptions

The expository mode assumes there is an essential body of content, skills, and values to be learned. It is assumed, further, that this learning has been pulled together into courses of study, textbooks, and other curriculum documents that form the core learning of the school curriculum. Teachers are prepared to teach this essential material. Teaching is assumed to be basically a transmission process. The teacher and the instructional resources serve as conduits for moving information, skills, and values from their sources to the learner. Teaching, therefore, is a variation of telling; learning is the receiving of information that has already been processed in terms of its importance and "learnability." Information and information-gathering skills are deemed to be important. Consequently, pupil achievement is measured either by the amount of information that can be recalled or how effectively information-gathering skills can be used.

Major Purposes

The major purpose of expository teaching is, clearly, to transmit knowledge and skills to the learner. If it is deemed important to get across particular information relating to science, mathematics, social studies, health, safety, and so on, this can often be done efficiently and effectively through an expository mode. Exposition does not necessarily concern itself with the social values of the learning experience. Its purpose is purely and simply getting across to the learner that which is specified by the curriculum requirements. For example, a teacher may want to teach a group of fourth graders that the major land masses and water bodies of the earth consist of seven continents and four oceans. The teacher displays a world map, points out relevant information, names and labels the continents and oceans, explains that the earth's surface is divided between water and land, and that these land and water bodies have names. Children are not necessarily involved in discovering anything for themselves; the essential information to be learned is presented to them.

Role of the Teacher

In the expository mode, teachers direct the learning program. They *are* the programmers. They must see to it that the prescribed learning is covered and that the children have mastered it. Teachers are an important data source and are an important component of the transmission line between instructional resources and the learners. They decide what books and other instructional materials will be used. Their role is to guide the learners to get the right answers—those that are a part of the required curriculum. In the expository mode, teachers' directions and explanations to learners must be crystal clear. Ambiguous questions and inconclusive explanations are a deterrent to learning.

Role of the Learner

In the expository mode, the learner is expected to meet requirements that are established by the teacher. This usually includes reading required material, answering assigned questions, discussing topics or problems presented by the teacher, and demonstrating skills deemed to be important. The learner is not required to exercise the same degree of self-direction as would be expected in the inquiry mode. The child is not necessarily encouraged

(Courtesy of Terri Malinowski.)

The effective teacher knows how and when to use the expository mode of teaching to good advantage. What is there about this photograph that suggests that the teacher has been successful in selecting the expository mode?

to go beyond the tasks outlined by the teacher, although this sometimes is encouraged by providing "extra credit" for additional work.

The role of the learner in the expository mode is often inaccurately described as "passive." Actually, learners can be and often are very active in the expository mode—reading, searching for answers to questions, using instructional resources, or going on field trips. Their activity, however, is directed toward requirements established by the teacher, rather than toward those initiated by the learners themselves.

Use of Instructional Resources

The expository mode requires that the learner get certain prescribed information from the instructional resources used. Typically, instructional materials will be used to respond to questions framed by someone *other* than the learner, that is, the teacher, the textbook authors, and so forth. Rather than seeking data in order to make their own interpretations, children will be looking for and learning the interpretations and summaries presented by the information sources. Instructional resources are best used to *summarize* learnings in the expository mode. There can be no question that the expository mode relies heavily on instructional materials that stress verbal learning as opposed to direct experience. The mode also uses instructional resources that are compartmentalized along conventional subject matter lines—reading, mathematics, social studies, science, and so forth.

Method of Evaluation

The achievement of learners in the expository mode is represented by the extent to which they have acquired the prescribed subject matter and skills that were transmitted to them. Tests that assess knowledge of informational content covered in the curriculum are appropriate, as are those that measure skills. Conventional standardized tests are a good example of evaluative measures based on the expository mode. Teacher-made tests designed to find out whether or not learners can reproduce correct answers are also consistent with the expository mode. The expository mode operates on the premise that there is a predetermined curriculum that children are supposed to learn. It follows, therefore, that the method of evaluation will be one that assesses the extent to which this learning has been achieved.

BUT HOW DO YOU DO IT, REALLY?

The National Council for the Social Studies was holding its annual convention in a nearby city and Miss Simmons, a first-year second-grade teacher, decided to attend. She found the experience both inspiring and instructive. She listened to some great speakers but was confused about some of the things she heard. One speaker emphasized that "Teaching is not telling. Children have to experience on a firsthand basis the cultural world that surrounds them. They need to find things out for themselves. They need to inquire and to discover."

The next day Miss Simmons attended another general session where the speaker was just as eloquent, just as distinguished, and just as convincing as the first one was. He told the audience, "You must consider how a culture is passed on from one generation to another. Is it likely or even reasonable to expect that the whole of culture will be rediscovered by each individual as a part of the growing process? I think not. Not even with the best schools and the most creative teachers could we reasonably expect that a child would discover all that he needs to know. We cannot rely on discovery as the means of transmitting the culture to children and youth. Culture cannot be discovered; it must be passed on or it is forgotten."[1]

1. How can Miss Simmons reconcile these two points of view?

2. Are the speakers necessarily in disagreement?

3. Do these sketches tell you anything about the importance of being able to use more than one mode of teaching?

The Inquiry Mode

To *inquire* means that one is involved in asking questions, seeking information, and carrying on an investigation. Inquiry strategies in teaching and learning, therefore, are those that involve learners

---

[1] *See* Jerome S. Bruner, "Some Elements of Discovery," in Lee S. Shulman and Evan R. Keislar, eds., *Learning by Discovery: A Critical Appraisal* (Chicago: Rand McNally & Co., 1966), pp. 101–114.

in these processes. To a large extent, the learner is responsible for providing ideas and questions to be explored, proposing hypotheses to be tested, accumulating and organizing data to test hypotheses, and coming to tentative conclusions. Inquiry can take many forms, but the problem-solving format suggested by the prominent American educator John Dewey near the turn of the century is one that is commonly used. This process involves five steps. Thelearner confronts a problem situation; what Dewey called a "felt need." The learner moves to resolve this need by searching for a solution. In the process, possible solutions or hypotheses are proposed and then a search is conducted for evidence that will support or reject them. On the basis of data and the testing of proposed solutions, the learner either comes to a tentatively held conclusion or rejects the hypothesis and continues the search until a satisfactory resolution of the problem is found. These five steps, e.g., (1) defining a problem, (2) proposing hypotheses, (3) collecting data, (4) evaluating evidence, and (5) making a conclusion, have become institutionalized in the so-called scientific method of problem solving.

Often overlooked is the fact that the procedure, as proposed by Dewey, includes two thought processes. The defining of the problem and proposing the hypotheses involve *inductive discovery.* In gathering data, applying and testing solutions, one engages in *deductive proof.* It is clear that problem solving of this type makes use of both inductive and deductive thought processes, even though it is commonly assumed that inquiry involves inductive processes only.

When inquiry is conducted in such a way that learners find out the meanings of concepts and form conclusions and generalizations from data they themselves have gathered, we may refer to such an inquiry as a "discovery experience." For example, in a science experiment dealing with the effect of light on a growing plant, the children may have two plants of the same variety, of similar size, and grown under the same environmental conditions. One is left to grow as usual in sunlight, and the other is covered. All other conditions of heat, moisture, and exposure are the same for the two plants. In a few days noticeable changes occur. From these observations, children conclude that sunlight is an essential component of plant growth. Throughout this process the teacher neither told them what would happen, nor what to expect. The teacher might have asked thought questions along the way in order to guide the inquiry, but the children themselves discovered the relationship. When educators refer to inquiry, they are usually referring to this kind of discovery learning. It is important to note that *discovery* used in this sense does not mean that children are uncovering new knowledge; they are discovering knowledge hitherto unknown to *them.*

Assumptions

Inquiry assumes that the school serves children best by teaching them to be self-directed, critical thinkers, and problem solvers. Therefore, inquiry is largely learner centered, requiring that the children be "actively involved" in learning, meaning that learners exercise initiative in the process. Inquiry involves a search-surprise element, and this characteristic makes it highly motivating. There is no fixed body of knowledge and skills that all must learn. The *process* of learning is perceived to be at least as important an outcome as is the *product,* e.g., what is learned. Learning should be kept open-ended—the achievement of goals being simply an intermediate step to additional investigation. Learners are therefore encouraged to wonder and imagine, and this curiosity leads to further inquiry. Learning, for the most part, is applied as it is acquired, not stored only for future use. Learners have individual learning styles, and these can best be accommodated when learners are responsible for their own learning. There is less need to focus on a search for "right" answers, because conclusions are tentative in terms of the data available at the time.

Major Purposes

The major purpose of inquiry teaching is to provide a means for the learner to develop intellectual skills related to critical thinking and problem solving. If thinking is to be the central purpose of American education, as many believe it should be, then ways must be devised to help individuals develop that capability. Inquiry is intended to do this by focusing on the development of such mental processes as identifying and analyzing problems, stating hypotheses, collecting and classifying relevant data, interpreting and verifying data, testing hypotheses, and coming to conclusions. It seeks to develop independence. Children are encouraged to find things out for themselves by applying principles of the scientific method of inquiry. Through inquiry, they should *learn how to learn.* Inquiry stresses discovering things for oneself.

Travel agencies advertise that "getting there is half the fun."

131

This is analogous to the inquiry process in that the inquiry or the search is both the means and the end. Inquiry carries its own reward, quite apart from what is learned in the way of content and skills. It is important to understand this aspect of the inquiry mode, particularly if one is concerned that certain subject matter be covered at certain grade levels. The purpose of inquiry is to provide training in the development of specific intellectual skills, not to cover specified elements of subject matter.

Role of the Teacher

Because inquiry is highly learner centered, the role of the teacher is that of guide-stimulator; a facilitator who challenges learners by helping them identify questions and problems, and guides their inquiry. The teacher provides an atmosphere that ensures freedom of exploration, good human relations, along with needed psychological support. Insofar as possible, the teacher tries to encourage independent habits of work. As needed, the teacher helps children find appropriate sources of information and is responsible for seeing that an adequate amount of appropriate instructional resources is available. The teacher restates and clarifies pupil responses, and suggests alternative interpretations of data. The situation is structured to the extent that inquiry can actually take place. That is, children are not wholly free to wander about on their own "doing inquiry." The teacher does not stress seeking *the* right answer but helps them find and validate appropriate answers. The teacher must be particularly skillful in asking the kinds of questions that encourage critical thinking and problem solving.

Role of the Learner

The inquiry mode places learners in a role that requires considerable initiative in finding things out for themselves. They must be actively engaged in their own learning. Naturally it is not expected that they will be left unguided in their inquiry searches, but it is expected that they will be encouraged to ask questions, to challenge what is presented to them, and to think about alternatives. Within limits, the learners, with the help of the teacher, set their own goals. Learners are free to explore broadly and are provided many opportunities for choice making. They are encouraged to range widely in their search for information. The role of the learner is not one of responding to questions posed by the teacher, but of asking questions and discovering answers to those questions through quests and searches.

Use of Instructional Resources

Contrary to what is often assumed, the inquiry mode does not require the use of specially designed instructional material. Any of the conventional resources, i.e., textbooks, supplementary books, films, pictures, field trips, resource persons, the library, can be used effectively for inquiry searches. Indeed, the learner is encouraged to use a broad range of data sources. In the inquiry mode, as in the case to the other modes as well, the question is not so much *what* instructional resources are used as it is one of *how* the children make use of them. Inquiry necessitates getting data in order to make interpretations. Presumably prior to the information search, the children and their teacher have raised questions and suggested hypotheses concerning the topic under study. The instructional resources are used to shed light on these queries. This suggests that there is no requirement that any particular instructional resource, such as the textbook, for example, be "covered" in the traditional sense. Also, there is no prohibition against the use of the textbook in conducting inquiries.

Method of Evaluation

Evaluation of learning in the inquiry mode focuses on the extent to which the learner is able to use the intellectual skills associated with this mode. Because the major purpose of inquiry is to generate and verify propositions, the learner should not be evaluated only on the ability to recall and reproduce information. Sometimes when an inquiry mode is used, the evaluation is based on the extent to which knowledge has been transmitted. This is an obvious confusion of purposes in the instructional and evaluation phases of the learning process. Standardized tests that focus on assessment of critical thinking and problem-solving skills are generally more appropriate for evaluating inquiry-based instruction than those tests that are primarily subject matter based.

The Demonstration Mode

Miss Giles is introducing cursive writing to a third-grade class. She finds it impossible to explain what is involved. Therefore, she makes use of the chalkboard. As she writes the letters on the board, she explains how each letter is formed. She points out to the children how they are to make specific curves, and how best to overcome any difficulties they might encounter. Miss Giles says, "Now watch carefully how I make the top part of the letter. I will do it a few more times." This teacher is *showing, doing,* and *telling.* These are the essential components of a demonstration mode of teaching.

Often demonstrations are developed on the spur of the moment when the teacher discovers the limitations of an explanation. Suddenly chalkboard erasers become ships in a harbor to clarify a social studies concept; pencils are grouped to illustrate a mathematics concept; playground balls are used to illustrate the positions of the sun, earth, and moon in a solar eclipse. Such improvised demonstrations are common in teaching. Whether they are preplanned or improvised, demonstrations can be effective in communicating to learners.

Demonstrations can be and often are combined with other modes of teaching such as exposition and inquiry. For example, a teacher may be conducting an experiment on magnetism in a science lesson. Magnets and iron filings are used to illustrate certain magnetic principles. The teacher may conduct the experiment by asking inquiry-type questions. "If I place this magnet under the glass with the iron filings on it, what, if anything, will happen to the iron filings? Why do you think so? Shall we try it and see?"

"Now then, why do the filings take this particular shape? What would happen if I turned the magnet around?"

Here we see the teacher demonstrating while conducting a lesson that is basically inquiry oriented. The learners are hypothesizing, applying prior knowledge to the present inquiry, and are testing their hunches through the demonstration procedure.

The same demonstration setting could be used in an expository mode. In this case, instead of asking questions the teacher would be telling the class what to expect, what to look for, what is likely to happen, and why things happened as they did. Such

---

DOES IT MATTER WHAT YOU CALL IT?

From the time of her first brush with the classroom as a student teacher, it was clear that Miss Marsh had a knack for asking questions that sparked the thinking of children. And they loved it! She would rarely come right out and tell them much of anything. She would rephrase and clarify what they said and in the process provided a cue or two that led them in the direction of what they wanted and needed to know. Now in her seventh month as a contracted teacher, her classroom was something of a science laboratory, a museum, a "fixit" shop, an art gallery, and a learning resources center all wrapped into one. Her pupils seemed always to be talking interestedly about what was going on in the classroom, and would often ask each other questions about projects and activities. A colleague told her one day, "How lucky you are to have such a curious and interested group of children. They've changed so this past year."

"Yes, they do seem interested in what we are doing, and they learn a great deal on their own. But I must get back to school this summer and learn how to do inquiry," replied Miss Marsh.

1. What is there about this sketch that suggests that Miss Marsh is already making effective use of the inquiry mode?

2. Why do you suppose Miss Marsh did not recognize as the inquiry mode that which she is doing?

3. What do you think of the comment of her colleague, to the effect that she is "lucky to have such a curious and interested group of children"?

---

demonstrations are usually used with more mature learners. With young children, most educators would prefer a more inquiry-oriented procedure, with greater direct learner involvement.

Demonstration modes, therefore, can be used to serve at least two educational purposes. The first is that they can be used to illustrate and dramatically present ideas, concepts, and principles in an engaging way. It is more interesting and provocative to see something happening than to listen to an explanation alone. Even professional actors depend on props and staging to get their ideas across to their audiences. The chances of misunderstanding are minimized if the learner can see as well as hear what is being explained. Oral explanations used alone are necessarily more abstract than when they are combined with a relevant demonstration.

But demonstrations provide values in addition to their facilitation of the learning of subject matter and content-related skills. Their second purpose is that they can develop critical thinking skills. This is especially the case in some aspects of science and social studies. The demonstration provides an opportunity for the learner to speculate on what will happen, how it will happen, and why it happens as it does. This is undoubtedly the greatest value in having young learners participate directly in demonstrations. By involving themselves in the demonstration, they are applying and practicing important thinking skills that should become a permanent part of their education.

Assumptions

The demonstration mode may accept portions of, or all of, the assumptions that apply to the inquiry or expository modes. Good teaching is perceived in part as good communication, and demonstration facilitates communication. It assumes that learning will be enhanced if the child is exposed to a functioning model or guide. This exposure will shape the learner's future behavior or attitudes, because there is an inclination to imitate the demonstration model. Through observing a demonstration, the learner engages in sympathetic behavior by visualizing and observing, perhaps even verbalizing subvocally, what is happening, and this strengthens the achievement of the desired behavior. Even when the teacher is conducting the demonstration alone, without direct pupil involvement, the child may be participating intellectually. The learner conducts the demonstration mentally, following along with what the teacher is doing. Learning is further facilitated through demonstration by focusing attention on the most critical aspects of what is to be learned. That is, a well-conducted demonstration is one in which the key ideas stand out clearly.

Major Purposes

The purpose of the demonstration mode is to show how something is to be done, how something happens or works, or how something should not be done. Demonstrations are used to improve communication. Many demonstrations are extensions of exposition; the only difference being that the demonstration stresses seeing in addition to hearing. Where there is the expectation of failure to understand an oral explanation, where there are frequent errors in learning, where the possibility of misunderstanding is high, the demonstration mode can help overcome these difficulties.

Role of the Teacher

The role of the teacher in the demonstration mode is to plan, organize, and execute the demonstration in such a way that the key ideas to be learned are made clear. The demonstration must be factually and technically correct and presented in a step by step sequence. The teacher must be able to show, in conducting the demonstration, what is to be learned. If demonstrating a skill, the teacher must be able to perform it proficiently. If equipment is involved, such as a motion picture projector, maps and globes, or science laboratory materials, the teacher must have those ready, and know how to use them for the demonstration. It is the teacher's responsibility to ensure that everyone in the class is able to see and hear the demonstration.

Role of the Learner

In the demonstration mode the role of the learner is to observe, listen, and follow the presentation carefully and attentively in order to understand what is being communicated. In some instances the learner may be required to participate in the demonstration, or to replicate it, using duplicate materials or equipment. Children may be asked to respond to questions at critical points in the demonstration, to provide feedback to the teacher, thereby showing the extent of their understanding.

Use of Instructional Resources

Instructional resources for this mode consist of whatever materials and equipment are needed to conduct the demonstration. The children may or may not need materials other than those used in the demonstration. Ordinarily there would be some follow-up to a demonstration, and for this purpose the conventional instructional resources can be used such as textbook assignments or special readings. Appropriate use of these materials would be similar to uses described in the sections on expository or inquiry modes, depending on which the teacher prefers.

Method of Evaluation

Any evaluative procedure that measures the extent to which the purposes of the demonstration have been achieved will be satisfactory. A written test may be given, but discussion is also useful in detecting understanding or misconceptions. The learner may be required to replicate the demonstration and explain it to someone else. The teacher should be observing pupil behavior, noting whether important points have been omitted, whether there is misunderstanding and confusion, whether the proper sequence has been followed, or whether any other deficiency is apparent that will require further clarification or reteaching.

The Integrated Curriculum Mode

Earlier editions of this book referred to the integrated curriculum mode of teaching as "The Activity Mode." Because all modes make use of learner activities, there has been some confusion about the use of the term *activity* in the context of a separate teaching mode. The term *integrated curriculum mode* more accurately describes what is meant because in this mode we see the entire classroom curriculum as being focused on learner activities or on projects that are intended to provide unity to the child's school experience. This mode has a strong kinship to the inquiry mode, is highly individualized, calls for a loosely structured learning environment, and is problem solving in its orientation. When the teacher decides to use the integrated curriculum mode, the entire classroom life will need to be planned in accordance with the philosophy that undergirds this method of teaching.

The integrated curriculum mode is not appropriate for everyone, but for those who can implement it successfully it does make possible the achievement of a wide range of educational objectives through highly motivating, learner involving, functionally related experiences. The following vignette is an illustration of the integrated curriculum mode in operation:

> The space in which the children work—it hardly seems appropriate to call it a "classroom"—exudes a feeling of informality, warmth, and activity. I visited the classroom each day

for two weeks during the time these fourth graders were learning about their home state in a unit entitled, "Under Five Flags." The classroom is loaded with instructional materials of every stripe, and the teacher encourages the children to make use of these materials on their own. She wants them to wonder, to imagine, to be curious about what they see, touch, and feel. Evidence of children's work is everywhere, much of it genuinely creative.

The children are working on several projects, all related to the central theme of the unit. Some activities are done in small groups, whereas other children work independently. The teacher is constantly moving among the children, challenging them with questions for clarification. She provides encouragement and offers suggestions. Much of her interaction with the class is on a one-to-one basis. Such contacts are not lengthy but they are frequent. The teacher seems to know what progress each child is making and what special assistance is needed. She maintains a flexible time schedule and will get small groups or the entire class together from time to time in order to take stock of things and to set new learning goals.

The topic "Under Five Flags" provides the central focus for much that happens in the room. Children make use of a wide range of information sources in the classroom and in the community. Some of the children are involved in an oral history project in which they record interviews with community residents. Elderly residents of the community have been invited to school to share their experiences, artifacts, and photographs of life in earlier times.

In order to carry out their information searches, the children have to do a considerable amount of reading, research, writing, notetaking, outlining, speaking, and listening. The teacher uses these occasions to teach the basic skills needed to accomplish such tasks. This gives the children clear purposes for learning them. In addition to learning and applying basic skills, the children made use of folk songs, creative art, and literature related to pioneer days in their state. Because of the different cultures that influenced the region while it was "under five flags," this provided a rich source of information for the children.

Parents and teachers who find conventional schools too highly structured, too regimented, and too adult dominated find the integrated curriculum mode attractive. They believe that this mode more nearly meets the emotional, social, physical, *and* intellectual development of growing children. They see it as a way of drawing the large number of disparate subjects and skills of the school curriculum into a functioning whole. They are attracted to the problem-solving aspects of this mode because they think such experiences are more closely analogous to life outside of school than are those provided by the conventional program. Finally, they see this mode as more democratic because the children themselves are involved in planning and decision making, and, therefore, it provides the children with better preparation for life.

The integrated curriculum mode has not been without its critics. Its apparent lack of organization, its informality, and the permissiveness allowed have been the main targets of critics. It is true that what goes on in classrooms operating under the integrated curriculum mode may bear little resemblance to traditional practices. At a time when the nation seems to be calling for more fundamental approaches to education, the integrated curriculum mode faces an uncertain future. It will doubtless continue to be available in alternative classrooms.

Assumptions

Like the demonstration mode, the integrated curriculum mode may accept portions of, or all of, the assumptions that apply to the inquiry or expository modes. Theoretically and philosophically, it is tied most closely to the inquiry mode. It assumes that children have certain natural drives, urges, and interests, and that they bring these to school with them. Rather than teaching a predetermined curriculum, the teacher explores the backgrounds and interests of the children, and out of this interaction, significant activities emerge. The activities selected should capitalize on these natural interests and inclinations. A rigid time schedule and the compartmentalizing of curriculum components are rejected because they run counter to the natural exploration of children. A rich and stimulating learning environment is essential in order that children may have many opportunities to explore interests and to learn from direct experience. The teacher serves as more of a guide, advisor, and expeditor than as a director of learning. Learning takes place best in settings that encourage social interaction and cooperation—children working with each other. Cross-age grouping is encouraged because children learn from each other, thus older children can help younger ones to learn.

Major Purposes

The purpose of the integrated curriculum mode is to teach children to become self-reliant, independent problem solvers, consistent with what is known about the nature of childhood. As such it involves children directly and purposefully in learning. It is designed to create a high level of interest in learning that will become personalized and individualized. It seeks to construct situations in which children can learn what they want and need to know, rather than what the curriculum specifies. Like inquiry, the purpose of the integrated curriculum mode is to stress the process of learning as opposed to specific subject matter and skills. Moreover, it is designed to capitalize on the social values of learning. Another of its purposes is to help understand and appreciate the extent to which school learning is integrated, rather than separated into a variety of discrete subjects and skills, as is the case with the traditional curriculum.

Role of the Teacher

In the integrated curriculum mode, the teacher's role can be described as that of setting the stage and providing the environment within which children can engage in learning activities in terms of their own interests, needs, capabilities, personalities, and motivations. This requires a warm and stress-free atmosphere. The teacher needs to structure and guide the explorations of children, but should do so without stifling their initiative. The teacher must be skillful and resourceful in being able to capitalize on the interests of children and to convert such leads into appropriate and workable learning activities. Also, the teacher must be imaginative in seeing the possibilities for other school-related learnings in the activities that interest children. The teacher must provide a carefully selected assortment of learning materials for children to handle, use for construction, manipulate, experiment with, explore, and puzzle over. The teacher should guide and provide. The teacher's role should be that of a catalyst to stimulate children's learning. In this environment, the teacher should also be a learner, along with the children.

(Courtesy of Terri Malinowski.)

Helping children discover things for themselves is an important part of the elementary school experience. What mode of teaching is represented in this photograph?

Role of the Learner

Here, more than in any of the other modes, we find the children centrally involved in the learning process. It is expected that they will initiate activities and that they will assume responsibility for their own learning. The exercise of *initiative* and *responsibility* is basic to the role of the learner in the integrated curriculum mode. Emphasis is on cooperation; therefore, children are expected to work harmoniously with others on their learning activities and projects. They are not expected to be seated at their desks completing assignments that have been prepared by the teacher. They will, instead, be working on a project or activity in which they are interested, and will be searching for answers to questions they themselves have raised. This necessitates a mind-set of curiosity and wonderment about the environment. Considerable intellectual and physical freedom prevails. Pupils may move about, ask any question they choose, and consult whatever data sources would seem to be appropriate.

Use of Instructional Resources

The integrated curriculum mode necessitates a wide variety of assorted learning materials. These should include the conventional ones—books, films, pictures, maps, and so on; but also included should be others, such as electric motors, branding irons, a computer, science equipment, carpenters' tools, historical artifacts, construction kits, art supplies, musical instruments, and audiovisual material. Indeed, anything at all that allows children to construct, explore, and manipulate might be a legitimate learning resource. A rich and responsive environment is essential to the success of the integrated curriculum mode. Because much of the learning is self-directed, these resources will be used to satisfy learner needs rather than to respond to requirements established by the teacher.

Method of Evaluation

Evaluation of learning in the integrated curriculum mode is more difficult than in the other modes because it may bear little similarity to traditional evaluative procedures. As in all cases, evaluation must be conducted in accord with the major purposes of the program. Therefore, in the integrated curriculum mode the teacher would be looking for such things as the extent to which the children are involving themselves in their own learning; how well they are sharing, cooperating, and assuming responsibility; how well they are able to attack and puzzle through problems as they confront them; how well they are able to use the tools of learning, i.e., reading, writing, spelling, and speaking, in solving problems and meeting their needs; the extent to which their work products show evidence of improvement; and the extent to which they are overcoming their learning deficiencies. Because these programs are highly individualized, emphasis will be placed on progress in terms of prior status, rather than in terms of comparing achievement with classmates or with nationally derived norms.

Study Questions and Activities

1. Which of the teaching modes present the greatest potential for classroom management problems for the teacher? Why?

2. Why is there such a diversity of views among lay persons—and even among teachers—about what constitutes good teaching?

3. It is often claimed that "teaching is not telling." If this is true, why do teachers continue to do a great deal of "telling"? What are appropriate uses of teacher explanations in teaching elementary school children?

4. In the discussion of teaching modes, the role of learners is sometimes described as "passive" or "active." List some things children do when they are "actively involved" in their learning. Does a child have to be doing something physical to be "actively involved"? Explain.

5. Why are demonstrations particularly important in learning skills?

6. What are some of the clear advantages of an integrated curriculum mode of teaching in a self-contained classroom?

7. Which of the teaching modes provides the greatest potential for achieving a wide range of learner outcomes? Explain.

8. This chapter does not discuss a teaching mode wherein the teacher combines exposition, demonstration, and inquiry over a two- or three-week time period. What is a topic that would lend itself to such a presentation mode? What aspects of the topic would be partic-

ularly well suited to each of the three modes? Could the integrated curriculum mode also be included? Why or why not?

For Further Professional Study

Blumenfeld, Phyllis C., Paul R. Pintrich, Judith Meece, and Kathleen Wessels. "The Formation and Role of Self Perception of Ability in Elementary Classrooms." *The Elementary School Journals,* **82** (May 1982), 401–420.

Bolster, Arthur S., Jr. "Toward a More Effective Model of Research on Teaching." *Harvard Educational Review,* **53** (August 1983), 294–308.

Joyce, Bruce, and Marsha Weil. *Models of Teaching,* 2d ed. Englewood Cliffs, N.J.: Prentice-Hall, Inc., 1980.

Orlich, Donald C., Robert J. Harder, Richard C. Callahan, Constance H. Kravas, Donald P. Kauchak, R. A. Pendergrass, Andrew J. Keogh, and Dorothy I. Hellene. *Teaching Strategies: A Guide to Better Instruction.* Lexington, Mass.: D. C. Heath and Company, 1980.

Zahorik, John A. "Learning Activities: Nature, Function, and Practice." *The Elementary School Journal,* **82** (March 1982), 309–317.

6

Organizing Groups of Learners for Instruction

THE QUALIFIED AND COMPETENT TEACHER . . .

1. Understands the rationale for using a variety of grouping practices.

2. Is sensitive to the importance of developing a group management plan.

3. Recognizes the importance of providing a balance of large group, small group, and individualized instruction.

4. Has knowledge of PL 94-142: the *Education for All Handicapped Children Act* and its implications for providing the least restrictive environment for handicapped children.

Performance Criteria

As a result of the serious study of this chapter, the student should be able to . . .

1. Discuss the advantages and disadvantages of the various ways children can be grouped for instruction.

2. Develop a group management plan to provide for large group, small group, and individualized instruction—based on the abilities, needs, and interests of children.

3. Identify a desired learner outcome that can be accomplished best through individualized instruction.

4. Identify a desired learner outcome that can be accomplished best through small group instruction.

5. Identify a desired learner outcome that can be accomplished best through large group instruction.

The self-contained classroom is the dominant organizational structure for elementary schools in this nation. It is a "one teacher-one classroom" plan that is based on the assumption that one adult should be responsible for the entire educational program of all children in his or her charge. Experts agree that teaching in a self-contained classroom is a difficult and challenging assignment, yet no satisfactory alternative has been devised as a way of teaching young children in this country or abroad. Some modifications of the self-contained classroom structure have appeared, the use of subject specialists being an example.

A music specialist and a physical education specialist may teach the class during the music and physical education periods on certain days of the week. The reading specialist, in some instances, provides assistance to the teacher of the self-contained classroom. The teacher in the self-contained classroom, however, instructs the children in all of the remaining subjects and is considered to be *the* children's teacher of record.

Team-teaching arrangements change the self-contained classroom into an organizational pattern in which two or three teachers share instruction for a group that is two to three times larger than the conventional classroom of twenty-five to thirty learners. Team teaching in a setting such as this requires classroom space for a large number of children. Many school buildings, however, are neither constructed nor equipped to handle this arrangement.

Other modifications of the self-contained classroom are based on the premise that quality education can occur only when instruction is individualized. Teaching machines and programmed texts were once very popular formats for individualized instruction during the 1960s. These devices did not meet with widespread acceptance for various reasons, some of which were philosophic and others economic. The development of learning programs for the machines and for programmed textbooks proved to be a costly venture, and there was a reluctance to invest in this approach. During the 1970s individualized instruction gained renewed vigor, largely because of the competency-based education movement. Born of a growing acceptance of "accountability" in the professional and public sectors, programmed instruction became a popular concept once again. It took the form of the "learning module" or "instructional package" containing carefully prescribed behavioral objectives enabling the pupil to master learning tasks in a "low-risk environment" and requiring only a minimum of teacher guidance. Individualized learning, accomplished through independent study, can promote the development of self-direction and self-reliance in children. Independent study activities, based on prepackaged materials that contain a high degree of direction, usually do not provide the child opportunity for decision making and, therefore, do little to promote these abilities. These materials may be excellent, however, for drill and review activities.

The classroom computer also is recognized as an important device for providing individualized instruction. Computer-assisted instruction can serve the teacher in the assessment of a child's learning difficulties and in providing remedial activities for these deficiencies. It can provide the learner with quick drill and reinforcement exercises. The classroom computer, with appropriate programming, also can assist the child in the development of problem-solving abilities and higher-order thinking skills. Computer-assisted instruction has found widespread use in elementary school classrooms. Because it is based on individual instruction, however, it does little to promote the development and growth of children's social skills.

Large group or whole class instruction has been promoted by advocates of *direct instruction* who believe it to be an effective way to produce improved pupil achievement.[1] Direct instruction usually occurs in those instances in which the teacher uses factual questions and controlled practice to teach a large group of learners. This represents a sharp contrast to individualized or small group instruction.

Recent classroom research has discovered additional relationships between deployment patterns of children within the class and learner gains in the basic skills.[2] The researchers concluded that grade-level differences of learners presented variables that affected the efficacy of certain grouping arrangements. Learners in the primary grades appeared to need a considerable amount of one-to-one interaction with the teacher in which practice and immediate feedback could be provided. Even though a great deal of practice occurred when learners were in small groups, it was important that the teacher gave attention to each child. Learners in the intermediate grades, however, were found to have less need for direct practice that was monitored by the teacher on a one-to-one basis. Older learners appeared able to attend to the teacher's presentations and to interact successfully with their peers. Consequently, a whole-class configuration became the format for teacher presentations of new materials. Remedial activities were conducted in small groups. The researchers found, however, that teachers needed to monitor and to provide feedback for each learner.

---

[1] See Allan C. Ornstein and Daniel U. Levine, "Teacher Behavior Research," *Phi Delta Kappan,* **62** (April 1981), 594.

[2] See Jere Brophy, "Successful Teaching Strategies for the Inner-City Child," *Phi Delta Kappan,* **63** (April 1982), 528, 529.

Rationale for Small Groups within the Classroom

We wish to emphasize the importance of children interacting with one another in the interests of their academic, personal, and social development. Teachers who share this point of view plan teaching and learning activities that provide a balance of individualized instruction, small group lessons, and whole-class experiences. Because group life remains the foundation of our society, children need experiences that prepare them to live and work in social groups. Teachers need to be skillful in organizing instruction that accommodates learners in both large and small groups.

Children's interest in learning is affected to a great extent by the degree to which they appreciate the intrinsic value of what they are expected to learn. It is also affected by the learning atmosphere. Pupils who are kept together consistently in a whole-class group do not have the opportunity to interact with one another and to participate in a wide variety of modes of teaching and learning. In classrooms in which children are provided with a variety of teaching modes, the learning atmosphere is apt to be more interesting.

Experienced teachers have learned that small group instruction also provides opportunities *to reach individual children.* They strive, therefore, to challenge each child by planning learning activities that occur in small group and large group situations as well as in individualized settings.

In the final analysis, small group instruction enables the teacher to:

1. Provide learners with opportunities to acquire socialization skills needed for participation in a democratic society.
2. Make efficient use of teacher time and effort.
3. Use modes of instruction that require pupil interaction.
4. Provide for individualized learning that occurs in a group rather than in an isolated setting.

Because the majority of beginning teachers will find themselves in a self-contained classroom, with or without modification, they should be prepared to plan and to instruct pupils in both large and small groups. Thus, they should be able to select the appropriate way to group children in order to accomplish the instructional objective. Experienced teachers know that placing children in small groups according to common interest can provide incentives for them to learn on their own. These teachers know that placing learners in small groups where the members have a common achievement level can enhance learning. They know that certain children work best when they are placed in a small group with others who can provide them with a good role model for learning. These teachers also know that certain learning tasks are best achieved by children in small groups.

To be able to provide learners with a variety of teaching and learning experiences, the teacher should have available a wide repertoire of activities and should systematically introduce them to the group. The expected outcome is that children will become increasingly self-selective in matching activities with their particular abilities and interests. A helpful way for teachers to classify activities for ready reference is to organize them as follows.

Suggested Activities For Small Groups	
Activities Based on Gathering Information	Reading; interviewing; map and chart study; computing; field trips; observing; viewing television, films, and slides; listening; experimenting.
Activities Based on Presenting Information	Oral and written reporting; creative expression through art, music, and drama; demonstrating; exhibiting.
Activities Based on Evaluating Information	Experimenting; valuing; questioning; role playing.

Teachers should recognize that most children like to participate in activities in which they feel successful. *All children, however, should develop an appreciation for a diversity of modes of learning.* They should develop an awareness of the importance of various study styles in helping them to broaden their ability to learn how to learn. The child who does only a few things well should have an opportunity to develop additional study skills and to acquire wider interests.

Small group instruction has received recent recognition as an effective vehicle for the promotion of *cooperative learning*—an instructional concept that changes the interpersonal reward structure of the classroom from competition to cooperation. Research on cooperative learning has discovered that generally it is effective for increasing pupil achievement, positive ethnic relations in desegregated schools, mutual concern among pupils, pupil self-esteem, and so forth.[3]

Cooperative learning through small group instruction may result from a classroom arrangement in which children select a subtopic from a study area established by the teacher. The children organize themselves into small groups consisting of two to six members. Each pupil works on a task; the results are then reported by the small group to the whole class and the teacher for evaluation. Another arrangement for cooperative learning through small group instruction obtains when pupils are arranged in small groups and are instructed to work on academic tasks and to hand in a single assignment as a group.

Teaching the Mildly Handicapped Child in the Regular Classroom

Historically, the accepted way of educating handicapped children was to provide special education in an instructional setting removed from the regular classroom. Such separation of the handicapped was deemed necessary to meet the unique needs of these learners. The isolation of handicapped children from the mainstream of public education is no longer permitted since the enactment of Public Law 94-142: *Education for All Handicapped Children Act* of 1975. Although the education of all handicapped children in regular schools is not yet a reality, the nation's schools are moving in the direction of implementing practices that *include* rather than *exclude* handicapped children from the mainstream of education.

---

[3] Robert E. Slavin, "Cooperative Learning," *Review of Educational Research*, **50** (Summer, 1980), 315–342.

PL 94-142

Many believe that this landmark act is the most important educational legislation in the history of the United States. The law is intended to benefit an estimated eight million handicapped persons. Its rationale is based on the extension of civil rights to the handicapped. The act also reinforces the 1954 Supreme Court decision in the *Brown* v. *Board of Education* case in its premise that segregation has harmful effects on those who enforce the practice as well as on those who are segregated. Federal support of the act in grants to the various states represents a large sum of money.

PL 94-142 requires that handicapped children be placed in the "least restrictive environment" for their instruction. This is identified as the regular classroom unless a different setting is more suitable for meeting the child's needs. If another placement is made it must be justified on evidence that it is expected to be more beneficial to the child than the regular classroom. The need is great for the professional development of teachers who can accommodate—in the regular classroom—children who are handicapped in one or more categories:[4] hearing impairments, orthopedic impairments, mental retardation, visual deficiencies, speech impairments, other health disabilities, serious emotional disturbances, and specific learning disabilities.

The teaching profession must attract teachers who are adequately trained and who have an accepting attitude toward handicapped persons. The entire school setting provides the mainstream for the child's learning environment. The teacher must be able to influence all school personnel and the nonhandicapped children in the positive acceptance of handicapped pupils. PL 94-142 promises to end the practice of providing special education in segregated settings. Each teacher now must assume some responsibility for the enrichment of the lives of handicapped children. No doubt there are persons who will be unable or unwilling to accept the challenge. The realities of the legislation must be faced in order to select prospective teachers who can meet the task successfully.

---

[4] For definitions of the various categories of the handicapped and for an explication of the discussion in this section, see Maynard C. Reynolds and Jack W. Birch, *Teaching Exceptional Children in All America's Schools,* rev. ed. (Reston, Va.: The Council for Exceptional Children, 1982).

Implications for Teachers

There are several aspects of PL 94-142 that every elementary teacher should understand and be prepared to implement. These may be summarized as follows.

1. *Provision of the Least Restrictive Environment for the Handicapped Child.*
The concept of a "least restrictive environment" is not generally well understood because of the use of "mainstreaming," which has been mistakenly taken to mean that all handicapped children are to be placed in a regular classroom. The wholesale dumping of handicapped children in regular classrooms does great disservice to them and to other learners in the regular classroom. PL 94-142 does not require that all handicapped pupils, regardless of their disabilities, be placed in the regular classroom as an appropriate environment. There are many handicapped children, however, who are capable of benefiting from instruction for the entire day in a regular classroom setting. For them, the regular classroom *is* the least restrictive environment for the realization of their potential for learning. Assignment to the regular classroom for a part of the school day and to a resource room for the remainder of time, a common practice, may be the least restrictive environment for other handicapped children. And, for those who are profoundly handicapped, a full-time assignment to a special room or even to a custodial setting may represent the least restrictive environment.

The goal is to move all those handicapped children who qualify into a regular classroom—the mainstream of public education.

2. *The Individualized Education Program.*
An Individualized Education Program (IEP) is required for each handicapped child. The IEP is to be prepared cooperatively by parents, educators, and other specialized personnel. It is a written document that contains statements about the educational objectives, instructional procedures, and evaluation of the learner's progress.

The IEP may be initiated by parents and/or school personnel. It is developed through planning sessions that may, on occasion, include the child.

In the final analysis, the IEP provides the teacher with a framework for planning the daily instructional program for the child. Because it also includes the expected learner outcomes, it enables

IT'S THE LAW

Federal law P.L. 94-142, the Education for All Handicapped Children Act, requires that all handicapped children receive a "free and appropriate public education." Here are some of the highlights of the law:

1. "Handicapped children are defined as: 'mentally retarded, hard of hearing, deaf, speech impaired, visually handicapped, seriously emotionally disturbed, orthopedically impaired, or other health impaired, or children with specific learning disabilities, who by reason thereof require special education and related services.' " (Sec. 602)

2. Public schools must seek out, identify and evaluate handicapped students or those suspected of having a disability.

3. Handicapped children must be educated with their nonhandicapped peers "to the maximum extent possible." This does not mean all handicapped children must be in regular classes, but it does mean that children should not be in segregated institutions or even in separate wings of a building any more than is necessary.

4. Before placing a handicapped child, a professional evaluation team consisting of a principal, classroom teacher, special education teacher and a parent must evaluate the child and make a placement decision.

5. The regulations add that teachers should not "put undue reliance" on tests which may discriminate against those with lesser sensory, manual or visual skills.

6. Parents must be informed in advance of any placement decision and may appeal in a formal hearing.

7. A written, individualized program of instruction must be developed by professional staff members in consultation with the child's parents. The program must be evaluated periodically—again, in consultation with the child's parents.

8. The confidentiality of all data and information pertaining to the child must be assured, and access to all the child's records must always be immediately available to his or her parents.

9. The child must be given access to all aspects of the school program normally provided for nonhandicapped children, including art, music, physical education, library science, and other special subjects or services.

10. All services to the handicapped child shall be provided at no cost to the parent.[5]

---

[5] *Your Public Schools* (March 31, 1980), Olympia, Wa.: Superintendent of Public Instruction, p. 10.

the teacher to assess the child's learning program on a long-range basis.

3. *Safeguards for Participants.*

Teachers should be aware of the provisions that are afforded by PL 94-142 for "due process" for the child, parent, teacher, or others who are involved in the screening and diagnosis of the child and in the preparation and evaluation of the IEP. The child and the parent are especially protected in such matters as confidentiality of the records (with parental access assured) and in the screening, placement, and evaluation of the child. All participants are provided with formal arrangements for the presentation of grievances concerning decisions or procedures. Such cases are reviewed to ensure that equity has been provided. Appeals can be made to state and federal agencies if satisfaction is not reached on a lower level.

Provision for the least restrictive environment under PL 94-142 will require the elementary school teacher to take on new roles in teaching children and in working with parents. The prospective teacher should take every opportunity to acquire knowledge and attendant skills that are necessary for the successful implementation of the *Education for All Handicapped Children Act.*

Management of Groups in the Classroom

Experienced teachers realize that a class is not necessarily a group. To be a group, children must have a psychological identity with one another. They also must have an *esprit de corps* that binds them together. A class does not inherently have these characteristics. The teacher should make the necessary provisions for the class to become a group. These provisions are based primarily on (1) establishing a group atmosphere in the classroom; (2) making provisions for individual differences; and (3) teaching the skills needed for effective group participation.

We turn once again to vignettes of Miss Baxter and Mr. Bond, as illustrations of how two teachers developed group management plans for their classrooms.

NOTE TO THE READER

1. As you read the following vignettes identify the techniques that Miss Baxter and Mr. Bond employed in teaching children in small groups.

2. Identify the learner outcomes that resulted from instruction in small groups that would have been difficult to achieve if they had been taught in a whole-class setting.

3. List the ideas you have gained from these vignettes about group management.

MISS BAXTER'S EXPERIENCES WITH TEACHING PRIMARY-GRADE-LEVEL CHILDREN IN LARGE AND SMALL GROUPS

Miss Baxter recognized that children need to develop effective group skills early in their school life. She also knew the importance of teaching the skills that are basic to effective group participation. She knew the importance of preparing learners for small group work by making certain they possessed the skills necessary for the performance of group tasks, and that they were ready for the level of social behavior necessary for the achievement of the tasks. She decided to begin small group work slowly by first building group spirit and effective social behavior on a whole-class basis.

Miss Baxter began on the first day of school to include children in the performance of certain duties related to the upkeep of the room. She wanted them to acquire a feeling of responsibility for the development and maintenance of the learning environment. She had also spent considerable time during the planning period each morning in helping children establish good speaking and listening habits, and in accepting each other's points of view. These experiences had convinced her that the children were capable of beginning to work in small groups.

Her First Group Discussion

Miss Baxter discovered during the first lesson, which was designed to introduce the unit of study, "Moving to a New Community," that the variability in the children's ability to carry on a group discussion was far greater than she had anticipated. She found that many children insisted on talking at the same time and that their responses to her questions were inclined to be irrelevant. She realized that the group discussion process would have to be structured more carefully to enable learners to accomplish planned objectives relative to the topic under study. Miss Baxter concluded that this group had the potential for participating in group discussion when the topic was limited in scope. She closed the lesson by having them suggest ways in which their discussion could be improved. The following rules were agreed on and written on the class chart.

Our Discussion Rules

Talk in turn

Speak clearly

Stay on the topic

Listen carefully

Respect the speaker

LAUGHTER AND LOVE IN THE CLASSROOM . . .

Children should have an opportunity to work in groups that are organized on the basis of criteria other than reading ability. They need to get acquainted with children they would not get to know very well at all, if groupings were based entirely on success in reading.

Teachers who make provision for multibased groupings for their pupils experience the rewards that come from hearing and seeing laughter and love in the classroom. This is because children are free to accept each other on new terms. They begin to appreciate one another because they are free from the pressure of having always to compete.

1. After you have read these vignettes on "Management of Groups in the Classroom," decide whether Ellen Baxter and Jim Bond provided their children with this kind of atmosphere.
2. Also determine what provisions, other than those made by Miss Baxter and Mr. Bond, you would make to create an atmosphere where laughter and love would be encouraged.

Miss Baxter decided to ask the more mature children to respond as to how well the class had observed their rules. The
idea worked very well, and she felt that she would continue
having individual children assist in the evaluation.

Making Provisions for Variability in Reading Levels

Miss Baxter, in a prior lesson, followed the picture-study activity
by asking the children to read silently to find answers to the
questions she had included in her daily lesson plan. In doing
so she discovered that the pupils differed widely in their skimming skills and in their ability to identify the main idea. She
realized that these differences would need to be considered carefully in the very near future, when the children would be expected to gather information from other sources related to the
unit of study. In a second lesson Miss Baxter decided that she
would provide some variety in the way pupils could gather additional information, and at the same time vary the level of concep-
tualization required. She planned two types of activities to accomplish this goal—one based on reading and another on picture
study. A search of the school library produced several copies
of a reference textbook containing a section on "Community
Life." She decided to make an assignment from it for one small
group; this would include a teacher-directed learning activity
based on picture study, followed by an art activity designed
to produce illustrations. The children would discuss pictures of
community life and then draw their own pictures of community
activities. Another small group, comprising learners who were
capable of reading independently, would be given a silent reading
assignment in the textbook based on "How Communities Satisfy
Basic Needs." These children would be provided with a short
list of study questions to guide their reading. They would be
called on to share their answers with the class at the close of
the information-gathering period.

Miss Baxter learned a lot about group management skills as
a result of the lesson. She had suggested that the small group
that was given an independent reading assignment spend fifteen
minutes on it. In her concern that the children develop habits
of self-direction, she had reminded them to observe the time
by referring to the clock and pacing their reading by it. But
she had become so engrossed with the picture-study activity
in the second small group that she herself had failed to watch

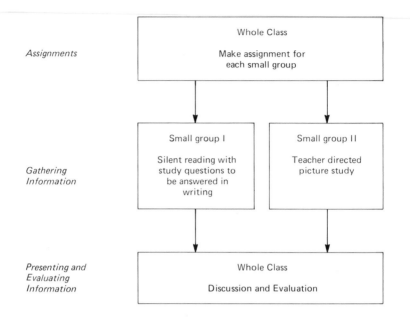

Assignments

Whole Class

Make assignment for
each small group

*Gathering
Information*

Small group I

Silent reading with
study questions to
be answered in
writing

Small group II

Teacher directed
picture study

*Presenting and
Evaluating
Information*

Whole Class

Discussion and Evaluation

the time. She suddenly became aware that the children in the other small group had either completed their reading assignment or had completely lost interest in it.

Miss Baxter managed to get the members of the reading group together again, and they sat quietly. But by that time several of the children in the small group with whom she had spent her time had also become noisy and restless. It was obvious that many of them had not prepared the illustration that had been assigned. She decided against having the children present their information. Instead, she conducted a whole class discussion and evaluation with the children, during which suggestions for improvement were made.

Later that evening, Miss Baxter reflected on what had happened. She realized that she was at fault. In the first place, she had not provided adequate supervision for the small group of independent readers. She also had failed to pace the lesson well. She wrote the following in her notebook:

> The lesson did not go well. Next time remember to provide each group with adequate supervision. The children just weren't ready to be left on their own in an independent reading activity. It's back to the "drawing board" for me.

Her Concluding Activities

After several days of work-study activities, Miss Baxter decided to plan with the children for creative learning activities that would conclude the first phase of the unit of study, "Moving to a New Community." She decided to schedule forty to fifty minutes for these lessons as more time would be needed to organize and supervise the various small groups of learners that would be involved in these activities. Having the whole class engage in each creative activity would be too time consuming and would fall short of enabling children to concentrate on activities that most appealed to their interests and abilities. Miss Baxter recognized the challenge of managing several small groups, all of which would be working at the same time. But she recognized that this approach would permit her to evaluate individual pupils on such criteria as skill development and personal-social adjustment as they participated in small group activities. It would also give her an opportunity to observe which children worked well together.

She referred to her sketch plan (as presented in Chapter 3) for the concluding activities she had anticipated using. With these ideas as guidelines, Miss Baxter and the children planned the following activities as a conclusion to the first phase of the unit.

1. Prepare a bulletin board display of "Communities Across Our Country."

2. Prepare illustrated stories of a family's experience in moving to another community.

3. Prepare a mural showing how our community provides for the four basic needs of its citizens.

4. Prepare wall charts with short explanatory statements on major inventions that have changed the communities studied in the unit.

5. Prepare dramatizations about a family preparing to move to a new community.

6. Plan a TV quiz program that would be based on answering the following questions:

    What is a community?

    How do communities differ in the way they satisfy basic needs?

    What are some reasons why families sometimes move to a new community?

163

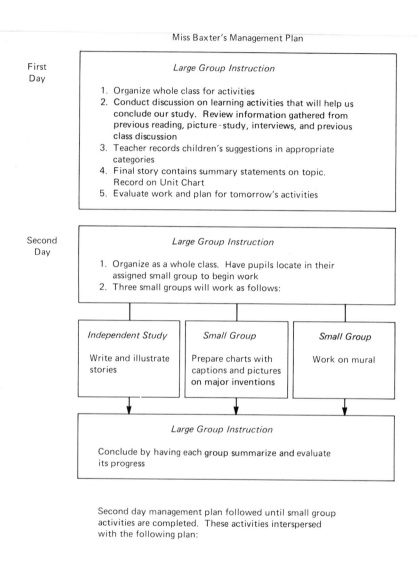

Miss Baxter's Management Plan

First Day

Large Group Instruction

1. Organize whole class for activities
2. Conduct discussion on learning activities that will help us conclude our study. Review information gathered from previous reading, picture-study, interviews, and previous class discussion
3. Teacher records children's suggestions in appropriate categories
4. Final story contains summary statements on topic. Record on Unit Chart
5. Evaluate work and plan for tomorrow's activities

Second Day

Large Group Instruction

1. Organize as a whole class. Have pupils locate in their assigned small group to begin work
2. Three small groups will work as follows:

Independent Study

Write and illustrate stories

Small Group

Prepare charts with captions and pictures on major inventions

Small Group

Work on mural

Large Group Instruction

Conclude by having each group summarize and evaluate its progress

Second day management plan followed until small group activities are completed. These activities interspersed with the following plan:

On Following Days

Modified Large Group Instruction

1. Keep large group together
2. Have pupils in groups of 3–5 dramatize a scene on a family preparing to move to a new community, with other children as an audience
3. Conduct a small group TV quiz

164

Miss Baxter's management plan for the lessons based on concluding activities for the unit of study is presented in the preceding chart.

MR. BOND'S EXPERIENCES WITH TEACHING INTERMEDIATE-GRADE-LEVEL CHILDREN IN LARGE AND SMALL GROUPS

At the intermediate grade level, children should be accustomed to working in small groups to accomplish various learning tasks. The teacher cannot take this assumption for granted, however. Before attempting small group work, the teacher should evaluate carefully the readiness of the class to perform well in a situation where more than one instructional group is working at the same time.

Instruction at the intermediate grade level is highly oriented to textbook learning. Children enter this level with a wide range of reading abilities, but textbooks are geared for the average reader. Furthermore, there is a heavier reliance on printed material as a means of learning the subject matter and related skills in social studies, literature, science, and mathematics than in the primary grades. Thus, the child must be able to read in order to learn. It is fair to say that reading is the predominant learning mode for children at this level. This is a concern to those educators who know that children's interest in school begins to decline appreciably at the intermediate grade level. We return to an earlier observation: pupil interest is directly related to the teacher's skill in providing variety in learning activities. The teacher who relies entirely on reading as a learning mode is restricting the avenues of learning available to children.

Mr. Bond knew all of this, and therefore was determined to provide his class with a variety of learning activities, even in the face of the school principal's admonition that the children must learn the essentials set forth in their textbooks. He also appreciated the difficulty that would be encountered because the problems, topics, and themes presented in the intermediate grade curriculum are far more abstract than those at the primary grade level. This, he knew, is as typical in mathematics as it is in the social studies. He concluded that, under these constraints, the best way for him to proceed would be to base his program on informational learning and attempt to provide the children with extended learning activities in the language arts and creative experiences—activities offering concrete, personalized learning opportunities. Let us return to his earlier planning for the social studies unit to learn how well he succeeded.

Mr. Bond's First Social Studies Lesson

Mr. Bond began by explaining to the children that he was interested in learning about their experiences in social studies during the previous year. Then he proceeded with the questions he had planned for this assessment. He learned several important facts as a result of the discussion:

1. The children were fairly skilled in group discussion. They talked in turn, listened attentively, and seemed to respect each other's responses. He concluded that part of this might be because, almost without exception, the class was intact from last year. He also surmised that their teacher had been somewhat successful in building a feeling of group spirit.

2. He concluded that the children had been largely restricted to a read-discuss-write mode of learning. Some of them said they enjoyed reading about the history and geography of their region, but they disliked "always having to discuss it and then write it out." Several others said they "got tired of taking so many tests" on it. Others said they were "tired of always having to read something."

3. Their responses to his question, "Why do you think it is important for us to study the United States and the other Americas?" were highly diversified, but most of the children had a strong degree of interest in the topic. Mr. Bond considered this to be a positive factor. It would be largely up to him to find ways to sustain their interest.

The activities he planned for introducing the children to the basic textbook convinced him that they had received very little instruction in study skills. Very likely their former teachers had made teacher-directed study assignments. Their reference skills seemed to be poor. There were, however, five or six children who always had the correct responses to his directions and questions. The majority of the group made serious efforts to respond, and seemed to be interested in what he was asking them to do. He observed an unresponsive group of four children who spent most of the time whispering to each other.

(Courtesy of Terri Malinowski.)

This teacher is directing the type of small group instruction that is used frequently in elementary school classrooms. Identify several teaching skills that are necessary for successful small group instruction.

Mr. Bond learned that he had planned too many activities for a single lesson. He did not have time for the last part of the lesson, when he had hoped to ask the class to match pictures of landforms with their probable locations on the regional map. Nor did he arrive at the place in the lesson at which he had planned an assignment for the next day. Instead, he asked the children for their comments about their book. He concluded they were impressed with its colorful layout and study aids. He decided to continue the following day where he had left off in the plan. During the next few days he would assess the children's ability to read the social studies, a content field that would introduce many new terms and concepts and require them to develop a number of map and study skills.

Making Provisions for Variability in Reading Levels

Mr. Bond realized the importance of teaching reading in a content field such as social studies. He knew that although children have learned certain skills during regular reading instruction, these skills must be reviewed, and retaught if needed, in the social studies unit. His plan for meeting the reading needs of the children follows.

1. Continue with whole-class reading in the textbook. The thrust in this part was aimed at having learners acquire selected map and study skills while they were being introduced to a few major concepts about the geography, climate, and resources of the Americas.

2. Children who had reading skills needed for independent study in the basic textbook would be assigned to a single reading group. This arrangement included three fourths of the class. He would follow the excellent suggestions contained in the Teacher's Manual for helping children to read effectively. The remainder of the class would be assigned to a second group, which would, on some occasions, do directed reading in the basic textbook, and on other occasions would read in selected reference books. These books would treat parallel topics, written on a less sophisticated conceptual level and with a simpler vocabulary. Because the range of reading ability in the second group clustered around a beginning-second to a late-third-grade level, he would need to change his approach and adjust materials for them.

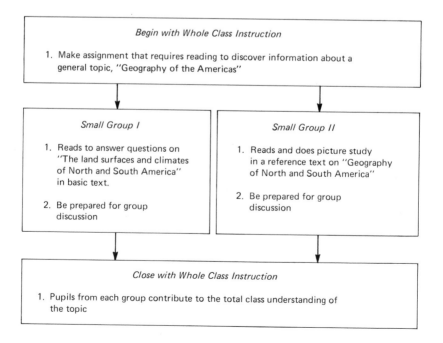

Because Mr. Bond had limited experience in the actual management of children in small groups, he determined to proceed carefully and to avoid a larger number of small groups, at least until he had the management of the whole class well established. With this model in mind, Mr. Bond tentatively identified other approaches to provide meaningful reading experiences for the class. Here are examples of these.

For Small Group I	For Small Group II
To individualize learning:	To provide variety in learning:
1. Research references, encyclopedia, *National Geographic*. Use to enrich reading in the children's textbook.	1. Directed oral reading with teacher in the children's textbook.
2. Picture study by individual children.	2. Picture study on a group basis.
3. Read selected fiction related to topic.	3. Silent reading in references that contain suitable concept and vocabulary load.
4. Read newspapers and other journals.	4. Teacher reads orally to group.

Mr. Bond felt the need to provide individualized reading experiences for children in small group I especially, because their reading differences ranged from a late-fourth-grade level to a few who could read material at the tenth-grade level. The amount of teacher guidance during the reading activities would have to focus on small group II, but he was aware that he could not neglect the other small group in this respect.

Providing Additional Opportunities to Gather Information

Too frequently, intermediate-grade level teachers tend to "equate research with reading." This is unfortunate because there are numerous other ways for children to gather information. Field trips, films, filmstrips, videotapes, interviews, television, and a study of photographs are examples of media that can be used in the gathering of information. At the intermediate grade level, where the variability of children's ability to read is much greater than at the primary-grade level, these additional learning resources offer children from the lowest to the highest level of reading achievement opportunities to work together in a small group that has the task of gathering information. There are many children who, although they have reading problems, are exceptionally able to interpret and make inferences on a very high level, when they are given the opportunity to use media that do not require a high level of reading ability. These learners need every opportunity to become contributing members of the group.

Mr. Bond planned to vary the membership of small groups I and II by mixing the children when the opportunity arose to gather information through learning resources that were not dependent on reading ability for interpretation. His basic model for group management still could be applied—only the membership of the subgroups would need to be changed.

This provision is very important for the psychological support of the poor reader and contributes to positive personal and social development of learners.

His Concluding Activities

Mr. Bond's sketch plan included activities that were to occur in the language arts and creative arts classes. They were intended to personalize instruction and to make social studies more meaningful to the children. To summarize briefly, Mr. Bond decided to have the children engage in a variety of extended learnings that included the following activities.

1. Visit the school library to locate information (reading materials and other media) on the geography of the Americas.
2. Prepare artwork to illustrate landforms and vegetation types that are characteristic of the natural regions of the Americas.
3. Prepare oral reports to present basic learnings. These are to include results of interviews on how physical features affect how people live and work in the community.
4. Use artwork to illustrate the major learning, including illustrations and maps of the regions studied.

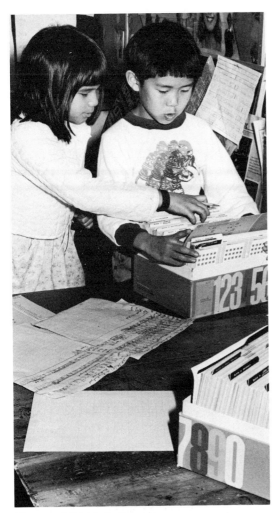

Successful teachers provide for individualized as well as group instruction. Identify situations in which the type of individualized learning shown in this photograph would be appropriate.

(Courtesy of Patricia A. Conrard.)

Study Questions and Activities

1. Why did Miss Baxter and Mr. Bond change their classes from whole group to small group instruction over a period of several days, rather than on a single day?

2. For what reasons did these teachers intersperse whole-class with small group instruction?

3. What classroom activities are particularly well suited to a whole-class configuration and which ones to small groups?

4. What criteria did these two teachers apply in evaluating the effectiveness of their small group instructional endeavors?

5. Give examples of how these two teachers made use of small groups to help individualize learning.

6. What ill effects might result from unwise grouping of children? What would you consider "unwise grouping of children" to mean?

7. Why are grouping policies particularly relevant in light of the current emphasis on mainstreaming mildly handicapped children?

For Further Professional Study

Corbett, H. Dickson. "To Make an Omelette You Have to Break the Egg Crate." *Educational Leadership,* **40** (Nov. 1982), 34–35.

Donmoyer, Robert. "Pedagogical Improvisation." *Educational Leadership,* **40** (Jan. 1983), 39–43.

Dunn, Rita, and Robert W. Cole. "Enter into the World of the Handicapped: P.L. 94-142 Opens the Door." *The Clearing House,* **53** (Jan. 1980), 241–243.

Garcia, Jesus, guest ed. "Integrating Social Studies, Language Arts, and Reading Skills." *Social Education,* **47** (Nov./Dec. 1983), 527–540.

————, and John W. Logan. "Teaching Social Studies Using Basal Readers." *Social Education,* **47** (Nov./Dec. 1983), 533–536.

Goodlad, John I. *A Place Called School: Prospects for the Future.* New York: McGraw-Hill Book Company, 1984, Chaps. 4, 5.

Leiter, Jeffrey. "Classroom Composition and Achievement Gains." *Sociology of Education,* **56** (July 1983), 126–132.

Orlosky, Donald E., ed. *Introduction to Education.* Columbus, Ohio: Charles E. Merrill Publishing Company, 1982, Chaps. 5, 6, 12.

Rowan, Brian, and Andrew W. Miracle, Jr. "Systems of Ability Grouping and the Stratification of Achievement in Elementary Schools." *Sociology of Education,* **56** (July 1983), 133–144.

Shepherd, Gene D., and William B. Ragan. *Modern Elementary Curriculum,* 6th ed. New York: Holt, Rinehart and Winston, 1982, Chap. 2.

Treffinger, Donald J. "Gifted Students, Regular Classrooms: Sixty Ingredients for a Better Blend." *The Elementary School Journal,* **82** (Jan. 1982), 267–273.

Walker, Decker F. "Reflections on the Educational Potential and Limitations of Microcomputers." *Phi Delta Kappan,* **65** (Oct. 1983), 103–107.

Guiding
Children's
Learning

7

THE QUALIFIED AND COMPETENT TEACHER . . .

1. Realizes the importance of the classroom environment in enhancing learning.
2. Is familiar with the potential of various instructional media.
3. Is skillful in framing, stating, sequencing, and pacing questions.
4. Understands the importance of diagnostic and corrective teaching in the elementary school.

Performance Criteria

As a result of the serious study of this chapter, the student should be able to . . .

1. Identify the salient characteristics of a suitable elementary school classroom environment.
2. Explain the rationale for a multimedia approach to teaching.
3. Incorporate a variety of media in a lesson plan.
4. Write a series of questions in an appropriate sequence for the development of a lesson for a grade of his or her choice.
5. Provide an appropriate reaction (i.e., acknowledging, cuing, probing, restating, and clarifying) to the response of a child to a teacher's question.
6. Perform a simple screening of a child's learning difficulties.
7. Plan an appropriate corrective procedure for a child with a learning problem.

The four topics discussed in this chapter, (1) the learning environment, (2) using multimedia, (3) questioning strategies, and (4) diagnostic and corrective teaching, embody skills and procedures that many successful elementary school teachers use on a daily basis. These topics are vast in scope and complex in their makeup. Many teacher education institutions offer separate courses that treat these topics in depth. We encourage the teacher to take such courses, preferably after gaining some experience in the classroom. For beginners, the basic concepts and skills discussed here will get them started toward the achievement of their most important professional mission, that of helping children learn.

The Learning Environment

Establishing an appropriate classroom environment is mentioned in several chapters of this book because of its central importance to teaching and learning in the elementary school. The classroom environment is a direct measure of the quality of human interaction that takes place there and, consequently, has an impact on how children learn. Some of the messages transmitted to children by the classroom environment are easily discernible— the furniture is comfortably arranged, children's work is displayed, there is evidence of pupil involvement in the life of the classroom. Other messages are more subtle; they lie beneath the surface of what immediately comes to the eye of the classroom visitor. These are the feelings that are projected from teacher to children and from the children to one another. These messages are also carried by voice inflections and statements of praise, and through "body language." These not-so-easily observable message systems of schools have been referred to as "the hidden curriculum," what John I. Goodlad refers to as "the implicit curriculum."[1]

THE HIDDEN CURRICULUM

The "hidden curriculum" is pervasive in a classroom and school and reflects the attitudes of the teacher, the administration, and the children. Without saying so directly, the teacher, through a combination of circumstances, conveys to the children much about the expectations and values that are prized. Through the "hidden curriculum," children learn the extent to which life at school suits them and their needs. Lessons learned through the informal interaction with other children may condition a child's social skills and human relationships for a lifetime. Children learn, often without being told, which models of behavior are highlighted for emulation. They learn which behavior is likely to gain favor and which is not. They know a great deal about how the teacher feels toward social issues, groups, and individuals, and, again, without ever having been told explicitly.

---

[1] John I. Goodlad, *A Place Called School* (New York: McGraw-Hill Book Company, 1983), p. 30.

178

Because it is not possible to eliminate entirely the effects of the "hidden curriculum," it is important for teachers to understand the concept and to come to grips with it. The teacher is the one who sets the emotional tone of the classroom. Because of the high social status of teachers in elementary school classrooms, children generally treat them with deference. This being the case, the teacher is in a position of considerable power when it comes to shaping the nature of the "hidden curriculum." Thus, the expression of a preference, an aside comment, a statement of surprise, or even a facial expression may strongly influence the thoughts and actions of young children.

CHARACTERISTICS OF THE LEARNING ENVIRONMENT

Three dimensions of the classroom environment need to be considered by the teacher: (1) the physical arrangement of the room; (2) the social relationships within the space; and (3) the psycho-

(Courtesy of Kay F. Engelsen.)

The classroom environment should provide the opportunity for children to broaden their interests. What evidence do you see in this photograph that the teacher has met this requirement.

logical suitability to the developmental level of children who occupy the space. These variables can be combined in numerous ways to make for a good learning environment. For example, some teachers prefer a more structured physical environment than do others, yet both arrangements are acceptable because the furniture in both cases is comfortably and functionally arranged for children's use. We can provide guidelines that will be helpful, but the classroom learning environment will always be a reflection of each individual teacher's personality, philosophy, teaching style, and competence. With that in mind, the following are qualities that supervisors look for in assessing classroom learning environments:

1. There is evidence of unity and cohesiveness; children willingly cooperate to achieve class goals; conflicts are resolved without continued hostility and rancor.
2. The teacher involves the children in making plans and decisions appropriate to their level of development concerning life and work in the classroom.
3. There is evidence of good interpersonal relations among children and the teacher.
4. The children are interested in what they are doing.
5. Individual differences among learners are recognized and respected; not all children are required to do the same tasks, in the same amount of time, all of the time.
6. The physical makeup of the room—the desks, tables, chairs, and so forth—indicates flexible use.
7. There is a plentiful quantity of good quality instructional materials suitable for a wide range of abilities and learning styles.
8. There is much evidence of children's creative work—constructions, murals, artwork, and written work—all of which suggests their active involvement in learning.

In recent decades, creative school architecture has produced facilities that are visually, acoustically, educationally, and psychologically appropriate to the lives and learning needs of children. The most indispensable ingredient, however, is still supplied by the teacher. It is the teacher who is critical in determining the quality of the learning environment for elementary school children. Notice how the teacher in the following vignette combines flexible use of space and a concern for the social, psychological, and educational needs of children with the use of diversified and appealing instructional resources in developing a classroom environment that is conducive to learning.

Mrs. Garcia provides a classroom environment that is plentifully supplied with materials related to the work of the children. This allows them to explore various aspects of topics on their own. She encourages the children to wonder, to imagine, to be curious about what they see, to touch, and to feel. Much of the work is done in small groups in activity areas and learning centers in the classroom. She supervises and directs the work of these groups and that of individual children in accordance with their need for assistance. She provides a minimum of supervision for those who are self-directed and capable of independent work. She often asks such questions as, "Where can you find the information you need? What evidence is there that proves your point? What do you think would be the best way to do that? Why do you think so? Can you think of another reason?"

Mrs. Garcia is usually physically close to those who read poorly or who are unable to work productively on their own. She arranges the small work groups in ways that encourage the involvement of those children who may be less interested or less capable than others. This helps them learn and provides avenues for greater acceptance of these children by the rest of the class. She maintains a flexible time schedule and will usually bring the entire class together for a summary and an evaluation session at the close of each day's work.

A visitor to this room is impressed with the abundance and variety of instructional materials. Mrs. Garcia makes use of basic texts, but there are also a great number of other reading resources available. She has three learning centers for the current social studies/science unit. One consists largely of books and other materials for children who are good readers and want to do individual study and research. Another center contains the audio and visual materials that are used: filmstrips and audio tapes that can be operated by the children. The third center consists of learning packets and other self-study material. In addition the room has interest centers that contain displays, artifacts, maps, a globe, an encyclopedia, study prints, and an abundant supply of magazines. Because these instructional materials are systematically arranged, they do not give the room a cluttered look.

There is a considerable amount of teacher participation on a one-to-one basis. Mrs. Garcia moves among the children as they work. In this way she is able to give assistance to children on an individual basis, make an adjustment in an assignment, or help a child find a needed book. She likes to think in terms of the performance capabilities of individual children and assigns responsibilities accordingly. Even though children are working on several projects and assignments at the same time, she seems to know where each one is, what each is doing, and what level of performance can be expected from each.

Looking about the room one sees much evidence of the children's creative work. Here is a small construction project underway. Over there we see a group preparing a mural. The bulletin boards have posted on them several pieces of written work and illustrations. It is apparent that these children are expressing their ideas and feelings through several channels of communication, and in the process their creative abilities are being tapped.

Using Multimedia

When children in the primary grades participate in "show and tell," they are using two of the oldest traditions in human communication and teaching. Until books were in widespread use, teachers conveyed ideas and made explanations orally, sometimes combining such presentations with showing or demonstrating for learners. It was out of this tradition that the lecture became so firmly established as a method of teaching. Later, as the implements of writing became available and affordable, teachers had learners write, or more correctly *copy*, material that the teacher had prepared.

Much of this changed after books could be manufactured at low cost. Learners no longer had to rely on the teacher as the chief source of information. This change had a profound effect not only on teaching methodology but also on the curriculum. Increasingly, reading became an instrumental skill of vital importance to success in school, and it remains so today. Teachers did not have to spend most of their time lecturing and explaining subject matter but could work more closely with individual children and small groups. They could engage their students in discussions and could challenge them to read their materials critically. Although teachers continued to talk to their classes, and do so today, the print tradition of conveying information to learners has been the dominant one in schools for a hundred and fifty years.

As time went on, new instructional technologies were introduced: pictures, models, charts, and artifacts. Much later came recordings, filmstrips, and sound motion pictures. By 1960 a wide range of new instructional resources had become available. These materials were used mainly to aid children who were unable to read well enough to get essential information from textbooks, or the subject matter was so complex that it was difficult for learners to understand it. This use of visual and/or auditory instructional material introduced the tradition of *audiovisual aids.*

When educators talked about "audiovisual aids," such references placed these media outside the mainstream of the curriculum. If they were "aids," not all learners needed them. Such "aids" could be regarded as nonessential or even "frills." Gradually, therefore, the audiovisual aids tradition gave way to the concept of integrating a variety of media and experiences into teaching or presentation modes. This use of media makes them an integral part of the teaching/learning process and places the emphasis on learners and learning rather than on technology. Teaching is thought of in terms of communication between teacher and learner. That communication can often be enhanced or "mediated" through the use of some device. The teacher does not rely on a single device or "medium" to carry the communication, but uses many appropriate and carefully selected resources and experiences to do the job. Thus, the notion of "multimedia" provides us with what amounts to sophisticated components of a comprehensive system of educational communication.

WHY MULTIMEDIA?

The chief purpose for using multimedia is to make it possible for learners to achieve the objectives of instruction more easily and effectively. We know that children do not all learn in the same way. Some are comfortable in using printed materials. Others are more visually oriented and are able to learn easier when concepts or skills are presented visually. Still others need to manipulate objects in order to understand relationships. The use of different media makes it possible to accommodate the various learning styles of children.

When a variety of media is used, the teacher can take advantage of the particular strengths of each one. There can be no question, for example, that some motion pictures can present some ideas more vividly and more clearly than can books. A film, however, cannot carry the rich descriptive detail that is provided in a story about winter life in colonial New England. Textbooks open certain avenues to learning; maps and globes open others. Manipulative materials in mathematics fulfill particular purposes; science equipment fulfills others. The library is an important learning resource, but so is the bulletin board, the community, and the classroom aquarium. There is no one best instructional resource; rather each serves a specific instructional purpose.

If we combine differences in learner needs with the unique strengths and limitations of each medium, the necessity of a multimedia approach becomes clear. Additionally, each subject and skill of the curriculum varies in abstractness and complexity; thus each requires the use of carefully selected instructional resources and experiences. Appropriate selection and use of media not only contribute to improved learning for greater numbers of children but also result in increased interest and enthusiasm for learning.

SPECIAL SKILLS

Through specific courses, laboratory self-study, student teaching, or classroom experience, the teacher must achieve proficiency in certain skills related to the use of multimedia.

Technical Skills

Inability to handle the technical skills associated with machine operation is often a deterrent to the use of certain media. Most teacher education institutions provide courses or "A-V Lab" experiences in which these skills are taught. Other than the computer, the operation of media for classroom use has been greatly simplified and should pose no problem for teachers.

(Courtesy of Patricia A. Conrard.)

Use of modern technology provides new avenues of creative expression for children. What possibilities for expressive activities do you see in this photograph?

Selection and Use

The professional use of media requires that the most appropriate experience be selected and used to achieve a specific purpose. Three considerations should be taken into account: (1) the nature of the learners; (2) the nature of the material to be taught; and (3) the special strengths or limitations of the instructional resource. Ideally, the teacher seeks to obtain the best "fit" among these three variables.

Keeping Abreast of Developments

Because educational communication is part of the rapidly growing "hi-tec" field, changes in it are occurring at a fast pace. What the teacher in preparation learns today will need to be updated on a continuing basis once the teacher is in service. Professional journals, such as *Instructor, Learning-Teacher, Media and Methods, Instructional Innovator,* and *The Computing Teacher* provide information about developments in the media field. Professional reading, attendance at professional conferences, and journals of the various subject fields (science, mathematics, social studies, reading, and so forth) are additional good sources of such information.

HOW WOULD *YOU* DO IT?

Mr Wills is considered to be a very good first year teacher, but in using media, things rarely work well for him. Right in the middle of a lesson he often discovers that he is missing some important piece of equipment or material needed to complete the presentation. Once, he was going to demonstrate how a candle extinguishes itself when covered with a glass jar. He had the candles and the jars all right, but he forgot to bring matches to light the candles. Another time, he planned to use an overhead projector, only to find at the last minute that the electrical cord was not long enough to reach the outlet, and he did not have an extension cord. On another occasion he wanted to use slides in a demonstration and found that he had placed the slides in the carousel upside down and backwards. The same thing happened once when he was to show a filmstrip. Situations like that always seemed to pop up at the last moment to surprise Mr. Wills and spoil his plans.

1. If you were Mr. Wills, what action would you take to avoid such unexpected contingencies?

2. How can this carelessness result in other more serious problems for Mr. Wills?

Questioning Strategies

Questioning is a natural way to learn and to satisfy one's curiosity. Whether in or out of school, people ask questions when they want to find out something. Questioning is also among the oldest and most commonly used practices in teaching.

In modern times thinking is often stated as a high-priority goal of education. If teachers are to help children develop the intellectual skilis associated with reflective thought, they will have to ask questions that trigger the use of such skills. Therefore, attention has been focused on so-called *higher level* questions—those that call for application of information, analysis, synthesis, interpretation of data, and so on. In this context, so-called *lower level* questions, those that require the recall of information or the reproduction of information, would not be appropriate.[2]

DEVELOPING SKILL IN USING QUESTIONS

Three subskills are a part of skillful questioning: framing and stating questions, sequencing of questions, and pacing questions. Let us consider each of these briefly.

Framing and Stating Questions

In framing and stating classroom questions, the first requirement is that they be appropriate for the subject matter and the purpose for which they are being asked. But even if they are satisfactory on those counts, questions may be faulty for technical reasons. The following guidelines will be helpful in avoiding such problems:

1. The question should be worded correctly. The grammar should be correct; the syntax easy to follow. Keep the questions short and the vocabulary simple. Avoid bookish terms and expressions.
2. Express the question clearly enough so that the child will know what is wanted in the way of a response.
3. Do not include giveaway clues in the question.
4. If the question begins by asking "What do you think . . . ?" or some similar stem that calls for the expression of an opinion, the teacher should be prepared to accept *any* response provided by the child.

---

[2] The idea of "levels" of questions has come from the extensive use of the taxonomy of educational objectives (cognitive domain) by Benjamin Bloom and his associates. Although the taxonomy was designed as a way of ordering educational objectives, it can be used for the classification and study of questions as well. *See* Benjamin S. Bloom, Ed., *Taxonomy of Educational Objectives: Handbook I, The Cognitive Domain* (New York: David McKay Co., Inc., 1956) and Francis P. Hunkins, *Questioning Strategies and Techniques* (Boston: Allyn & Bacon, Inc., 1972), pp. 33–61.

5. State questions in a tone of voice that encourages children to respond.

6. The question should be stated in a way that stimulates children's thinking rather than leading them to an expected answer.

To avoid the difficulties suggested by these guidelines, it is recommended that, during the development of a lesson, beginning teachers write out the questions they plan to ask. When the beginner counts on improvising questions while teaching a roomfull of children, the questions are likely to come out badly. It is often helpful to make and listen to a tape recording of one's teaching in order to self-evaluate questioning skills.

Sequencing of Questions

If ideas are to be *developed* in the course of a lesson, questions must be properly sequenced. Idea development means that the lesson has direction: the questions lead somewhere. One cannot ask a series of questions at random and expect that ideas will build cumulatively. In the sequence of the following questions, notice how each question builds on the one that precedes it. The questions are based on a story of a young man's visit to an abandoned house.

1. Can you give an overall description of the house Charlie went to visit?
2. What was there about it that made him uneasy?
3. When did he first discover that something was out of the ordinary?
4. Why do you think he did not leave at that time?
5. At what point was he absolutely certain that someone else was in the house?
6. What, exactly, happened that made him know he was not alone?
7. Why could he not go for help then?
8. What can we learn from Charlie's experience about going into strange or unfamiliar surroundings?

Even if the reader is not familiar with the story, essential elements of the story line can be inferred from this sequence

---

HOW WOULD YOU SAY IT?

The following five questions are poorly stated. Identify what is wrong with each one, then restate it correctly.

1. Indian people lived how on the Plains before the coming of the Europeans?

2. At what point in a musical selection does the "finale" come?

3. Can you list the steps in doing the experiment from start to finish beginning with the last step first?

4. I don't think it was a very good idea to use those colors for the picture, do you?

5. What would happen if, but, of course, you would never want to do anything like this, you were hiking along and you suddenly stepped on a rock, twisted your ankle and couldn't walk any further, and you had to get help but there was no one around?

6. If you saw a hot-air balloon one day as you were playing with your beach ball, what do you think would make it stay in the air?

---

of questions. Asked in a random order, the questions would not produce this effect.

Perhaps the easiest way to learn how to ask questions sequentially is to teach a process that has a fixed sequence, such as following a product through its manufacturing process, or discussing how an item gets from where it is produced to where it is used. Science experiments that necessitate a specific sequence lend themselves well to learning how to sequence questions, as do some operations in mathematics. With increased experience the teacher will become sensitive to whether or not the questions being asked are in an appropriate order. This aspect of questioning is much like building a sequence for a computer program. Indeed, the teacher in the classroom *is* the programmer much of the time. Accordingly, if learning is to proceed efficiently, the teacher should provide questions that will deal with small increments of learning in a progressively more complex sequence.

Pacing the Questions

Pacing has to do with the rapidity with which questions are asked. Two problems are commonly associated with pacing. One is that the questions are asked too rapidly. Little or no time is allowed for the development of ideas associated with a question before another one is asked. Short answers are expected and encouraged, rather than elaborate responses. The second problem has to do with the small amount of time given to respond. Teachers seem to feel that unless children respond immediately, the question needs to be restated, clarified, or the learner provided with a cue. Given more time, children will often come forth with a thoughtful response.

The position taken here is that teachers should slow the pace of questioning. They should not be hasty in providing cues, nor should they too quickly restate and clarify questions. The atmosphere should encourage reflection rather than quickness of response. Questions are designed to provoke thinking, and thinking requires time.

HANDLING PUPIL RESPONSES TO QUESTIONS

How a teacher handles the response of a child may be as important as the question itself, in terms of productive learning. As a general guideline, the teacher's comment following a response should be such that it leaves the child with the feeling that he or she would like to respond again to another question. Let us examine some of the ways a teacher might deal with responses of pupils.

Acknowledging a Pupil Response

There are a half-dozen or so common expressions that teachers use to acknowledge pupil responses. Among these are "all right," "uh-huh," "yes," "okay." These are noncommittal, nonevaluative utterances that simply recognize that the pupil has responded. (Of course, these might be accompanied by nonverbal clues that carry powerful evaluative messages, such as an approving or disapproving facial expression, tone of voice, or body movement.) Responses of this type, i.e., simple acknowledgments, are often effective if the teacher is encouraging a discussion of the question. When a pupil response is recognized in a noncommittal way, the class knows that the matter is still open and others may contribute their ideas to the discussion.

When listening to tape recordings of their classes, teachers are often surprised—and embarrassed—at how often they use the same expression over and over in acknowledging responses. A teacher may say "all right" a hundred times a day and not even be aware that he or she is using that expression. A teacher needs to strive to develop some variety in the acknowledgement of pupil responses.

Evaluative Statements

Some teachers seem to think they must evaluate every response with a "Yes, that's right" or "No, that's not right." Of course teachers need to evaluate the work of children, and incorrect responses should not be ignored. But there is much that is wrong with a procedure that necessitates an evaluative comment from the teacher each time a pupil answers a question or makes a comment in class. First, the teacher does not always know whether a response is right or wrong. Moreover, many responses cannot be categorized as being totally right or wrong. Also, this procedure tends to encourage the kinds of questions for which answers can be evaluated only in this way. Finally, some children will not participate in questioning of this type, because they do not want their responses evaluated negatively in front of the whole class. Rather than risking such a contingency, they simply will not participate; and if called on, will say they do not know.

Restating and Clarifying

Not every pupil response needs to be restated and clarified, but this is a good practice from time to time. It is especially appropriate when the response has been spoken so softly that it could not be heard by the entire group. Also, the teacher may know that further clarification will be helpful in either promoting continued thinking about the question or in providing more precision to the response. For example, in a science lesson the teacher may ask, "If I have a gallon of water and I pour in a quart of oil, what happens to the oil?" A child responds by saying, "It goes to the top." The teacher restates and clarifies, "You say it goes to the top. Do you mean that the oil will float on top of the water?" The child continues, "Yes, it separates. The oil floats on top of the water." Here, through the use of another question, the teacher is clarifying in order to verify that the child's response has been understood.

191

(Courtesy of Mary Wilbert Smith.)

The children in this photograph are participating in a small group activity at a science learning center. How can the use of artifacts contribute to the enrichment of instruction?

Probing

It often happens that a child's response is only a partial answer to the question, and the teacher wants to encourage a more complete answer. This can be done by probing for additional information. Such statements as these can be used for that purpose:

1. "Can you say a little bit more about that?"
2. "But why do you suppose he turned back?"
3. "Can you explain why it happened?"
4. "You said 'yes'; now tell why you think so."
5. "That is correct, as far as you have gone, but there is yet another very important point you haven't mentioned."

In probing for a more complete response, the teacher should not press too hard, thereby making the child so anxious and nervous that he or she cannot respond at all. Needless stress-producing probing can easily become counterproductive.

"RAISE YOUR HANDS, PLEASE!"

Should a teacher "call" only on volunteers who raise their hands? Experts disagree on this matter. Some believe a random selection of respondents is best because all must then prepare themselves intellectually to answer the questions. They feel that a fixed pattern of questioning is not effective because children prepare themselves to respond only to those questions they know they will be asked to answer. In terms of learning, research studies indicate that the fixed pattern of questioning produces better results because it ensures that all children will be involved in the question-answer transactions.

1. Provide anecdotal examples from your own experience that illustrate limitations and advantages of various methods of soliciting responses.
2. Should the teacher be sensitive to the pupil anxiety that is induced through the use of certain questioning procedures? What impact might a fixed pattern of soliciting answers have on a child who is a stutterer, or one who does not speak English well? Discuss.

Cuing

It may happen that the teacher asks a question and draws a blank—a sea of empty faces. This has happened to all teachers at one time or another. It may mean that the question was poorly stated or it may mean that the children simply did not know what it was that the teacher was asking. When this happens, the teacher should not provide the response, but instead should give them a few leads, *cues* that will guide their thinking along the lines being proposed. This involves more than simply repeating the question or even rephrasing it. In cuing, the teacher provides small amounts of additional information.

EXAMPLE:

Teacher: Why is it that the candle went out when we placed a jar over it?
Pupil: It doesn't get any air.
Teacher: (Probing.) Yes, but what is it in the air that is needed to keep the candle burning?
Pupil: (No response.)

AND YOU SAID . . .

In the following four situations, imagine that you are the teacher. In these situations the teacher asks a question and a pupil responds. The response, however, is in some way inadequate. You are being asked to supply what you would say next, in order to move the instructional sequence along.

Situation I

Teacher: You enjoyed the poem so much yesterday that I thought we could share another one today. What was it that you liked most about the poem we read yesterday?

Pupil: Rhymes

And YOU said: _____

Situation II

Teacher: Now you notice that this line (pointing to a line showing the amount of food produced) on our graph goes up, but this other line (pointing to a line showing number of people living on farms) goes down. What does this tell us about how farming has changed?

Pupil: It tells us that people moved away. They got other jobs.

And YOU said: _____

Situation III

Teacher: An electric generator produces electricity by the rotation of a coil in a magnetic field. It needs some source of energy or power to rotate the coil. Thus we see that an electric motor uses electrical energy to produce mechanical energy. A generator, however, uses mechanical energy to produce electrical energy. What forms of mechanical energy do we use to produce electrical energy?

Pupil: (No response; dead silence.)

And YOU said: _____

Situation IV

Teacher: In our social studies we have been learning about how people get the things they need to live in our community. You remember we learned two new—and big—words. (Children respond enthusiastically, "consumer" and "producer.") Yes, you remembered well. Now who can tell us something about these words?

Pupil: All consumers are producers.

And YOU said: _____

Teacher: (Cuing.) Do you remember when we learned about rust . . .

Pupil: (Picking up on the cue.) Oxygen! The candle needs oxygen to burn. It goes out when it has used up the oxygen.

Notice, in this example, that the teacher did not give the answer. The teacher simply provided a small hint that pointed the learner's thinking in the appropriate direction. In this case, the child was able to respond even before the teacher completed the cuing sentence.

QUESTIONS THAT FOCUS ON SPECIFIC PURPOSES

The teacher must be skillful in selecting appropriate questions in terms of purposes or the results are likely to be disappointing. For example, teachers sometimes report their inability to involve pupils in discussions. An examination of the kinds of questions they are asking often provides clues as to why they are having this problem. If the questions asked require a yes or no answer, or call for the recall of a specific answer, there is little to discuss. Discussion questions must be those that will allow for some divergence of views, and those that open possibilities for creative interaction.

Procedural Questions

Teachers ask many questions that have to do with classroom procedures, the clarification of directions, transitional inquiries, or rhetorical queries. Some of these questions are a necessary part of teaching, of course; but often they amount to little more than time-fillers while the teacher is gathering his or her thoughts. They may even take the form of a threat. ("Do you want me to change your seat?") Frequently no pupil response is given; indeed, none is expected. Teachers usually are not even fully aware of the extent of their use of questions of this type.

EXAMPLES:

1. Does anyone have a question?
2. Are you ready for the next point?
3. How many of you will be having lunch here today?

4. Will someone review for us what we planned to do during our music period today?

5. Do you think we can figure out a better way to return the bats and balls to the storeroom?

6. Is there anyone in the group who has so little to do that he or she wants me to assign additional work?

QUESTIONS TO CHECK LITERAL COMPREHENSION

In content fields such as social studies, science, and health, it is necessary for the teacher to know whether or not children are extracting the essential information presented in the material they are required to read. Questions used to check such literal comprehension should encourage good study habits; they should focus on important concepts and ideas rather than on inconsequential detail. For example, if too many trivial fact questions are included, the child may assume that those facts are all that is important in the material. Perhaps it is best to include a variety of questions—some calling for identification of important facts and ideas; others requiring greater breadth of understanding. The questions should be constructed in a way that will help children identify the most relevant information presented in the material.

EXAMPLES:

1. What terms are the most important for understanding this selection?

2. What costs are included in the price you pay for shoes?

3. After reading the passage in your science book, make a list of all the pollutants mentioned. Can you divide the list into two groups, one listing *natural* pollutants and the other *people-made* pollutants?

4. Can you draw a diagram to show that you understand the number relationships in a problem of indirect measurement?

5. In each of the paragraphs, can you find the cause and effect relationship between the items?

6. What characteristics of the countries of the Middle East would justify grouping them together as a region?

7. Exactly what happened at each of the four stages of the experiment?
8. What are the five fire-danger spots in a home?

Reflective or "Thought" Questions

Reflective questions are those that are open-ended and require higher-level thought processes. Their purpose is to stimulate the creative imaginations and thinking abilities of learners. A reflective question may *not* have a right answer, in the sense that one and only one response is acceptable. Reflective questions are often tied to decision making, thereby requiring the consideration of several alternatives and the consequences of each. Reflective thinking includes such mental processes as application, analysis, syntheses, and evaluation.

For generations teachers have admonished their pupils to "think." Even today it is fairly common to hear teachers say, "Now think, boys and girls. Think real [*sic*] hard!" Simply telling a child to think is not a satisfactory way to develop thinking

(Courtesy of Joel Schwarz.)

The teacher in this photograph is using a puppet as a prop to stimulate a dramatic activity. What are other examples of resources that a teacher can use to encourage creative expression?

abilities. What is needed are activities, situations, and questions that require the use of intellectual skills such as comparing and contrasting, noting cause and effect, considering alternatives, and drawing conclusions based on information.

EXAMPLES:

1. In the early years of our country, many people had comfortable homes and a good life in the thirteen states along the Atlantic. Why do you suppose some chose to leave all that behind and go to the West, which promised a hard and often dangerous life?

2. Scientists think some chemicals are so dangerous to human health that they should not be used for insect and disease control. Can you think of conditions when they might be used even though they are dangerous?

3. What businesses and what kinds of work would be in greater demand if everyone worked only four days a week?

4. How might the story have ended if the family had visited Aunt Sophie and Uncle Charlie one day sooner?

5. Why are some drugs sold only when prescribed by a medical doctor?

6. Do you think it would be wise to protect only those animals that are useful to human beings? Why or why not?

7. Why must the control of air and water pollution go beyond a single community or a single state?

PUPIL QUESTIONS

The kinds of questions pupils ask should tell the teacher a great deal about the effectiveness of classroom management procedures and about the conduct of instruction. For example, a preponderance of questions that call for reassurance and teacher approval (e.g., Am I doing this right? Is this what you want us to do? Is it all right if I make my picture sideways?) might indicate the general feeling of insecurity, a feeling that there is considerable risk in doing things that displease the teacher. It could mean, too, that the teacher has developed a high level of pupil dependence on him or her. It might also mean that the teacher's directions are not clear, and that the children do not understand precisely what is expected of them.

Sometimes teachers become annoyed when children ask end-less procedural and permission questions (e.g., May I sharpen my pencil? Please, may I get a book? May I take this book home?). Yet the teacher should recognize that he or she may be contributing to the problem. If children are not provided opportunities to develop self-direction, and to assume responsibility for a certain amount of decision making, it can be predicted that they will turn to the teacher to get authority to engage in routine procedures.

Children are likely to model their question-asking behavior after that of the teacher. By listening to the teacher's questions, they sense what the teacher believes to be important. Thus, if they hear the teacher asking mainly recall and memory questions, they might naturally assume that such questions are the most important ones. If, on the other hand, the teacher tends to ask provocative questions that enhance higher-level thinking skills, the children are likely to follow the teacher's example.

Diagnostic and Corrective Teaching

The challenge of teaching is to secure the best "fit" between individual learner interests, capabilities, and learning styles *and* the presentation strategy—and to do this in the setting of a classroom group. But no matter how well the teacher individual-izes instruction and how sensitive the teacher is to the special needs of children, learners respond differentially to presentations, and some will need corrective teaching to enable them to pro-gress. A relatively minor learning problem, or a missed lesson because of absence on the day the material was presented, may, if left unattended, escalate into a serious learning handicap for a child. What is needed, therefore, is an alert teacher who is able to spot difficulties and correct them in order to avoid their taking on serious proportions.

In our discussion of diagnostic and corrective teaching, we are not referring to children with extraordinary learning needs or to those who have disabilities that may impair their ability to learn. We are, rather, referring to ordinary boys and girls who, for one reason or another, are not progressing as well as could be expected. Such children usually will respond well to corrective teaching because their learning problem is not related to serious psychological or physical impairments.

THE TEACHER AS DIAGNOSTICIAN

When teachers teach but children fail to learn, there is a natural inclination to blame the learners. The assumption is that learning would be improved if children would "just work harder," or "be more attentive during presentations," or "have better home backgrounds," or "would care more about learning." No doubt these concerns are valid up to a point. Most certainly the learner has a responsibility to do those tasks and assignments that are needed to learn. But teachers themselves must shoulder some of the responsibility for the children's failure to learn. Presentations are not always as clear as they could be, or as captivating as the teacher would like them to be. Moreover, presentations are not always well suited to the learning styles of some children.

A good elementary school teacher is constantly making assessments of children's learning both in terms of specific objectives to be achieved and in terms of the overall goals of the school. Most of these assessments are based on astute observations of children's behavior. The teacher notices that a child is not able to use recently taught word-attack skills; another is unable to compute simple problems in mathematics; a third is losing interest in school. It is from these observations that the teacher forms judgments about an appropriate program of corrective teaching.

Good teachers do not assume that children learn new concepts and skills simply because they have been taught. They teach and reteach as needed. If one presentation is not clear, good teachers will try another approach. They present complex concepts in varied settings, and they provide adequate drill and practice for skills. The teacher is as much of a diagnostician as a presenter in the day-to-day work of the classroom. The teacher's assessments of children's behavior is critical to many decisions that need to be made each day—how to group, what materials and media to use, which children need more practice, which ones need special help. Much of what we call effective teaching consists of diagnostic assessments of situations and shaping the instructional program in accordance with them. The insight and judgment of the classroom teacher are critical in doing this well.

In taking a diagnostic approach to teaching, the teacher is cautioned against the practice of labeling children, a practice that continues to be rather widespread. Labels are of dubious value and are often detrimental to a child's learning. Quite clearly, labels mark children with stereotypic characteristics that may or may not be appropriate to specific cases. Besides, attaching a label to the behavior does not in and of itself do anything to correct the learning difficulty. In fact, identifying a child as being "aphasic," "dyslexic," "autistic," "mentally retarded," "a stutterer," or "low SES" may contribute to the complexity of the problem. What *is* important is to know enough about the child's learning problem to be able to develop a suitable program of instruction that will enable him or her to resume progress.

DIAGNOSTIC AND CORRECTIVE PROCEDURES

The teacher who is oriented to diagnostic and corrective teaching is constantly monitoring the responses of children and adjusting the instruction in accordance with such observations. As the teacher becomes involved in more formal diagnostic work, three questions can serve as guidelines for that process: (1) What evidence is there that a learning problem exists? (2) What is the *specific* learning difficulty the child is encountering? (3) What level of corrective work is required? Let us examine each of these more carefully.

What Evidence Is There That a Learning Problem Exists?

Let us assume that a teacher is examining the scores of children in a class and finds that, with one exception, mathematics, the children's scores are consistently high. This is a clear indicator that a learning problem exists in the mathematics area. If the test results are reported as mean scores, it may be that the scores of a few low-achieving children are depressing the average for the entire group. On the other hand, it may be that most of the children scored relatively lower on math than they did on the other parts of the test battery. The teacher will need to explore this situation in detail.

The case described in the foregoing paragraph is different from that of another class where the teacher finds the children's achievement scores low on *all* subtests. The teacher will need to know if this is because the group as a whole is less capable than an average class, or because of poor teaching in prior years, or because the test was given under adverse conditions, or for

Child's name_____Age_____Birthday_____

Grade_____ School _____ Teacher_____

CLASSROOM SCREENING CHECKLIST*

Please check one of the columns after each item listed. Check a column, 1 through 5, depending on the frequency of occurence of that particular behavior. A mark in the one column indicates low occurrence and a mark in the five column indicates continual occurence. Columns 2-4 indicate intermediate levels of occurence.

It should be remembered that no single item on this checklist by itself should be considered as being indicative of a child with learning disabilities. It is the over-all pattern of items checked or not checked that should be evaluated.

AUDITORY DISCRIMINATION AND ORGANIZATION	Seldom 1	Occasionally 2	Generally 3	Frequently 4	Almost Always 5	Comments:
1. Doesn't seem to listen to daily classroom instructions or directions (often asks to have them repeated whereas the rest of the class goes ahead).						
2. Can't correctly recall oral directions when asked to repeat them.						
3. Doesn't seem to understand spoken words (may recognize the words separately but not in connected speech).						
4. Mild speech irregularities (can't pronounce words at his or her grade level).						
5. Immature speech patterns (still uses baby talk).						
6. Unable to learn or pronounce the sounds of letters (can't associate proper phoneme with its grapheme).						
7. Has trouble telling time.						
8. Doesn't understand the calendar (what day follows Wednesday, what month follows September, etc.).						
9. Has trouble organizing written work (seems confused).						

*Developed by the Washington Education Association for an inservice course. *Used by Permission.*

CLASSROOM SCREENING (cont.)

VISUAL DISCRIMINATION AND ORGANIZATION	1	2	3	4	5	Comments:
1. Avoids work requiring concentrated visual attention.						
2. When doing work requiring visual attention, he may move his head or trunk excessively (instead of moving his eyes).						
3. Is slow to finish written work (doesn't apply self, daydreams a lot, falls asleep in school).						
4. Difficulty in copying, both at near and far point.						
5. Reverses and/or rotates letters, numbers, and words (writes or reads p for q, b for d, u for n, saw for was, 6 for 9, 14 for 41, 327 for 723, left for felt).						

LARGE AND SMALL MUSCLE COORDINATION						
1. Unnecessary tongue and facial movements when using hands for writing, cutting, etc.						
2. Poor coordination (can't skip or hop on one foot or may have difficulty kicking a ball, jumping rope, walking a line, etc.).						
3. Accidentally breaks and tears things (clumsy, awkward).						
4. Indications of directional confusion (confuses left-hand with right-hand side of paper or eye movements indicate a right to left pattern of reading movement).						
5. Difficulty with small muscle activities (writing, cutting, tracing, tying shoe laces, etc.).						
6. Improper pencil grasp (clutched in fist, held too lightly or presses so hard as to break the lead and tear paper; this may include poor handwriting compared with peers).						
7. Poor eye-hand coordination including: drawing of a person, printing or writing on lines, difficulty in copying tasks.						

ACADEMIC PERFORMANCE	1	2	3	4	5	Comments:
1. Does very poorly on spelling test as compared with peers.						
2. Loses place more than once while reading aloud for one minute.						
3. Quits or substitutes words while reading material aloud (omits more than one out of every ten).						
4. Reads silently or aloud far more slowly than peers (word by word while reading aloud).						
5. Points at words while reading silently or aloud.						
6. Can't sound out or "unlock" words.						
7. Can read orally but does not comprehend the meaning of written grade-level words (word-caller).						
8. Can't follow written directions, which most peers can follow, when reading orally or silently.						
9. Difficulty with arithmetic (e.g. can't determine what number follows 8 or 16; may begin to add in the the middle of a subtraction problem; can't seem to learn addition, subtraction, or multiplication facts).						
VERBAL EXPRESSION						
1. Errors in oral expression: confuses prepositions such as over, under, in, out, etc. Also, seems to know an answer, but has or seems to have much difficulty explaining himself.						
2. Transposes sounds in words (says nabana for banana).						
3. Has much difficulty in using the right word to accurately express the meaning of an answer in a subject matter area.						

CLASSROOM SCREENING (cont.)

BEHAVIORAL CHARACTERISTICS	1	2	3	4	5	Comments:
1. Underactive (seems lazy, couldn't care less) in classroom and on playground.						
2. Overactive (can't sit still in class), may have a short attention span.						
3. Tense or disturbed (bites lip, twists hair, high strung).						
4. Easily distracted from school work (can't concentrate with even the slightest disturbances from other student's moving around or talking quietly).						
5. Cannot apply the classroom or school regulations to own behavior whereas peers can.						
6. Excessive inconsistency in quality of performance from day to day or even hour to hour.						
7. Seems very bright in many ways but still does poorly in school.						
8. Doesn't get along with most peers (unusually aggressive, can't make or keep friends, poor loser).						
9. Unusually shy or withdrawn.						
10. Cries easily or often for no apparent reason.						
11. Seems quite immature (doesn't act his/her age).						
12. Easily frustrated with school work.						

ADDITIONAL COMMENTS:

_____

_____

_____

_____

This checklist was included in a teacher inservice course entitled "Handicapped Placement and Program Planning" by W. R. Pickles and nine teachers for the Washington Education Association.

some other reason. In any case, the low scores alert the teacher to the possibility of learning problems that seem to be pervasive with that group of children.

The use of standardized achievement tests is only one way—and perhaps not even the most important way—that a teacher is alerted to the presence of learning problems. The teacher's best tool for this purpose is skillful observation of the children's behavior. To assist in this process, the teacher should make notes of observations, should keep records of each child's progress, and should systematically keep samples of children's work. A child's progress in learning subject matter and skills is likely to progress in spurts from one week to the next. But over a period of several weeks or months, each child should show signs of progress. Failure to do so means that there may be a learning problem. Similarly, if a child does not show interest in schoolwork or does not pay attention, or has behavior difficulties, the teacher should suspect learning problems.

Teachers should be particularly observant of children's responses when skills are introduced. Skill competence is built on practice, and if a child is not performing the skill properly, he or she will be practicing it incorrectly. It is not uncommon to find children in the upper grades who are handicapped in their use of skills because they are performing them in inefficient or incorrect ways—simple mechanical errors in writing, inability to write a single complete sentence, incorrect spelling of most commonly used words, inability to do simple mathematics problems, faulty methods of work (e.g., add, when the need is to subtract), and so on.

The accompanying "Classroom Screening Checklist" can be used to systematize the observations of children's behavior to help determine whether or not a learning problem exists.

What Is the *Specific* Learning Difficulty the Child Is Encountering?

After a teacher has identified a general area of learning difficulty, it will be necessary to locate as precisely as possible the limitations and deficiencies the child is experiencing. It is not adequate to know that a child is a "poor reader." In order to provide the child with corrective instruction, the teacher will need to know the precise nature of the reading problem. For example, does the child have limited word recognition techniques? Does the child not comprehend what is read? Is the child not able to

(Courtesy of Terri Malinowski.)

In this photograph the teacher is diagnosing the children's ability to do visual discrimination. What specific areas of the school curriculum require the ability to discriminate visually?

use aids to reading? Does the child have a limited sight vocabulary? The reason children often do not progress rapidly in "pull-out" corrective teaching settings is because the instruction does not focus precisely on the learning problem. No amount of drill and practice on sentence comprehension, for example, is going to help a child who does not have a repertoire of word-attack skills.

What Level of Corrective Work is Indicated?

After the teacher has pinpointed the learning problem, some analysis should be made of its probable cause. The sources of causes could be many; some reside within the learner, some with the classroom and school, and others are external to the school. Recent research has underscored the powerful impact of the family background of a child on school learning. The teacher needs to recognize this, without at the same time using it as an excuse to justify poor achievement. Not all children from impoverished home environments do poorly in school.

The classroom teacher uses a "large mesh screen" in sifting learning problems and their causes. This does not mean that what is done is unimportant; quite the contrary. If the classroom teacher does not pick up learning problems of children, they will likely go undetected. At the same time, we should recognize that the classroom is not a clinic and the teacher is not a remedial specialist. The teacher must be able to make a judgment as to the level of corrective help that will be needed to get the child "on track."

Generally speaking, learning problems of children can be sorted into three levels of complexity. The simplest ones are those that can be handled within the classroom by the regular teacher. For instance, a child was absent from school just at the time the class was taught how to multiply fractions. When the child returns, the teacher spends some time with him or her on an individual basis, and the child is shortly multiplying fractions as well as his or her classmates. Most learning difficulties are of this level of complexity. All that is required is an alert and observant teacher who cares enough about individual children to provide them with the help they need to overcome minor hurdles in the learning process.

A second level of complexity of learning problems relates to those that require more time or more specialized teaching than the classroom teacher is able to provide. Children with such specific learning difficulties have, for one reason or another, not been able to respond satisfactorily to group instruction presented by the regular classroom teacher. For example, a child may have had a problem of vision corrected by being fitted with glasses. Because the problem has been of long standing, the child has accumulated learning deficits that need to be overcome. The classroom teacher does not have time to provide such corrective instruction. Thus, the child is "pulled out" of the regular class for special instruction targeted on the needed work. When the child is able to function on a par with his or her classmates, the corrective work is terminated.

Occasionally, teachers encounter children with learning difficulties that far exceed the complexity of the two types just described. In these cases, the learning problem is often a symptom of some deeply rooted physical, neurological, or psychological disorder. The capability to deal with problems of this type may often exceed the professional scope of practice of the regular classroom teacher and the building remedial teacher. To provide intensive one-on-one tutoring instruction is not likely to be fruitful because such instruction is targeted on the symptom rather than on the cause of the difficulty. Children with learning problems of this type require the highly specialized diagnostic and corrective services that are provided in a referral agency such as a Psycho-Education Clinic.

The classroom teacher's responsibility, therefore, is to be able to sort out the various learning difficulties in accordance with their complexity and to take appropriate action in each case. By far the greatest number of learning difficulties will be attended to in class on an ongoing basis by the regular classroom teacher. A few children may need more intensive corrective work that the teacher may not have the time or skills to provide. These children will be referred to the building remedial teacher for special tutoring for a short time each day until they have overcome their problem. If such teachers are not available, some other arrangement will need to be made to provide the child with the needed individual help—parents, aides, volunteers. In the case of those children with the most severe learning difficulties, the teacher's responsibility is to see that an appropriate referral is made. This involves consultation with the principal, the parents, and the person in charge of the district's psychological service's office.

The teacher's professional judgment and competence are always tested in sorting out the severity of learning difficulties. It cannot be assumed that all learning problems can be attended to within the context of the busy classroom. On the other hand, the teacher cannot refer to someone else all children with learning problems. Teachers develop the skills of diagnostic and corrective teaching through experience, technical preparation, and maturity as professionals.

Study Questions and Activities

1. Provide examples of positive and negative learning outcomes that are achieved through a school's "hidden curriculum." What implications do you see in this for the work of the classroom teacher?

2. Using the eight points on page 180 as a guide, observe an elementary school classroom. Discuss your observations with your classmates.

3. Is it likely that reading will become less important to school learning as a result of the use of other media? Why or why not?

4. Often overlooked as media for learning are community resources. Make a short list of resources in your community that could be used by an elementary school class.

5. Select a short passage from an elementary school science or social studies textbook. Write five questions that check literal comprehension of the passage. Then write five reflective or thought questions based on the same passage. Which ones are easier to construct? Discuss.

6. You are the teacher of a child who has been achieving satisfactorily in mathematics. In correcting his written work, you notice that the child answered incorrectly every problem involving the division of fractions. How would you go about finding out what the difficulty is? How would your approach be different if you discovered that *all* the children answered such problems incorrectly?

7. Single out a child for individual study using the Classroom Screening Checklist on pages 202–205. When you have completed your observations, discuss your evaluations with the child's teacher. Were your observations consistent with those of the teacher? On what items was there the greatest discrepancy? How do you explain that?

8. Visit a school in your area to become familiar with the kinds of educational and psychological referral services available for children with learning difficulties that cannot be handled by the classroom teacher.

For Further Professional Study

Beck, I. L., and M. G. McKeown. "Developing Questions That Promote Comprehension: The Story Map." *Language Arts,* **58** (Nov.–Dec. 1981), 913–918.

Blankenship, Colleen, and M. Stephan Lilly. *Mainstreaming Students with Learning and Behavior Problems: Techniques for the Classroom Teacher.* New York: CBS Publishing, 1981.

Brophy, Jere E. "How Teachers Influence What Is Taught and Learned in Classrooms." *The Elementary School Journal,* **83** (Sept. 1982), 1–13.

Brown, James W., Richard B. Lewis, and Fred F. Harcelroad. *AV Instruction: Technology, Media, and Methods,* 6th ed. New York: McGraw-Hill Book Company, Inc., 1983.

Hunkins, Francis P. *Curriculum Development: Program Improvement.* Columbus, Ohio: Charles E. Merrill Publishing Co., 1980.

Hyman, Ronald T. "Questioning for Improved Reading." *Educational Leadership,* **39** (Jan. 1982), 307–309.

Johnson, Clark. *Diagnosing of Learning Disabilities.* Boulder, Colo.: Pruett Publishing Company, 1981.

Salvia, John, and James E. Ysseldyke. *Assessment in Special and Remedial Education,* 2d ed. Boston: Houghton Mifflin Company, 1981.

Classroom Management Skills

The term *classroom management* focuses attention on that cluster of skills needed to plan, organize, administer, and implement an appropriate program of instruction. Classroom management is not a goal to be achieved, but a set of procedures and conditions that make it possible for the teacher and learners to attain valid educational goals and objectives. It has to do with the emotional tone of the classroom, with daily procedures and routines, with the deployment of pupils, with the setting of standards of conduct, and with the system of rewards and punishment that prevails. Good managers are not always good teachers, but the inability to manage a class in ways that facilitate instruction is usually a "fatal flaw" to the success of a teacher.

Classroom Management As Related to Teaching

Each year since 1969 the Gallup Poll has conducted a national survey to measure attitudes of Americans toward their public schools. When asked to respond to the question, "What do you think are the biggest problems with which the *public* schools of this country must deal?" Americans mentioned "lack of discipline" more frequently than any other problem in fourteen out of the fifteen years the survey has been conducted.[1] Classroom management is popularly, but not altogether correctly, referred to as "control" or "discipline." It is the one component of teaching that worries beginning teachers more than anything else. It is also what experienced teachers often find most exhausting. New teachers want, above all, to be successful. They also want their pupils to like them. Yet they know that they cannot achieve either of these goals unless they are able to succeed in classroom management. They may recall experiences they had as pupils in a classroom where the children were unruly and boisterous. Perhaps the principal had to be called to quiet them. Maybe they remember that one or more teachers had to terminate during the year because of management problems. Now that they are beginning student teaching, or facing their first teaching position, they are apprehensive about the complex challenges involved in managing a classroom.

There can be little doubt that skill in classroom management or "control" is a major factor contributing to the success of the teacher. More time is spent on it in student teaching supervisory conferences than on anything else. It is the one aspect of a teacher's credentials that principals are most interested in examining. It is the one part of a teacher's behavior that parents are most concerned about. When a teacher is in difficulty on the job, the chances are good that the problem can be traced to classroom management.

The beginning teacher is likely to disassociate what is thought to be "teaching" from classroom management. Teaching is regarded as conducting reading, spelling, and mathematics lessons, developing concepts in social studies, doing science experiments,

---

[1] Reported in *Phi Delta Kappan,* 65, No. 1 (September 1983), 28–51.

and so on. In an almost naive way, the teacher may rely on the pupils to conduct themselves appropriately—to move about in an orderly fashion, to move quietly from one grouping arrangement to another, and to treat each other courteously and respectfully. When they do not do so, the teacher regards their behavior as misconduct requiring disciplinary action. Classroom management is perceived primarily in the negative sense—correcting misbehavior, keeping a watchful eye for evidence of mischief, and disciplining pupils. This approach, although fairly common, is likely to cause the teacher some difficulty because it neglects to take into account the important part that classroom management contributes to successful teaching.

It is clear that management and instruction are two sides of the same coin we call teaching. Successful teaching cannot take place without both of these elements. The interaction of these two components of teaching means, also, that they affect each other. Skillful management facilitates the conduct of instruction. Inspired and interesting instruction reduces the likelihood of management problems.

We take the position here that classroom management must be perceived positively rather than negatively. The teacher needs to develop a management system that builds habits of responsible self-direction in children. Such a system also produces and maintains an environment in which teaching and learning are facilitated. Good classroom management procedures must be planned, just as the instructional components of teaching are planned. Through planning, a teacher can anticipate and avoid problems. Let us now consider some of the characteristics of a well-managed classroom.

1. *Good classroom management enhances the mental and social development of children.*

Getting "control" of a class, in the sense of the teacher's ability to wield power over children, should not be much of a problem for an adult. A situation can be created where the teacher has absolute control over everything that takes place in the room. The teacher uses threats of low grades and failure, ridicule, punishment, rigid rules, and keeps pupil activity controlled to the point that children cannot move or talk without permission. This may be justified on the grounds that it is the only way the teacher can maintain order and therefore conduct instruction. But these repressive tactics can be detrimental to young children.

We are learning that a positive self-concept is not only important to learning but is vital to the total development of the individual. In the type of distrustful setting just described, children may not develop good images of themselves. Moreover, the pressures that build up in some children as a result of an authoritarian atmosphere in school erupt, either in or outside of school, in various forms of aggression, tears, withdrawal, bedwetting, nail-biting, or other more serious forms of maladaptive behavior.

The elementary school should be a laboratory for the social growth of children. Here the child learns to give and to take, to share with others, to interact with peers, and to develop a degree of responsible independence. The child learns social skills partly through instruction, but mainly by having opportunities to participate with others in social situations. Programs that have children working continually on an individual basis do not provide adequately for the social dimension of a child's learning. One cannot learn social skills except in social settings.

Good management will reflect itself in a room where children are comfortable intellectually, emotionally, and socially. Here, the teacher as an authority figure is recognized and respected but is not feared by the pupils or perceived as a constant threat to their self-confidence. This room is a confidence-building place, where children grow in their competence as human beings.

2. *Good classroom management facilitates the achievement of instructional goals that suit the developmental level of children.*

Mr. Campbell is working with a group of eight third-graders on phonetic skills in a reading lesson. Meanwhile, the remaining twenty-four third-graders are moving about the room, talking loudly; occasionally there is an altercation that necessitates Mr. Campbell's intervention. The noise level is high. The pupils in the reading group often ask to have things repeated because they cannot hear, or are not paying attention to what is being said.

This is a serious matter because the pupil behavior resulting from Mr. Campbell's poor management is interfering with the instructional program. Phonetic analysis depends on fine sound discrimination, and, therefore, pupils must be able to hear those sounds. This would be difficult, perhaps even impossible, in the situation described. Moreover, Mr. Campbell himself cannot attend properly to the lesson because of the commotion in the room. And the pupils not in the reading group are reinforcing behavior patterns that contribute neither to good study habits nor to social skills.

In order to establish conditions that make possible the conduct of instruction, it is necessary to develop a systematic method of organizing classroom activities. The teacher will need to steer a course somewhere between Mr. Campbell's lack of organization and the other end of the continuum, characterized by rigidity and teacher dominance. For most classrooms, a schedule of events of the day will be needed. These will probably not vary much from day to day. Children like this. They like to know when each of their classes is to take place. They know when there is to be quiet time and when there is activity time. This type of flexible, but planned, organization of the day makes it possible for the teacher to do his or her job and the children to do theirs, in order that the goals of instruction can be achieved.

Developmental differences in children require that teachers select learning goals and presentation modes that are appropriate for the grade level. Young children need considerably more one-on-one interaction with the teacher than do older ones. Learning objectives for younger children need to be more explicit, and their work must be closely monitored in order to correct for level of difficulty.

3. *Good classroom management provides intellectual and physical freedom within specified limits.*

If children grew up knowing the subject matter and skills of the curriculum, and were completely socialized, well-mannered, and well-behaved, there would be no point in sending them to school. The object of school is precisely to teach children such subject matter and skills. If children are to learn them, however, they need to be in a secure environment where they can be free to try to do new things. Not only that, children should be encouraged to do so without having to fear, or be embarrassed by, making mistakes.

Although children should be as free as possible to explore intellectually and be allowed a great deal of physical freedom as well, they need also to learn that no one is totally free. There *are* rules and regulations that apply in every classroom, no matter what the teacher's personal philosophy may be on this issue. For example, the teacher cannot, and must not, allow children to do things that injure others, that are inhumane, or destroy the property of others. Such behavior is simply not permitted.

When teachers pretend there are no rules or fail to make them explicit, it can be predicted that they will have a stormy time of it. When there are no rules, no one knows what is expected. Children may run wild, and in the process may injure themselves or each other. Even when there are explicit rules, children will test the outer edges of them. They seem to need to search out the limits of freedom, within which they then know they must function. In cases where the procedures are made known, the testing will be more focused. Where procedures and rules are not known, the testing takes the form of trial and error—to see what the teacher's tolerance level is.

4. *Good classroom management allows children to develop skills of self-direction and independence.*

This point is an extension of the previous one. It is a curious fact that teachers often expect children to develop self-direction and independence without permitting them to practice the skills needed to achieve these characteristics. Children are not likely to gain self-direction and independence in classrooms that are almost wholly teacher directed and teacher dependent. What is needed is a good balance: providing sufficient guidance and direction, on the one hand, and allowing children to experiment with independence and self-direction on the other. The tendency is either to be too highly teacher directed or to be overly permissive. Neither provides an appropriate setting for learning.

5. *Good classroom management allows children to share some responsibility for classroom management.*

Involving children in some aspects of the management of the classroom provides them with practical experiences in contributing to policy and decision making.

Such involvement also gives children a sense of ownership of the classroom. Insofar as possible, the feeling should be generated that it is not only the teacher's room but the pupils' room as well. Of course, this will not be easy to do if the teacher makes all the rules, makes all the decisions, and makes no effort to involve children in the management aspects of classroom life.

This is not to suggest that the teacher can evade responsibility for the conduct of the classroom by turning the management over to the children. This has been tried many times, and it usually fails because children lack maturity for such responsibilities. It is asking more of them than can reasonably be expected. The teacher, being the most mature person in the classroom, must provide the leadership and guidance needed to make the operation function. In point of fact, the teacher is legally accountable for what goes on in the classroom.

6. *Good classroom management works toward a warm, but firm, relationship between the teacher and children.*

Sometimes beginning teachers, especially in the middle and upper grades, believe they can develop a close "buddy" relationship between the children and themselves. Informality is encouraged by allowing them to call the teacher by his or her first name or even a nickname. Social distance is removed by the teacher, who assumes somewhat of a peer relationship with the children. This rarely works well; it usually means that in the process the authority of the teacher is compromised.

The other extreme is represented by the teachers who feel they cannot "get too close" to the children—they must maintain an appropriate social distance. They talk in a stilted way. They do not relax because they feel if they did the children might take advantage of them. They are careful never to reveal much of the informal aspects of their personality. They develop and maintain the traditional stereotypic role of the teacher.

Good teachers extend their warmth and "human-ness" to children. They work with children in ways that show they enjoy young people. At the same time they maintain the basic firmness needed and, what is more, *wanted* by children. Children expect the teacher to behave in certain more or less conventional ways. When teacher behavior strays too far from this expectation, children do not know how to deal with it.

7. *Good classroom management results in positive learner attitudes toward the class.*

When the school situation is what it should be, children like to go to school. They may complain, but this is out of deference to a culturally institutionalized attitude that children are supposed to dislike school. Given a choice, most children would prefer to go to school than to stay home. After all, their friends are there, and a child's natural curiosity does not make learning completely distasteful.

Also, children will usually develop a strong identity with the class, if conditions are right. There will be in-group and out-group alliances formed, but this is to be expected. In general, children will take pride in their class.

If children genuinely dislike school, if there is a high level

WHAT DO YOU THINK ABOUT THIS?

Long before the opening of school, Mrs. Badger had decided what behavior standards she wanted in her classroom, and had constructed a set of rules concerning pupil conduct. She felt uneasy about this, however, because she remembered what one of her professors had said about children being more willing to respect and accept rules and standards if they had a hand in the formulation of them. Mrs. Badger resolved her dilemma in the following way:

On the first day of school, she explained to the children that she was sure that all of them wanted to do their best work. If this were to happen, there would need to be rules and standards. If everyone did anything he or she pleased at any time, without consideration for others, no one could get anything done, and the room would not be a very pleasant place. The children, of course, understood and expected this. She went on to explain that because rules and standards affected everyone, she thought they should help her make the rules. This too, received a favorable reaction. It was agreed that children would suggest rules and standards, and when they were accepted by the group, Mrs. Badger would write them on the chalkboard.

As suggestions were made, Mrs. Badger would involve the class in a discussion of each one. She was careful not to reject any suggestion, but when one surfaced that she had already decided was one she wanted, she would say something like "Now, that's a good idea!" By the time the period was over, the rules and standards adopted by the class were those Mrs. Badger had decided on three weeks before the opening of school, but the children seemed pleased with "their" rules.

1. Do you find anything objectionable about Mrs. Badger's procedures?

2. What would you predict to be the lasting effect of rules generated in this way?

3. Can you suggest an alternative procedure to that of Mrs. Badger's?

of unexplained absenteeism, or if there is a great deal of conflict and aggression in the classroom, one should suspect that there may be something wrong with management procedures. This does not mean that school experiences must in all cases be fun.

It does mean that overall, school is a pleasant rather than an unpleasant place to be.

Control and Discipline

The term *control* is often used as a convenient catch-all for what is more correctly called classroom management. Control implies restraint, regulation, regimentation, and the direct use of power. Popularly, it is sometimes referred to as "keeping the lid on"— appropriately so, in those classrooms that operate as pressure cookers. "You have good control" is usually regarded as a compliment to a beginning teacher. One is never sure whether the meaning is intended in the broad sense (to cover all of classroom management), or in the literal sense, that of keeping pupil behavior so curbed that the classroom is teacher dominated. Used in the literal sense, the term *control* can easily be given unwarranted importance, becoming an end rather than a means.

Control should not, in itself, be a goal of teaching—nor should management, for that matter. These should be perceived as processes used to accomplish other more important tasks. A negative example is a third-grade teacher who has "perfect control" of a class: the class is quiet, individuals are immobile, no one speaks out of turn, and so on. In order to achieve this calm, the teacher has the children doing relatively meaningless "busywork" at their seats, while she attends to other matters. These "other matters" may have to do with preparation of lessons and materials, teaching small groups or individuals, or taking care of business relating to pupil accounting, reporting, or the lunch program. To achieve this level of restraint, the teacher does indeed need to control most of the physical and intellectual activities in the classroom. One must, of course, ask whether these kinds of training procedures are appropriate for life in a democratic society.

An objectionable aspect of the control concept is the implication that it is the teacher who is wholly responsible for maintaining an orderly classroom. This runs counter to the idea that children need to learn responsible habits of self-direction. They need to learn to conduct themselves properly, not to please the teacher, but because in so doing they develop greater maturity and independence. Of course, children cannot do this entirely

223

(Courtesy of Terri Malinowski.)

What is there about this photograph that indicates that this teacher is skillful in managing the classroom? What evidence is there that this teacher is able to do more than one teaching task at the same time?

on their own. Left unguided they are likely to become unruly and mischievous. Learning to take care of oneself should be an important outcome of the school experience. It is not likely to be achieved if the behavior of the learner is always controlled by the teacher.

The term *discipline,* like control, is often incorrectly used to mean various aspects of classroom management. "She has good discipline" usually means that the teacher maintains an orderly classroom. Discipline also connotes punishment. "Strong discipline" is used to describe teacher behavior that is rigid, firm, unbending. There is an adversary quality to this meaning of discipline. When teachers say, "Anyone who leaves the room without permission will be disciplined," they mean that the offender will be punished. In this sense, discipline means both punishment and corrective treatment.

A more acceptable use of the term would describe discipline as an imposition of controls on oneself in order to develop character, efficient habits of work, proper conduct, consideration for others, orderly living, or control of one's impulses and emotions, as when the teacher says, "We will need to discipline ourselves not to talk unnecessarily if we hope to finish this project by the end of the day." Discipline as internally imposed control, i.e., self-control, is, of course, a worthy objective. But in order to develop discipline, the learner must be given some independence; and in the process of experimenting with such independence, the teacher's guidance will be needed. Neither highly structured, teacher-dominated environments, nor those that are completely permissive, facilitate the development of self-control and self-discipline.

Classroom Climate

The term *classroom climate* is not in as widespread popular use as are management, control, and discipline. Climate has to do with the emotional tone and quality of human relations that prevail in the classroom. Classroom climate may be described as being relaxed, pleasant, flexible, rigid, autocratic, democratic, repressive, or supportive, and so on. Classroom climate results from a composite of the interactions and transactions that take place in the room. Consequently, it is related to the management procedures used by the teacher.

Teachers often deal with a class as if that conglomerate of individuals were a single individual. Consider the kinds of statements teachers make to class groups: "Now, class, I want you to turn to page 53." "The class should now pay close attention to what is being said." "If the class does not stop talking, we will be late for lunch." "I will need to have the attention of the class." These are just a few instances of the teacher's referring to a class of individuals as if they were a single individual. It is important to stress that a class is a *group,* and in successful group management, it is group psychology rather than individual psychology that is relevant. Groups develop their own characteristics, as *groups,* quite apart from the individuals who comprise them.

Because of the special characteristics of pupil groups, teachers must secure from them their implicit consent for management procedures. In other words, the children must be willing to cooperate with the teacher or the system cannot function. Without their willing cooperation, an adversary relationship develops between the class and the teacher. When this happens, the classroom climate becomes so tense that even the smallest issue can, and often does, become the cause of a major confrontation. If such relationships are prolonged, the teacher becomes ineffective and would probably be forced to terminate.

WHAT WOULD YOU HAVE DONE?

It was the first really warm, spring day that Middleton had had that year. In fact, it was downright hot. And the schoolchildren loved it! After a long cold winter and a damp and rainy spring, it seemed as though summer had arrived with one big burst of sunshine, and energy that had welled up during the many dreary months seemed to have released itself like a mountain of water flowing through a broken dam! During the noon hour the children played hard, ran and yelled and had a great time in the welcomed sunshine. Now the "first" bell had rung and several hundred very reluctant children found their way into the building and to their respective classrooms, still talking loudly, perspiring profusely, and with flushed faces.

Mr. Gardner scheduled math immediately following the lunch hour. Today the children were hardly ready for the concentration needed for a math lesson. Mr. Gardner saw the hopelessness of the situation confronting him and immediately decided to alter his schedule.

1. Do you think this was a wise decision on the part of Mr. Gardner?
2. Can Mr. Gardner forget about math each time the area has a beautiful day?
3. If this is a persistent problem, what might Mr. Gardner do to deal with it on a long-term basis?

Typical Classroom Problems

It is a mistake to believe that the removal of certain children, so-called troublemakers, will in itself solve problems of classroom management. Far from it. If the management procedure is unsound, there will be problems arising no matter what the composition of the group. This leads us to the conclusion that disruptive behavior is often a function of the social dynamics of the class itself.

In the case of teachers assessing the emotional and psychological problems of children, two types of teacher attitudes prevail. On the one hand, there are teachers who see nothing disturbing about any behavior of any child. "There are no problem children, only children with problems." "No child's problem is so great that it can't do with some love and affection." "A wanted child is a loved child, and a loved child is a happy child." These are only a few of a bagful of clichés that have been generated regarding the handling of behavior problems of children. Although the clichés contain valuable kernels of conventional wisdom, they do not serve as well as plans of action for working with children who have deeply rooted psychological problems. The attitude that all that is needed is "plenty of love and affection" is a naive approach to complex problems of pupil disruptive behavior. Love and affection are important, of course; most of us can do with more of both. But there is considerably more to the management of classroom problems than love and affection.

The second teacher attitude that prevails vis-à-vis the behavior of children is one of suspicion. The smallest infraction of a rule of conduct is interpreted as psychological imbalance. There is a low tolerance for anything except the most straitlaced behavior. This attitude is especially unfortunate because it may create problems where there are none. Children who are in good mental and physical health can be expected to be lively and active. They naturally find the classroom environment restraining, even under the best of conditions. There will be conflicts between children and groups of children. All of this and more is to be expected, and to interpret as emotional disturbance such normal expressions of child behavior is not a professionally sound judgment. Teachers are neither psychologists nor psychotherapists and should resist the temptation to "overpsychologize" the problems of children in their classroom.

As a part of their professional preparation, teachers need to be able to make some assessment, in a general way, of the potential seriousness of the behavior of children with whom they work. No single checklist of behaviors is sufficient for this pur-

TABLE 1
*Classroom Management Problems in Terms of Behavioral Descriptions**

Distinguishing Characteristics	Behavior Descriptions
1. *Lack of unity*	The class lacks unity, and conflicts occur between individuals and subgroups, as: when groups split; argumentative over competitive situations such as games; boys against girls; when groups split by cliques, minority groups; when group takes sides on issues or breaks into subgroups; when hostility and conflict continually arise among members and create an unpleasant atmosphere.
2. *Nonadherence to behavioral standards and work procedures*	The class responds with noisy, talkative, disorderly behavior to situations that have established standards for behavior, as: when group is entering or leaving room or changing activities; lining up; cleaning up; going to auditorium; when group is working in ability groups; engaging in committee work; when group is completing study assignments; receiving assignments; correcting papers; handling work materials; when group is engaged in discussion, sharing, planning.
3. *Negative reactions to individual members*	The class becomes vocal or actively hostile toward one or more class members, as: when group does not accept individuals and derides, ignores, or ridicules children who are different; when group reacts negatively to members who deviate from group code; to those who thwart group's progress; or when a member's behavior upsets or puzzles members of the class.

pose. Through training and the careful observation of children, teachers will begin to detect signals warning of possible danger. They will learn to discern what can be ignored and what deserves further careful watching. Once a problem is suspected, it should be discussed with the school psychologist, counselor, or guidance officer, if there is one. A parent conference may help the teacher learn what the child's behavior is like at home and how consistent the in-school and out-of-school behavior is. Often it is wise

Distinguishing Characteristics	Behavior Descriptions
4. *Class approval of mis-behavior*	The class approves and supports individuals, as: when they talk out of turn; act in ways that disrupt the normal work procedures; engage in clowning or rebellious activities.

5. *Easily distracted; prone to work stoppage and imitative behavior*	The group reacts with upset, excited, or disorderly behavior to interruptions, distractions, or continual grievances, as:
	    when group is interrupted by monitors, visitors, a change in weather;
	    when members continually have grievances relating to others, lessons, rules, policies, or practices they believe are unfair; and when settlements are demanded before work proceeds.

6. *Low morale and hostile, resistant, or aggressive reactions*	The class members engage in subtle, hostile, aggressive behavior that creates slowdowns and work stoppages, as:
	    when materials are misplaced, pencils break, chairs upset;
	    when books, money, lunches are temporarily lost;
	    when there are continual requests for assignments to be repeated and explained;
	    when children continually complain about behavior of others with no apparent loss of friendship;
	    when children accuse authority figures of unfair practices and delay classwork by making claims.

7. *Inability to adjust to environmental change*	The class reacts inappropriately to such situations, as:
	    when a substitute takes over;
	    when normal routines are changed;
	    when new members transfer into the class;
	    when stress situations cause inappropriate reactions.

* Reprinted by permission.

for a child to have a thorough physical examination when there are unexplained changes in behavior. In any case, the teacher needs to know enough about the development of children to be able to assess the seriousness of observed behavior. A child should not be sent to the school psychologist for minor infractions of rules of conduct, but neither should serious signs of maladaptive behavior be ignored.

Management problems in the classroom are usually a result of the collective behavior of the children, rather than the result of the actions of one or of a few. Individual children may engage in disruptive behavior, but when this happens repeatedly, it means that the behavior is approved or even encouraged by the group. For various types of management problems to persist, there must be covert, or even overt, reinforcement from the group. In other words, there is consensus in the group that supports the behavior. This, of course, is rarely expressed openly.

What kind of management problems are most common in classrooms? Lois V. Johnson and Mary A. Bany collected hundreds of descriptions of incidents of classroom problems over several years. These incidents, according to the authors, are very similar—year after year, teachers describe the same troublesome behavior. "Children talk at inappropriate times, they delay work processes, engage in disputes and conflicts, react with indifference and lack of interest, and fail to follow prescribed procedures. They quarrel, fight, resist, protest, and fail to cooperate."[2] In order to deal with these problems in terms of analysis and remediation, Johnson and Bany classify classroom management problems as shown in Table 1 (see pages 228 and 229).[3]

Organizational Aspects of Management

The way a classroom is organized will not, of course, eliminate management problems. But actions can be taken that will move the teacher a long way down the road toward preventing problems and toward resolving them when they arise. In this regard, there are two principles that are so important that they need to precede all else that is said on this subject:

---

[2] Lois V. Johnson and Mary A. Bany, *Classroom Management: Theory and Skill Training* (New York: Macmillan Publishing Co., Inc., 1970), p. 45.
[3] Ibid., pp. 46–47.

1. The first few days of the school year are critical in setting the standards of behavior in a classroom,

and

2. Preventing problems from arising is always easier than correcting them once they have occurred.

WHEN VIEWS COLLIDE

Mr. Watson, a beginning fourth-grade teacher, has a very "loose" classroom. He is much opposed to anything that suggests conformity behavior. In his classroom there are few rules, and there is nothing that even approximates a schedule. He believes that children need to grow up as independent, self-directed human beings, and that this can never be achieved when they learn to be blindly obedient to rules. "Our whole society is too regulated," he says. Mr. Watson is a sensitive and warm person, devoted to the children he teaches.

Mr. Watson is a constant source of problems for the principal. His attitudes run along more conventional lines than do Mr. Watson's, although he too is a sensitive and humane person. He is bothered by the "noise and confusion" in Watson's room. He is irritated by complaints from parents who are bothered by the laxness in "discipline and control" in Watson's classroom. The principal has urged Watson to "tighten up," to set some rules and standards of conduct and hold the children to them. He also wants Watson to prepare a daily schedule and follow it. "For heaven's sake, Mike, get some control in that room," he says. Watson resists all of these suggestions, and three months into his first year of teaching, it is clear that he is on a collision course with his principal.

1. What are your views as to the goals Mr. Watson has set for his class?
2. What are your views as to the effect of rules and standards on the development of overconformity, something Mr. Watson was very concerned about?
3. Does the principal have a legitimate concern in this situation?
4. Speculate on various ways this problem might be resolved. (One way, obviously, is that Mr. Watson be dismissed, but provide other alternatives.)

The first day of school and the ones that immediately follow are the times when children are most aggressive in testing the teacher's management capability. If the teacher is lax in establishing standards of conduct during these first few critical days, it will be almost impossible to do so later in the year. Experienced teachers know that it is easy to become more permissive as the school year progresses without compromising standards of conduct, but that it is enormously difficult to become more strict once a permissive pattern has been set. Because beginning teachers want pupils to like them, they are reluctant to take a firm stand on pupil conduct for fear they will offend the children. This form of indulgence is almost always a mistake. The time for firm, strict, and formal—but always, of course, fair—teacher action is during the first few days of the school year.

Several suggestions are presented in the remainder of this chapter that deal with the prevention of behavior problems. In a way, the firmness being suggested as appropriate at the beginning of the school year is a prevention strategy. An interesting, stimulating, instructional program, combined with the rewarding of expected behavior, is a much more effective deterrent to disruptive pupil behavior than is punishment, or the threat of punishment, of misbehavior. When pupils know clearly what is expected, when teachers follow through on pupil expectations, and when they do not permit a gradual erosion of standards of conduct, the behavior of pupils can usually be kept within manageable levels. Of course, no class is totally free of behavior problems all of the time.

Schedule

Teachers create all sorts of management problems for themselves simply by not planning and observing a daily schedule of events. It is probably true that classrooms of the past have been too tightly scheduled. Part of the rigidity of classrooms comes about because of too close adherence to a time schedule. "Schools are run by bells and ditto machines," the critics say, and to a degree the criticism is well taken. The inflexibility created by clinging slavishly to a minute-by-minute schedule can hardly be condoned; however, this is not the same as saying there should be no schedule.

Because of the ordinary requirements imposed on the teacher to attend to various areas of the curriculum, it is possible to block out large periods of time to be devoted to reading, social studies, science, mathematics, language arts, and so on. The schedule can be tentative, to be changed from time to time during the year, if this seems necessary. Also, the schedule can be perceived as reasonably flexible. If on some days a few more minutes of time are needed to complete an important task, such time should be taken. If, however, every lesson exceeds the budgeted time, or does not require the amount of time allotted, this is evidence of weak planning, poor pacing of the lesson, or an inaccurate estimate of the time needed.

When a teacher has a schedule and observes it reasonably closely, this ensures that all of the children and all areas of the curriculum will receive the attention each deserves. When teachers are careless about scheduling classroom events, days may go by without finding time for some subjects. What usually happens is that favorite subject areas of the teacher get the lion's share of time; those the teacher is less fond of, or those in which the teacher is not particularly strong, get shortchanged. Also, if the teacher works with subgroups within the class, some groups may not get an adequate amount of the teacher's time. If this happens once in awhile, it is not a serious matter, but if it occurs regularly, it cannot help but be detrimental to a well-balanced instructional program, and will therefore contribute to management problems.

Routines

Closely related to the setting of a schedule is the establishment of routines that regularize activities that occur day after day in a classroom. Included are entering and leaving the classroom, taking roll, collecting lunch money, moving from one grouping configuration to another, going to the restroom, getting books and supplies, coming to order after recess, checking out athletic equipment, and so on. There should be routine ways of doing these routine activities, and others like them, simply to avoid altercations, bickerings, and conflicts that are inevitable when they are handled on an ad hoc basis.

As with scheduling, there has been some criticism of the use of routines. This criticism is not without justification. Traditional classrooms were undoubtedly overroutinized. For example, in outmoded dismissal procedures, the teacher might expect all children to be seated upright, with hands folded and resting on top of the desk. With a series of taps on the desk with a ruler, the teacher would signal that the children were to turn, stand,

and pass in rows. It is against antiquated procedures of this kind that criticism of routines is leveled. Routines should approximate ways of behaving and acting that are normal and natural for children. They should not require stilted and regimented behavior, such as one would expect in a military or prison environment.

When routines are reasonable and are implemented sensibly, the children do not find them objectionable. As a matter of fact, they get some security from knowing what is to be done and how they are expected to do it. Almost invariably, substitute teachers are reminded by the pupils as to how things are done in their classroom; they object strongly when alternative ways are suggested.

Clarity of Directions and Goals

Management problems can be reduced by giving clear directions. When directions are carelessly given, or are ambiguous, children will not know what they are to do and consequently will ask to have directions clarified or repeated, sometimes several times. This annoys the teacher, who may then establish a rule that directions will be given only once. This is generally not a good idea, because it is patently unfair. Besides, there are times when, for obvious reasons, directions will need to be repeated. The teacher is then placed in the position of having to violate one of the classroom rules. If the teacher is careful about having the attention of the class before directions are given, and is skillful in giving directions clearly and completely, it is not likely that directions will be misunderstood. It is helpful for teachers to tape-record themselves in order to evaluate how clearly they give directions or make explanations.

Human beings find it annoying to be asked to do things without knowing the reasons for doing them. Children in school often are assigned tasks without the least idea as to how the specific activity fits into the larger framework that serves as a long-range goal. Time taken to explain what is to be done and where the activities lead is usually time well spent.

Physical Arrangements

There is much in the arrangement of a classroom that can either contribute to or alleviate management problems. Most authorities on modern methodology advise against straight-row seating.

There are good reasons for this, chief among them being the formality and rigidity that such arrangements suggest. Unfortunately, a completely satisfactory alternative to the traditional arrangement has never been accepted. There is no one "best way" to arrange pupil stations in a classroom. Most would agree that the arrangement should be kept flexible, and that learners be deployed in ways most suitable for accomplishing specific tasks.

Because teachers often form subgroups within their classrooms, and because these smaller groups might, to some extent, represent ability levels, the teacher may be tempted to place children in clusters based on their ability or level of achievement. The teacher might reason that there will be less shuffling around when moving from one subgroup to another. (In a sense, it is the teacher who moves from group to group, rather than the children who move in the direction of the teacher.) And on the surface, this seems to make good sense; however, three strong reasons argue against this arrangement. First, it is likely to create problems in trying to build unity in the total class group. Second, although the teacher probably cannot disguise the fact that the groups represent high-, middle-, and low-achievement levels, seating children accordingly is to them a constant reminder of their position in the class. Third, from what is known about self-expectation and self-image, it is reasonable to assume that such an arrangement does not work to the advantage of slower-achieving children.

Teachers are often bothered by children interacting with each other at times when this distracts from what others in the classroom are doing. Constant whispering, talking, and visiting are encouraged by some seating arrangements. If a teacher has a low tolerance for pupil interaction, he or she should not seat children close to one another. When they are seated side by side, it is perfectly natural for them to talk to each other. Therefore, if the purpose is to encourage social interaction, they should be seated close together; if the reverse is wanted, they should be separated. But the teacher cannot have it both ways.

Perhaps it is best not to have *a* single room arrangement but to move seats from one configuration to another, depending on the nature of the task. For independent study it is better for a child to sit and work alone, in order not to be distracted by others. For group discussion or other group activity, children will have to be seated close to others. It is unreasonable to place children in situations that encourage a maximum amount of in-

WHAT'S WRONG HERE?

Miss Fox knows that if she is to succeed as a beginning teacher she must have good "control" in her classroom. She is determined, therefore, not to allow the slightest infraction of room conduct to go unnoticed. When children enter the room, she is usually seen standing at the door, where she can monitor the behavior of children in the hallway and in the classroom at the same time. She likes to think of herself as a "no nonsense" teacher who will not put up with any "foolishness" from her fifth graders. Many of her comments to the pupils during the day run along this line:

"Stop running in the hall, boys."

"Now settle down quickly, boys and girls."

"Karen, what are you doing over there? Please take your seat."

"I want it quiet in here—What are you two talking about over there? Is that Billy's book you have, Cindy? Give it back to him and get on with your own work."

"Everyone listen carefully to the directions, because I will give them only once."

"Clear everything from the top of your desks except the book we will be using. (Pause.) Mark, put that ruler away. Sally—the pencil inside your desk! Jim, the waste paper goes in the basket."

Although the children have nicknamed her "Hawkeye," they really do not dislike Miss Fox. But they often talk about the good times they had with Miss James the year before, and this bothers Miss Fox.

The classroom gives the outward appearance of orderliness, yet one senses an unnatural tenseness about the room. There is more carping and petty bickering among children than one would expect. They comply with Miss Fox's expectations, but there is little evidence of cooperation among them or between them and Miss Fox. When the principal visited her classroom, she advised Miss Fox to try to develop a more positive approach to room management but did not provide examples of what this entailed.

1. If you were Miss Fox, what would you do to implement the principal's recommendation?

2. What behavior can one expect if teacher talk is mainly directive, negative in content, and perhaps hostile in tone?

3. Do you think Miss Fox likes being a teacher?

teraction, then admonish or berate them for whispering and talking.

The teacher should not be seated much of the time during the day, therefore it matters little where the teacher's desk is located. The elementary school teacher will be moving about the room, supervising, clarifying, answering questions, and providing individual instruction. In conducting instruction in small subgroups, in working with individuals, or in supervising seatwork, the teacher should habitually be positioned in such a way to monitor the behavior of the class. The children should be aware of the teacher's presence.

Personal Dimensions of Management

Just as the physical arrangements of the classroom may facilitate or obstruct classroom management, so may the personal characteristics of the teacher. Teachers, like everyone else, have their personal strengths and liabilities, assets and peculiarities. Although there doubtless is value in modeling one's behavior after that of an outstanding teacher, or even role playing in early experiences in teaching, the teacher must be his or her own person. The greatest contribution the teacher makes lies in what is brought to the classroom in one's own unique personality. Therefore, what is said here should not be construed to mean that all teachers need to fit into a prescribed or established mold that is supposed to represent teacher behavior.

The concepts of *with-it-ness* and *overlapping* are often used in discussing the subject of classroom management. These concepts were identified and so labeled by Jacob S. Kounin and his associates as a result of their research and are described in Kounin's book, *Discipline and Group Management in Classrooms.*[4] With-it-ness has to do with the teacher's intuitive sense of knowing what is going on in the classroom. When the teacher is "with it," he or she is especially skillful in monitoring the behavior of

---

[4] Jacob S. Kounin, *Discipline and Group Management in Classrooms* (New York: Holt, Rinehart and Winston, 1970), p. 79.

(Courtesy of Patricia A. Conrard.)

Examine this photograph and then list the specific things the teacher would have had to do in advance in order to have the children engage in this activity. Keep in mind that there are at least another twenty children in the classroom.

the entire class and in processing feedback from members of the class that indicate when intervention is needed. In this way it is possible to stay on top of things and defuse potential trouble spots before they become serious problems. As has already been noted, preventing behavior problems is much more critical to successful classroom management than is correcting disruptions once they occur.

The concept of *overlapping* means that the teacher is able to do more than one teaching task at the same time. For example, while Mr. Trimble is conducting a reading lesson with one group of third graders, he notices that there is some confusion about a seatwork assignment that another group is supposed to be completing, and in yet another part of the classroom a child is raising her hand for permission to go to the restroom. The teacher nods his head to the girl and then moves to the group having trouble with its seatwork. A clarifying statement from Mr. Trimble gets the group back on track, and he returns to the reading group to find that it is ready to discuss the passage. All of this happens in about two minutes. Much of teaching is like this because of the dynamic character of elementary school classrooms. The teacher must be able to do more than one thing at a time and must also have eyes that scan all activity in the room all of the time. Obviously, Kounin's concepts of *with-it-ness* and *overlapping* are closely related.

Verbal Behavior of the Teacher

Professional literature on teaching is generously sprinkled with statements such as "teaching is not telling" and "teaching is more than talking." In spite of this, there is a considerable amount of evidence, based on observations in countless numbers of classrooms, that teachers do a lot of talking. Some estimates indicate that almost 70 per cent of classroom instructional time is spent in talk by the teacher. Teachers evidently have a low tolerance for silence.

Not only do teachers do a lot of talking, but what they say and how they say it often contributes to rather than reduces management problems. Much of what the teacher says has to do with directing work and behavior, relating opinions or ideas about content and procedures, reminding children of the teacher's authority, and using that authority. It is well known that utterances of this type strengthen the domination of the teacher over the children, consequently *increasing* the dependence on the teacher. This, of course, leads in a direction away from building self-direction and responsible independence. It makes the teacher *more* responsible for the conduct of the children in the classroom and the children *less*. For good classroom management, the situation should be reversed. That is, the teacher should do as much as possible to make learners self-directed and responsible for their own conduct.

In order to move away from domination of children and toward a more independent relationship between them and the teacher, the teacher needs to be aware of the effect of his or her own verbal behavior on them. As this awareness deepens, the teacher will encourage and praise more appropriately. Rather than evaluating every response, the teacher will be more inclined to accept what is said, clarify if necessary, and restate responses. Support will be given to the ideas and feelings of children. Research on the reaction of learners to teacher verbal behavior, spanning the past fifty years, shows clearly that both the learning potential and classroom conduct are greatly influenced by statements made by the teacher.

Quite apart from the *content* of the teacher's utterances, the tone, modulation, and volume of the teacher's voice itself bears on classroom management. Children are quick to detect impatience or insincerity in the tone of the teacher's voice and are likely to react negatively. Similarly, shouting at a class to get attention or to give directions works as a deterrent to good management. Making a tape recording of one's teaching from time to time helps remind the teacher of areas where improvement is needed in teacher talk.

Appearance

There can be no question that a teacher's appearance and bearing have much to do with success in classroom management. Successful teachers project an appearance of quiet confidence that communicates security and competence. When the teacher's behavior is such that it appears as though there is some uncertainty about what to do next, pupils are sure to sense this quickly and will take advantage of the teacher's insecurity. It is paradoxical that often rather small, slight teachers have little difficulty managing classes and maintaining control whereas large, athletic-type males may find themselves in unmanageable circumstances, even with young children. The teacher's "commanding presence," in the benign sense, helps explain these differences.

No doubt there are wide individual differences in personality traits among teachers that make it easier for some and more difficult for others to develop a secure, competent demeanor. Nevertheless, any teacher can work toward the improvement of this characteristic. Professional competence can be strengthened through sound scholarship and thorough planning and preparation. Part of the teacher's insecurity may come from fear of being unprepared to handle ideas or questions that may come up. Confidence in one's own competence, and preparation, will do much to dispel such fears. Also, the beginner can model the behavior of a successful, fully competent inservice teacher. In this connection, role-playing strategies may be helpful in establishing an appropriate presence with a class.

Warmth in Interaction

The teacher in the elementary school is without question the most influential and powerful personality in the classroom. The teacher's behavior will set the qualitative pattern of interactions in the group. If the teacher is warm and caring, the chances are that these traits will be modeled by the children. Conversely, if the teacher is domineering, arbitrary, carping, and critical, children are likely to reflect those behaviors, too.

Wholesome classroom management procedures cannot be developed in an environment lacking in trust and respect. Because control problems loom so large in teaching success, the beginner may take a mistrusting and suspicious attitude toward children. Such mistrust is apparent when the teacher is constantly casting his or her eyes about the classroom, looking for children who may be up to mischief; is quick to reprimand the slightest infraction, to be sure no one "gets away with anything." There is an exaggerated fear that misbehavior, if left unattended, will undermine the teacher's authority. When teachers assume such distrustful attitudes, children will usually not disappoint them. If the teacher goes to a class expecting trouble at every turn, he or she is likely to find it. In such settings it is reasonable to assume that events come under the influence of the self-fulfilling prophecy.

Nonverbal Communication

Educators are beginning to appreciate the powerful influence of unspoken cues provided by the teacher in communicating with children. Sometimes overt, but more often quite subtle, these nonverbal cues may range from a gesture to a facial expression, to simply the expression of a mood. For example, a restless child may be calmed by the reassuring smile of an understanding teacher. Or a teacher may place a hand on the shoulder of a child who seems to need emotional support. Or a teacher will show enthusiasm in his or her eyes as the child is relating what is considered to have been an exciting experience. Some authors have referred to this system of communication as "the silent language."

It may be that teachers communicate more profoundly through such nonverbal cues than in any other way. Words are always manipulated to come out the way the teacher thinks is most appropriate. But true feelings and attitudes are laid bare by those unspoken messages that flow between human beings, and which children, in their innocence, are so skillful in decoding. It is these signals that tell the child whether or not the teacher is, indeed, a concerned and caring adult. It is this unspoken message that will have much to do with the management of the teacher's classroom, and will, in the long run, be the deciding factor in whether or not the classroom is to be a fertile seedbed for the growth of an enlightened and sensitive humanity.

Study Questions and Activities

1. Suggest five things you can do as an elementary school teacher to reduce problems of classroom management.
2. Flexibility seems to be an essential quality of elementary school classrooms. Provide specific examples that illustrate flexibility in the classroom.
3. Why should children be involved in goal setting in a class? Does the same apply to the development of behavior standards? Explain.
4. Table I has two vertical columns; one is headed *Distinguishing Characteristics* and the other, *Behavior Descriptions*. Develop a third column entitled *Suggestions to Deal with This Problem*. Discuss your suggestions with an experienced teacher and report reactions to your college class.
5. Interview three teachers, one each from grades K–1–2, 3–4, and 5–6, to find out how they schedule the daily activities in their classes. Secure a copy of their daily schedules. Having conducted the interviews and secured daily schedules from the three teachers, respond briefly to the following questions:
   a. What common elements flow through the grade levels?
   b. How does the amount of time devoted to the various subjects and skills change through the grades?
   c. What differences are apparent to you from one grade level to another in these daily time schedules?
6. Good classroom managers are not necessarily good teachers. Why not? Is the reverse also true? That is, are good teachers necessarily good classroom managers? Discuss.
7. Explain the concepts of "with-it-ness" and "overlapping" as applied to control and discipline in the classroom. Do these concepts help explain the phenomenon of the teacher "who has eyes in the back of her (or his) head"?
8. A teacher punished a child for tardiness by assigning him twenty additional math problems. What effect do you think such an experi-

ence might have on the child's attitude toward mathematics? If a teacher punishes a child, should the punishment be logically related to the misbehavior? Discuss and provide examples to illustrate your points.

For Further Professional Study

Brophy, Jere E. "Classroom Organization and Management." *The Elementary School Journal,* **83** (March 1983), 265–285.

Duke, Daniel L., ed. *Helping Teachers Manage Classrooms.* Alexandria, Va.: Association for Supervision and Curriculum Development, 1982.

————, and Adrienne Maravich Meckel. *Teacher's Guide to Classroom Management.* New York: Random House, Inc., 1984.

Emmers, E., C. Evertson, and L. Anderson. "Effective Classroom Management at the Beginning of the School Year." *The Elementary School Journal,* **80** (May 1980), 219–231.

Jones, Vernon F.; and Louise S. Jones. *Responsible Classroom Discipline: Creating Positive Learning Environments and Solving Problems.* Boston: Allyn and Bacon, Inc., 1981.

Lasley, Thomas J. "Research Perspectives on Classroom Management." *Journal of Teacher Education,* **32** (March–April 1981), 14–17.

Schloss, Patrick J. "The Prosocial Response Formation Technique." *The Elementary School Journal,* **83** (Jan. 1983), 220–229.

Spaulding, Robert L. "A Systematic Approach to Classroom Discipline." *Phi Delta Kappan* (Part I Sept. 1983; Part II Oct. 1983), 48–51 and 132–138.

Wayson, William, Gary G. DeVoss, Susan C. Kaeser, Thomas Lasley, Gay Su Pinnell and the Phi Delta Kappa Commission on Discipline. *Handbook for Developing Schools with Good Discipline.* Bloomington, Ind.: Phi Delta Kappa, 1982.

Helping Children Learn Essential Skills

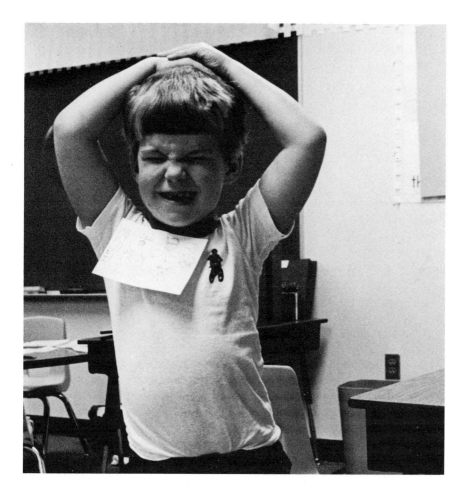

If one who has never thrown a dart throws one at a target and scores a bull's eye, we could hardly say that this was a demonstration of the skill of dart throwing. We would describe such a performance as a lucky shot; what has come to be called "beginner's luck." We would also say that such an experience is an example of chance success rather than of skilled behavior. A skill is a physical act or an intellectual process, or a combination of both, that can be performed in a consistently proficient way in repeated performances. Important in this definition are the conditions of *consistency, proficiency,* and *repeated performance.* Let us examine them in greater detail.

Whether something is judged to be done proficiently, that is, whether it is done well or poorly, depends on how well others perform the same act. This means that the norms or standards of performance are developed by observing the same performance by a large number of individuals. If someone were to do something totally new; something that had never been done in the whole history of the human race, there would be no way to judge how well or how poorly it was performed. Standards of performance are also related to the age and maturity of the individual. For example, we would be pleased to see a five-year-old child use his or her fingers to solve a simple mathematics problem, but this would not be acceptable behavior by a student of normal intelligence in a high school algebra class. In evaluating the proficiency of the performance of a skill, therefore, we must be familiar with the *norms,* the usual levels of expectation that apply to persons of similar age, experience, and cultural background.

The condition of consistency requires that the behavior can be reliably predicted. The individual, for example, does not perform superbly one day and miserably the next. Such a performance would be judged to be too erratic to meet the requirement of consistency. When skills are learned sufficiently well, the individual will be able to perform them consistently over a long period of time, providing the person engages in some amount of maintenance practice. For example, it would be extremely unusual for a child who was an excellent reader in the spring of one year to return to school in the fall having difficulty in reading. In fact, such a circumstance would be so rare that one would suspect that the child had suffered a physical or psychological accident during the summer. Inconsistent performance of a skill usually means that it was not learned well enough in the first place. More thorough learning will increase the reliability of performance.

The requirement of repeated performance eliminates the possibility of chance success. It is possible that almost any Saturday morning duffer can occasionally make a hole-in-one, but it takes a skillful person to play par golf week after week. In school-related skills, a child might by a stroke of chance provide insight that solved a difficult problem, but this does not mean that he or she possesses the intellectual skills necessary to perform similarly in repeated experiences. Obviously, the requirements of consistency and repeated performance are closely related.

Skills in the School Curriculum

A major portion of the elementary school instructional effort deals with teaching skills. This is necessary because skills open doors to other learning. Skills represent the tools of learning. Even though it is not clear whether low school achievement is a cause or an effect of inadequately developed skills, the evidence is clear that the two go hand in hand. The school records of poor achievers show a consistent pattern—failure to learn to read, inability to communicate orally or in writing, little or no ability to deal with simple quantitative relationships, inadequately developed work habits, poor social relations.

School learnings are often classified as (1) understandings (knowledge), (2) attitudes (values), and (3) skills. These are frequently discussed in terms of (1) cognitive learning, (2) affective learning, and (3) psychomotor learning. This breakdown has merit for purposes of analysis and study, but it is confusing when applied to the realities of classroom teaching and learning. Not all skills involve bodily movement as is suggested by the term *psychomotor*. Some skills are entirely intellectual, as for example decision making, analyzing data, or distinguishing between fact and opinion. In almost all cases, skills that are part of the school curriculum require that the learners think about what they are doing when they are learning and applying skills. Thus, we can conclude that most school skills have a cognitive component. Finally, skills do have an affective dimension in that the individual has feelings about how well one likes or dislikes what is being done. These relationships can be illustrated through an example from the field of reading.

Tim is a skillful reader. As we watch, his eyes race across the page with obvious interest in what he is reading. With the exception of his eye movements and his turning the page at intervals, we see no movement. When he completes the passage, we ask him detailed questions in order to check if he comprehended what he read. We find that Tim answers all of the questions correctly and he also provides some examples of application of ideas that were not included in the passage. Finally, we ask him how he liked what he had read, and he replies, "Just great! Wow! I could read that stuff all day!" Clearly this skill involved cognitive as well as affective components.

Certain segments of the curriculum are designated as skill areas. For example, reading, spelling, handwriting, oral and written expression, and certain aspects of mathematics are usually thought of as basic skills. They are deemed to be of such importance that a special curriculum sequence is designed to ensure their development. They are "basic" in the sense that most of whatever else children do in school calls for the use of these skills. If the children cannot apply them in functional settings, they are severely limited in the progress that can be made in any field of study.

Another important group of skills are those that are an integral part of the various content fields. Each subject-matter area places demands on the learner to use the specialized skills associated with that field. For instance, one reads social studies content differently from the way one reads directions for conducting a science experiment. Moreover, neither of these situations requires precisely the same reading skills that are needed to read a problem in mathematics. The same could be said for other skills as well. Social studies has its map and globe skills, science its special laboratory equipment, and mathematics has its special signs and symbols. Each has its own peculiar and relatively complex vocabulary. Additionally, each has its own basic study skills requiring the use of particular data sources.

Although the elementary school curriculum in most cases provides a sequential program of instruction for the basic skills (i.e., the three *R*s), the special skills related to the separate subject-matter fields are ordinarily not provided with as much systematic attention. More often than not they are treated in a hit-and-miss fashion. This is a major limitation of the skills curriculum in many schools. The usual assumption is that the basic skills transfer directly to the content fields. Although the professional literature has consistently called attention to the importance of the specialized skills related to each of the subject fields, teachers continue to emphasize content mastery and neglect the content-related skills. This is unfortunate because of the ephemeral nature of content learning as compared to the rather long-lasting quality of skills. Skills are among the most permanent learnings.

Complex skills such as reading, map reading, using resources, and using oral and written language consist of many component elements that are themselves subskills. Word recognition is a subskill of the larger skill we call reading. Using phonetic clues is a subskill of word recognition. Using initial consonant blends

(Courtesy of Terri Malinowski.)

For young children even simple motor skills require a high degree of concentration. Name three motor skills that are a regular part of the school curriculum and which the teacher must assist children in learning.

THERE IS NO MYSTERY ABOUT IT . . .

Dr. Dorothy Fisher is a much sought-after speaker for workshops, institutes, inservice programs, and other professional meetings of teachers. She is an articulate and dramatic speaker who has the capacity to greatly inspire audiences. Besides that she is a competent reading specialist. One day she was visiting with a colleague whose specialty is social studies education.

"Tell me, Dorothy," he said, "Which of the new reading programs produce the best results in terms of pupil achievement? There must be differences among them because some schools consistently produce better readers year after year. I'm not talking about differences that are attributable to differing school populations. Schools that serve similar populations show dramatic differences in reading achievement scores."

"The schools that produce the best readers are the ones that get kids to do a lot of reading," she replied. "Programmatic differences are almost inconsequential except as they differ in getting children and books together. Children who read well do a lot of reading. Those who read poorly do little reading. Of course, instruction is important, too, but it is the actual reading—and a lot of it—that builds genuine independence and skill in reading, and really makes the difference between good readers and so-so readers, barring some psychological, neurological, or physiological impairment."

1. What principles of skills teaching is Dr. Fisher talking about?

2. Is there any reason why every elementary school in the country could not do precisely what Dr. Fisher says is needed to produce good readers?

is a further refinement of the skill of using phonetic clues. In planning a skills curriculum, these component elements must be identified and then programmed to be taught at appropriate times. The performance of the larger skill may be greatly impaired because the child is unable to perform adequately one or more of the subskills. For this reason it is important to have regular checks on the progress of children as they move through the skills program. Where deficiencies are apparent, reteaching or corrective teaching should be instituted. This is particularly important in the case of a child who may have been absent from school at a time when instruction was being provided on a critical subskill.

Ideally, in a skills curriculum, learning experiences will be arranged sequentially, to move the learner from simple variations of the skill to complex ones, over a period of several years. In such sequencing it is essential to provide plenty of opportunities for children to apply their newly acquired skills in functional settings. The basic skills, as well as those taught in the subject areas, should be used frequently. This is the most important way skills are learned. The teacher should keep in mind that in spite of many different approaches to the teaching of reading, the best readers are always found in those classes and schools where children do a lot of reading. While this example uses reading to illustrate the point, the implications apply to any skill. Nothing is as damaging to skill development as is the failure to use the skill regularly.

Guidelines for Teaching Skills

General principles and procedures for teaching skills are not applied in exactly the same way to all skills. Nevertheless, the same basic principles are present. In applying these principles, the teacher is cautioned not to allow skill teaching to become routine and ritualized. Also guidelines have to be interpreted in ways that are consistent with the developmental and trait differences among learners. With these precautions in mind, let us examine what is involved in the teaching of a skill.

Meaningfulness

As is true with most learning, the process is facilitated if the learner understands what the skill is all about, what is involved in performing it, how it will be used, and "what it's good for." Demonstrations of skills are effective for showing meaningfulness and for illustrating a good performance. Demonstrations are frequently used in teaching skills that involve physical movement. For example, the music teacher demonstrates how to use the arm in moving the bow in playing the cello. Or the physical education teacher shows how to dribble a basketball. The primary-grade teacher demonstrates how to move the hand and fingers in handwriting. Not all skills are so easily demonstrated. In the case of skills that are mainly intellectual, it is necessary to show the results or effects of skill use, rather than the skill itself. For example, the teacher can show that one can arrive at a correct answer in mathematics, can locate a place on a map, or can find a specific book in the library through the use of certain skills.

Establishing meaningfulness serves several purposes that enhance learning. The most important among these is that it helps the learners understand how the skill can be *useful* to them. Unless this happens, the learners are not likely to involve themselves thoroughly enough in the process to learn the skill. Meaningfulness also helps learners know what constitutes a good performance of the skill.

Learner Involvement

If skills are to be learned at a high level of proficiency, the learners must involve themselves heavily in the process. Skill learning requires practice and application. When learners invest themselves thoroughly in learning the skill, they constantly seek ways to practice and apply it. Contrast this with other learners; ones who devote only a minimum effort to the skill and give that time grudgingly. One can take any skill as an example— reading, writing, playing a musical instrument, doing physical activities, or learning magic tricks. The individual who is self-directed and highly motivated to learn a skill will proceed much more rapidly and efficiently than one who is not. A key to good skill teaching, therefore, is thorough involvement of learners in the process.

Practice

Practice is an absolutely essential requirement in learning a skill. It does not matter how meaningful the teaching has been, or how well the learners understand what they are to do, they are not going to be able to perform proficiently unless they practice the skill. Through practice the learner develops the ability to respond with ease and confidence. There can be no question that lack of practice is a major factor in poorly developed skills.

However, if practice is to be a productive exercise, it must take place under certain conditions. Poorly conducted or halfhearted practice sessions can have a detrimental effect on the learner's performance. This would occur if the learner is allowed to practice incorrect responses, or if the practice session encourages poor habits of work.

Although "practice makes perfect" is often used as a guideline for teaching and learning skills, it is *improvement* rather than perfection that is the appropriate outcome of practice. Furthermore, the *desire to improve* is a very important condition of practice. A learner who goes through the motions of a practice exercise but whose heart is not in it will have a difficult time improving performance. It may even produce the reverse effect, because the experience is generating bad feelings, or what is called "negative affect," toward the skill. This means that the learner will not only engage in the practice session in an unproductive way but will avoid situations in which the skill is used. This obviously takes the learner farther away from developing proficiency in performance. Thus, highly motivated short practice sessions, with a strong intent to improve, are usually more productive.

The improvement of a skill may mean performing it with greater ease and precision, or it may mean doing it with greater speed. If improvement is sought in the preciseness of the responses, a conscious effort needs to be made to eliminate unnecessary movements and errors. The teacher would need, therefore, to show or tell the learner in what ways the performance is faulty. Exact repetition of the skill is *not* a good format if this type of improvement is sought. Instead, the learner must know how responses can be improved and work on those specific deficiencies in practice sessions. But if the improvement sought is increased speed of response, it would be appropriate for the learner to practice by repeating the performance in more or less the same way, trying to do it with increasing rapidity. In either case, improvement will be enhanced if the learner keeps a record of the improvement made in practice sessions.

In the early stages of skill learning, it is important to have the performance carefully supervised. This is to ensure that the learner is doing it correctly. Left unguided, the child may practice incorrect responses, which of course means that these errors will need to be unlearned before progress can be made. Once the child is able to do the skill, frequent short practice sessions will promote improvement. When the performance has reached an acceptable level, periodic practice sessions, along with opportunities for application, should be enough to maintain proficiency.

Feedback

One of the most important elements in skill learning is that the learner be provided evaluative information concerning the performance. This kind of information is called *feedback.* In skill learning, the learner receives feedback on successes and failures, and thereby can make the necessary adjustments in order to improve performance. When the feedback tells the learner of successes and that what is being done is correct, it is referred to as *positive.* When the feedback tells what is incorrect, that the performance is faulty, that the learner is going in the wrong direction, it is referred to as *negative.*

Generally speaking, positive feedback is more productive in maintaining a high level of motivation and promoting successful performance than is negative feedback. Success experiences are positive and predictable in their effect on the individual, whereas individuals are more variable in their response to failure. Some regard failure as a challenge; others are crushed by it, but almost everyone responds positively to success.

Finally, an important difference between the two types of feedback is the extent to which they guide the improvement schedule. Because positive feedback emphasizes what is correct, the performance can be replicated to ensure continued success. In negative feedback, the learner is simply told what is being done is incorrect but is not provided direction as to how to improve. This can result in a trial-and-error sequence of experiences unless the teacher provides additional guidance and direction. Negative feedback is needed, but it should be coupled with specific suggestions as to how the performance can be improved.

One of the most important sources of feedback is the teacher. This is the strongest argument in favor of reduced class size. Fewer pupils make it possible for the teacher to supervise and provide feedback. Besides the teacher, learners often get feedback on their performances from each other. If handled sensitively, this can be an important means of facilitating skill attainment. By using self-correcting materials, and by keeping careful records on trials, the learner can obtain a considerable amount of feedback on performances. Also, electronic devices are able to provide learner feedback.

Application

Essential to skill development is the opportunity to use the skill in a functional setting. Unless this is done, learning the skill will seem to be disassociated from the real world. For example, writing and spelling should not be thought of as being used, and useful, only during certain periods in the day or week. Writing, spelling, and reading skills should be applied frequently throughout the day in all other subjects—excellent settings in which to practice basic skills.

The traditional attitude toward skill development might be described as "learn-now-apply-later." Great emphasis has been given to basic learning skills in the elementary grades, the idea being that they would be used in later grades or in later life. This attitude has a detrimental effect on skill improvement in two important ways. First, it separates skill teaching from practical application in the early stages; and second, it shortens the length of time that skill instruction is given. The learning and application of skills must go hand in hand. In reading, for example, we would say that the child should learn to read and read to learn at the same time. These two processes should not be separated.

Whenever it is assumed that skills are taught in the lower grades and applied later, there is a tendency to discontinue, prematurely, systematic instruction of skills. Consequently, many students complete school with their basic skills at a functional level of about the fifth or sixth grade. If skills are to be improved and refined, instruction in some skills should be continued into, and in some cases, through high school. The application of skills should begin from the moment they are introduced in the primary grades. In this way a good balance can be maintained between direct instruction and functional application throughout the entire program.

Maintenance

When skills are used and applied regularly, there will be little problem in maintaining them at a satisfactory level. Problems arise, however, when a skill is taught and then not used for a long time. Through disuse the child loses whatever proficiency may have been developed. This usually means that the next time there is a need for the skill, a considerable amount of reteaching must be done. In cases where skills are maintained through regular use, the teacher should check from time to time to make sure that the pupils are performing the skill correctly and to provide reteaching as needed. This will ensure that faulty habits are corrected before they become a permanent part of the pupil's response pattern.

Basic Skills—The Three Rs

As we know, the elementary school has had responsibility for teaching the basic skills of reading, writing, and arithmetic from colonial times to the present day. Great importance is attached to these skills because they deal so fundamentally with basic literacy. A person who does not have a respectable command of basic literacy skills is greatly handicapped in doing school-work, and will be limited in choice making in life outside of school. Even though these skills are often dubbed "the three *R*s," they involve a vast array of skills and subskills that make it possible for the child to become a fully communicating human being. If a teacher desires to have a strong program in the basic skills, the following requirements must be met.

1. *The program is structured, systematic, and sequential.*
In situations where we find casualties in the learning of basic skills, we often see what might be called a "nonprogram" in basic skills. Instruction is entirely incidental to the informal activities of the classroom. Children write when they express a "need." They read when they have an interest in reading. They learn to write and spell because they want to communicate something in written language. All of this is commendable up to a point. Certainly we want basic skills to be used in purposeful ways, and no doubt some children can learn basic skills this way. But for most children, this approach is much too haphazard and opportunistic. It suggests that complex skills can be taught and learned on a catch-as-catch-can basis, with a disregard for the sequence in which the learning occurs. The outcomes of this approach, if widely applied, are predictable—there will be many children who do not learn the basic skills well enough to meet the requirements of school, to say nothing of life outside

of school. This is not to say, however, that there are not a few especially talented teachers who, using this approach, can achieve remarkable results with children.

To reduce the risk of having children not learn basic skills, the teacher should plan a systematic, structured, and sequential program of instruction in each of the basic skills. This means that time will be devoted to such instruction on a regular, planned basis. The various components of the skills will be taught sequentially, leading from simple to complex variations of the skill. The teacher will use well-prepared instructional materials produced by a reputable author and publisher. The specific skills to be developed can be and are identified. Pupil achievement is appraised behaviorally. These are qualities that characterize a structured and organized program.

The teacher has a right to expect the school district to provide curriculum documents that detail the structure and sequence of the basic skills program. Such a document should spell out specifically what skills are to be attended to and what level of attainment is expected. If such documents are not available, the teacher should study the teacher's manuals that accompany the reading, language arts, and mathematics texts used in the school. These manuals will acquaint the teacher with the organization and structure of the skills program developed in the children's material. Although the teacher will probably not want to follow such a textbook program precisely, it will provide an organizing framework around which the teacher can build the basic skills program.

2. *The program is interesting and stimulating to the children.*

Instruction in basic skills can easily fall into an uninspiring routine, one that varies little from day to day, and which becomes mindless and dull. For example, each day at the prescribed time, children go to their places and the lesson picks up where it was left the day before. And the ritual is repeated day after dreary day. Little wonder they, and their teacher, too, find this type of a program little short of drudgery. It would be unusual to expect any dramatic achievement to result from such uninspired teaching.

What is needed in effective skills instruction is the enthusiasm and interest that children bring with them in their early days of school—the time when learning to read, to write, to spell their names, and to do a little simple arithmetic represents a major success experience for them. How exciting it is for children to learn basic skills at that point in their school life! The child who exclaims, "I can READ!" has discovered whole new worlds opening to him or her. And what wonderful worlds those are! But as the years pass, much of this early enthusiasm wanes. And by the time the child reaches the middle grades, the teacher must conscientiously work at keeping the programs interesting and stimulating.

In order to maintain a consistently high level of interest, the teacher should make use of a variety of practice formats. In addition to the conventional practice exercises, generous use can be made of activities that involve practical application of skills, contests and games, visual and auditory aids, mechanical and electronic devices, and other vehicles that children find interesting. Variety seems to pay big dividends in keeping the practice session spirited and intellectually vigorous.

Experimental programs in skills teaching often report impressive gains in achievement when they are first introduced. Undoubtedly, the novelty of trying something new and different has the effect of making the instruction more interesting and exciting for both the teachers and children; consequently this is reflected in improved pupil achievement. Such success, in turn, has the effect of further inspiring teachers and pupils to work even harder, thereby propelling the multiplier effect. Perhaps *this* is the major contribution of innovative efforts to school programs.

3. *Frequent evaluations are conducted to ensure continuous progress.*

Progress in skill development (increased proficiency of performance), is a continuous, gradual, and cumulative process. The rate of improvement is irregular, progressing rapidly for awhile, then slowing to allow for the integration and consolidation of skills. Skill development does not take place by stages marked off by grade level, birthdays, or levels of schooling. Because progress is continuous and gradual, it is often referred to as "developmental."

The term *developmental,* however, is *not* meant to imply that skill growth occurs as a natural unfolding process, similar to the physical growth and development of a child. Without instruction and/or a conscious intent to learn and improve, skill growth will not occur at all. Skill development can be arrested at any point, for one of any number of reasons. It is essential, therefore, that frequent checks be made of the child's progress, with the results recorded for future reference. We need not be particularly concerned about the amount of improvement in a child's skill from day to day or week to week. But we should be very concerned if we see no progress over a period of a few months or in a school year. Nonetheless, the frequent evaluations—day to day and week to week—will alert the teacher to problems a child might be having. These can be corrected before they seriously impede the child's progress.

Cases are frequently reported where children have advanced to the third or fourth grades before it is discovered that they are having a reading or a writing problem or a problem with mathematics. There can be little excuse for this kind of oversight. Of course there will be pupils in these grades, and even several grades beyond, who are deficient in basic skills, but they should have been detected early in the school life of the child. After a child has been in school for a year or more, there should be no surprises for the professional staff regarding a youngster's skill development. When proper attention is given to evaluation, difficulties are diagnosed early and appropriate measures taken to correct them. There are of course children with complex learning difficulties that require highly specialized corrective measures. But the overwhelming number of learning problems of children are relatively simple to diagnose and to correct.

4. *The program must be individualized.*

There is much about the nature of the school setting that discourages the teacher from individualizing instruction in skills. The teacher has twenty-five or more children with whom to work. Often these children are of the same age and may not be too different from one another in physical appearance or size. This is especially the case in the primary grades. Moreover, tradition reinforces the idea that the teacher teaches a *class* rather than *individual pupils* who just happen to be grouped together. It is only when the teacher begins looking at children individually that differences between and among them become apparent.

The range of individual differences between and among children who have been randomly selected for grade groups in the elementary school is well documented. Children of the same chronological age differ in their rate of learning, in their interest in learning, in their learning styles, in their motivation to learn, and in almost every other relevant variable on which we have data. The challenge to the teacher is to devise methods of teaching that will accommodate the individual needs of children in group settings.

Individualizing instruction in skills does not mean that each child is to be shunted off to work alone on a workbook exercise. Individualized instruction can and, most often, does take place in small groups that have been formed to meet specific needs. The groups are temporary and flexible. There is no particular procedure or formula that can be recommended to the teacher, except that instruction probably cannot be individualized if the class is taught as a whole group day after day. The teacher needs to make a careful study of individual children in the class. By so doing, the teacher will get to know the achievement level of each one and will know what special help each requires. Then, by careful grouping of children, the teacher can provide each one with the kind of instruction that best suits him or her. Naturally, there will be many times when there will be a need for a one-on-one relationship between teacher and learner. Much of the time, however, instruction in skills can be productively conducted in small groups of five to eight children.

5. *Methods and materials should be used that stress purposeful and functional use of skills.*

The teaching of skills should *not* be separated from situations in which the skills are to be used. A major limitation of many skills programs is that they are isolated not only from life out of school but from other school learning as well. To be most effective, basic skills must be applied to other school learning and must be an essential component of the child's total school experience.

6. *The program encourages habits of independence on the part of learners.*

Many years ago (1948), the late Professor W. S. Gray published a book entitled *On Their Own in Reading*. This is a particularly appropriate title, not only for a book on the teaching of reading, but for any of the basic skills. As soon as possible, children should be "on their own" in reading, writing, spelling, mathematics, and in all of the subskill components that make up these basic skills. If this is to happen, they will need to be presented with many opportunities for the application and use of newly acquired skills. By using them, the children develop independence in their use. And as independence is gained they are constantly reinforcing and practicing the skill, thereby relying less on the school and the teacher to provide these enriching and extending experiences. The object or ultimate goal of the skills program is, of course, to make all children independent and truly "on their own" in the use of basic skills, and as soon as possible.

IS THERE A PREFERRED WAY?

Mr. Barto sets aside specific time periods during the day when he teaches basic skills such as reading, writing, spelling, handwriting, oral and written expression. He feels this is the best way to provide individual assistance to children and keep track of their progress. Beyond that, he does not do much with skills teaching.

Miss West does not provide specific time periods for these skills but lengthens her science and social studies periods and teaches the basic skills as needed in functional settings in connection with these units. She feels skills should not be taught in isolation, but in situations where they are used.

Mrs. Brookover combines what Mr. Barto and Miss West do. She has specific periods of short duration for systematic and sequential instruction, but also makes a big point of having children apply these skills in science, social studies and, where appropriate, in all areas of the school curriculum. She believes that both types of experiences are needed to ensure the satisfactory development and maintenance of skills.

1. Why does Mrs. Brookover's approach have advantages over those of Mr. Barto and Miss West?

2. Which of the three methods is potentially most vulnerable to the neglect of skills teaching? Which is most vulnerable to meaningless teaching? Why?

3. Assuming all three teachers have the same grade, and that the children in all three groups are roughly equivalent in their ability to learn, do you think there would be significant differences in standardized test scores among the three groups on a skills test?

Study Skills

In order to develop some degree of independence as an inquiring and self-instructing human being, the child must be able to use skillfully various resources and procedures. We refer here to the work-study skills, or simply, study skills. They are essential to successful achievement in the subject matter areas of the curriculum, and are central to any type of information gathering and data processing outside of school.

Variations of study skills may be spread along a continuum from simple to complex. The instructional program will introduce simple variations of these skills in the primary grades and spiral toward increasingly complex variations of them as the child moves through school. Thus, when primary-grade children are asked, "What happened first? What happened next? Then what happened?" the teacher is acquainting them with the arrangement of ideas in sequence, an important subskill relating to organizing material. Let us examine the study skills more closely.

1. *Finding and acquiring information.*

The deaths of former Presidents Truman and Johnson occurred within a short time of each other; both died during the winter months. Suppose this matter came up in a discussion by a fifth-grade class, and the question arose as to whether or not both former Presidents died during the same calendar year. If no one knew the answer, and it became important for the class to find out, where would they look? What source would be used, and how would they go about finding out what they want to know? Could such information be obtained from the textbook? If so, how would one go about locating it? By using the Contents? the Index? the Appendix, if there is one? Or can this information be obtained in the encyclopedia? If so, what is the best way to find it? Or does one have to use the library, and if so, what special references or reference aids are needed?

This example illustrates that procedures for finding and acquiring relevant information can be time consuming and unproductive unless the individual knows where and how to look for what is wanted. Children must be provided instruction, practice, and opportunities for application of skills relating to the useof tables of contents, card catalogs, indices, glossaries, appendices, tables of maps and illustrations, and others. They must learn what kinds of information are available in each, and how each of the various aids is organized and used. For example, an index is arranged alphabetically but a table of contents is arranged topically.

Skills relating simply to the efficient use of a book are also important in finding and acquiring information. For instance, paging through a chapter and noting the sideheads will often bring the reader quickly to the part containing the information sought. Of course, skimming is an essential subskill relating to the productive search for specific data. Children need to be taught to skim quickly over printed matter in search of specific items of information. This is a subskill of reading having to do with varying the rate of reading for the purposes to be achieved.

Beyond initial instruction, teachers must devise exercises calling for the use of these skills on a regular basis. This will achieve two purposes. One, it will provide maintenance practice and, two, it will alert the teacher to any problems learners are having. That is, it will serve diagnostic and evaluative purposes. For example, the teacher may have children use their social studies textbooks to locate a specific fact. If some are observed using the table of contents instead of the index, or worse, if they begin at the front of the book, page through it looking for the fact, the teacher knows that these children need help in developing more efficient information-search skills.

There are many skills relating to the use of general and special references that are critical in the collection of data relevant to a problem, topic, a question—or other research activity. General

(Courtesy of Herb Williams.)

This photograph illustrates how skills, such as careful observation, contribute to concept development. Provide other examples that illustrate how skills and conceptual learning are related.

and special references are the dictionary, encyclopedia, *World Almanac,* atlases, *Who's Who,* and the *Statesman's Yearbook.* Children need to learn what the sources are and what general or specialized information each will yield. Thus, they learn that if they wish to find information on many topics, a general, all-purpose encyclopedia is a helpful reference. But if this source is to be used efficiently, the user must be able to apply such subskills as recognizing alphabetical arrangements, key words, letters on volumes, indexes, and cross references. Therefore these specific subskills must be identified, taught, practiced, and used in functional settings.

2. *Reading and interpreting maps, graphs, charts, and other pictorial material.*

The extensive use of illustrative material today makes it imperative that individuals know how to read and interpret these visual devices. They are widely used because of their impact on the reader; they communicate with a minimum amount of effort—even to the individual with limited reading ability. Moreover, visual devices can communicate concepts, relationships, and data that would be extremely difficult, if not impossible, to comprehend in other ways. For example, imagine how difficult it would be to explain world rainfall patterns without the use of a map. A diagram illustrating the concept "chain reaction" is considerably easier to understand than an oral explanation, and greatly reduces the possibility of misunderstanding.

If children are to develop their skills in the use of these devices, a systematic program of instruction is needed throughout the grades. This program would consist of (1) formal and direct instruction on the component subskills and (2) many opportunities for practice and use of them. Too often it is assumed that children can learn these skills simply by using them in practical settings. As a result, they often learn them in a hit-and-miss way, if at all. The use of each of these visual devices involves skills that can be arranged along a continuum of complexity, and instruction should be programmed accordingly. Of course, children in the primary grades cannot read a complicated world map. But they can begin to learn that space can be represented symbolically— through the use of simple layouts and maps of the local area that they themselves make. When the primary-grade teacher uses stick-figure drawings to illustrate a point, the children are being provided an opportunity to learn chart-reading skills.

The use of various visual devices often relates to the subject matter of mathematics, science, social studies, health, and the language arts. Therefore, the special skills needed for their use should be taught within the curriculum of those subjects. There will be considerable carryover from one subject to the other. For instance, if children learn basic concepts and skills having to do with bar graphs, in the mathematics program they should have little difficulty applying these skills to data in science and social studies. Nevertheless, it cannot be assumed that this will happen automatically; the children need to be shown how to make specific use of these skills in each of the subject-matter fields.

3. *Organizing information into usable structures.*
Locating and collecting an abundance of information and data is of little consequence unless the individual can organize it in practical ways. There are well-established procedures and skills for this purpose. Among them are

outlining
preparing charts
making a time line
classifying pictures
arranging ideas, events, or facts in a sequence
making a data-retrieval chart
identifying a central issue
placing data in graph form
writing a summary
recognizing trends in data
taking notes
keeping records
evaluating information
processing data through analysis and interpretation

Such a list of skills presents a formidable challenge to the teacher, who may conclude that the task is overwhelming, impossible. No one could teach all these skills and do much of anything else! But of course, these skills are neither taught nor learned all at one time, or even in one year. The child's competence in the use of these skills is cumulative. The process begins when the child enters school and continues as long as he or she is in school. As is true with most skills, each of these has variants that are arranged in a simple to complex sequence in the curriculum. The primary-grade teacher who asks, "What is the one big idea we should remember from this story?" is helping the child to distinguish relative importance among ideas. This will be helpful to the child later on, when beginning to organize ideas in outline form.

Skills related to the organization of material can frequently be applied throughout the school day. Because this is so, the teacher may assume that direct instruction on them is not necessary. Or perhaps only a minimum level of instruction is provided, again the presumption being that the child will extend and refine these skills through functional use. This can lead to poorly developed skills or to the restricted attainment of them. To ensure that children will move toward more mature and sophisticated use of these operations, some direct instruction should be given on them each year, along with many opportunities for their practical use.

4. *Following directions.*

Following directions is a skill frequently used in life outside of school and, interestingly enough, is one that is either poorly performed or ignored until one gets into difficulty. Who knows how many cakes, cookies, or other delicacies have been disasters because the baker did not follow directions precisely! Postal authorities report that the public is incredibly incapable of following even the simplest directions on mailing procedures. In the use of coin-changing machines, it is not uncommon for users to stuff currency into the coin receptacles! Information accompanying new appliances, toys, and garden equipment always admonishes the buyer to *Read Directions Carefully Before Using,* further reminding us of our general carelessness in following directions.

In school, following directions is a commonly applied skill. There are directions for reading maps, for conducting science experiments, for taking tests and examinations, for constructing models, for using special equipment, and many others. These are times when there is an obvious need to apply the skill; it is at those times that the skill should be taught. Part of the teacher's responsibility is to monitor the behavior of children to be sure they *do* follow directions and procedures exactly in those situations where precision is essential. Poor habits in following directions can be reinforced by the teacher's lack of attention. But the teacher must not insist on precision to the point that it overshadows more significant educational outcomes.

THE NEED FOR A SMOOTH TRANSITION

In school, things went quite well for Jimmy until he reached the fourth grade. He was a sensitive, quiet, well-behaved boy and enjoyed the relaxed and informal program in the primary grades. Now the amount of reading he was being asked to do increased considerably from what it was the year before, and Jimmy was not a very good reader. Besides, he had to find things in the encyclopedia and in the library, and he did not know how to find what he was supposed to be looking for. He couldn't pick out a main idea, nor could he write a summary sentence. It just seemed as though nothing in school made much sense to him anymore. He was so discouraged that he would sometimes just sit and stare out the window. One day his teacher said to him, "Jimmy, you will just have to improve your work-study skills." He didn't even know what she was talking about.

1. How might the teacher have been more helpful to this child?
2. Why is the fourth grade such a critical year in terms of work-study skills?
3. If Jimmy's problems are left unattended, what would you predict his future in school to be?

Intellectual Skills

The development of children's thinking has been taken seriously as an educational goal by teachers, educators, and curriculum planners. Today much is said and written about "process" outcomes; often the reference is to intellectual processes. Children's textbooks, methods of teaching books, curriculum books, and curriculum guides, especially in the fields of science and social studies, show heavy emphasis on inquiry and other reflective processes. Little wonder, therefore, that intellectual skills are being highlighted in many programs.

Intellectual skills are involved in most of what one does when in a conscious state. As used here, however, the term applies to processes that are included in the application of intelligence to the solution of problems. Some authors have referred to these as *critical thinking skills,* others call them *inquiry skills.* Still other terms have been applied to this cluster of skills—reflective thinking, scientific thinking, creative thinking, reasoning, discovery learning, and investigation-oriented learning. Of course, information-processing skills such as interpretation, comprehension, and analysis are also important intellectual skills. Freedom of inquiry implies a commitment to intelligence and the rational process.

The phases or aspects of reflective thought developed by Dewey have served as the basis for much of the theoretical work in problem-solving and inquiry-teaching.[1] Out of *How We Think* have come the following five basic components of problem solving: (1) recognizing that a problem exists; (2) defining and delimiting the problem; (3) formulating hypotheses concerning the problem; (4) gathering data and drawing conclusions based on those data; (5) testing the conclusions and noting the consequences of the conclusions. In one form or another, these now famous five steps in problem solving have been widely cited in educational literature. Although problem solving and inquiry are not necessarily identical processes, the basic Dewey format is apparent in much of the work associated with inquiry teaching. There is a striking similarity between the familiar problem-solving steps developed years ago and the inquiry models developed by contemporary educators.

The use of structured problem solving and/or inquiry models has often resulted in the formalizing and ritualizing of these processes. Some speakers have amused teacher audiences by ridiculing the structured problem-solving procedure. For example, reference is made to the Nobel award-winning scientist who gets up in the morning and says to himself, "Today I am going to solve a problem. Therefore, I must remember the five steps required in scientific problem solving." This is ridiculous, of course, but it does illustrate the extent to which sound procedures can be distorted through faulty application.

The use of intellectual skills in problem resolution does not mean that one necessarily follows five (or any other number) of formal steps, as is implied by these structured procedures.

---

[1] John Dewey, *How We Think* (Boston: D. C. Heath & Company, 1933), p. 106.

270

(Courtesy of Terri Malinowski.)

Intellectual and social skills are referred to as "tools for learning." What subskills would be needed for the application of the skills shown in this photograph?

The individual who develops curiosity and skepticism will develop a system of defining and resolving problems. But if the learner is to develop any discipline in thinking, it is likely that some importance will be attached to such processes as defining and identifying problems, gathering and organizing relevant data, forming hunches and hypotheses, testing these against the reality of the data, coming to conclusions, and behaving in accordance with these conclusions.

The teaching of intellectual skills requires, above all, a low-risk classroom environment, one that encourages and supports diversity of thought, curiosity, and skepticism. This degree of intellectual openness will allow for the free flow of ideas that can be analyzed, discussed, verified, rejected, or accepted. An environment in which intellectual skills develop and flourish is one that values creativity, flexibility, and inventiveness. It rewards imaginative, unusual, novel responses. It supports and encourages pupils to engage in risk-taking ventures, as opposed to rewarding and praising of pupils for their search for the conventional, accepted, "right" answers. Given a classroom with this kind of intellectual configuration, the teacher may want to use the following suggestions. They have been used with success by classroom teachers:

1. Involve children in decision making in the classroom, dealing with such matters as methods of work, how to allocate time, classroom management procedures, unit activities, and so on.
2. Use role playing, simulation, and games to provide a setting for firsthand experiences in problem analysis and resolution.
3. Make generous use of "if-then" type questions that necessitate deriving consequences from given antecedent conditions.
4. Provide frequent opportunities for choice making, keeping in mind that choice requires alternatives from which to choose. If there are no alternatives, there can be no choice.
5. Provide instruction and experience in the use of structured problem solving and inquiry models.
6. Encourage children to become independently curious, eager to explore, and poke around in things with which they are unfamiliar.
7. Make it easy for them to be curious about their surroundings by providing a classroom filled with materials that provoke curiosity.
8. Make frequent use of reflective-type questions, as discussed in Chapter 7.
9. Encourage children to explore value dimensions of decision making, i.e., have them learn how their feelings interfere with their judgment.

Socialization Skills

When a person learns role behavior that is appropriate to social life in a culture, when one can satisfy one's needs through social discourse and interaction with others, we say that such a person has become *socialized.* In specific terms, this means that one knows how to use the language in communicating with others, behaves in accordance with the mores and folkways of the culture, has internalized the core values and beliefs of the culture and reflects those in his or her behavior, and that the person is able to modify behavior to suit specific social settings. For our purposes, this is an adequate definition of socialization, but it is by no means complete.

There may be specific applications of the socialization concept. For example, we may speak of political socialization as the process that shapes the learner's political belief system. Or we may say that the child has been socialized in the life of the school, meaning that he or she can perform social roles satisfactorily in the school setting. Some authors also write of "sex-role socialization." Sometimes the term *enculturation* is used in place of *socialization* in describing this process of acquiring, incorporating, and internalizing culture.

It is obvious, of course, that the total school program is concerned with socializing the youngster. The socializing process begins early in the child's life in the home and is continued and extended in contacts in the neighborhood, the community, and most especially the school. The forces that shape the socialization of a child are so powerful and pervasive that the process takes place whether or not it is willed and planned. But the nature and extent of this socialization may or may not conform to the expectations of the larger society, and this may make considerable difference with respect to the child's chances for success in the school's social environment. For some children the social environment of the home and the school may be similar; for others the two may be vastly different. In terms of school success, the child who is familiar with some of the protocols of the school culture has a great advantage. Those children who do not have a social readiness for school are likely to be identified as ones who present behavior or "discipline" problems when, in fact, they simply have never learned the needed social skills. This suggests that the teachers, especially in the lower grades, will need to build school readiness in those children who require it. This usually means more explicit directions, closer supervision, more frequent reminders of social expectations, and affirmative intervention in the formation of social and work groups in the classroom.

We deal here with a limited aspect of socialization. Indeed, we are confining our discussion to only three dimensions of socialization skills because it is known that these can be influenced by the school environment. These skills are those involved in (1) social interaction; (2) cooperative group efforts; and (3) conflict resolution. Clearly, these must be considered among the most important skills in the life of a human being because they profoundly affect how one deals with fellow human beings. Learning these social skills is also basic to much of one's personal happiness and stability. The person with deficient social skills is often one whose life is characterized by bitterness, cynicism, loneliness, and distrust.

SKILLS OF SOCIAL INTERACTION

In order to relate effectively to other human beings, one must first of all feel good about oneself. The way one feels about oneself is usually referred to as one's *self-concept*. We think of this in terms of self-esteem or self-image. Helping children build good self-images is probably the single most important thing a teacher can do in terms of the total development of a young human being.

There is overwhelming evidence that those children who have poor images of themselves are not only likely to be low achievers; they show other evidence of maladaptive behavior. It is not altogether clear whether one is the cause or the effect of the other, but it is reasonable to assume that it could be either, depending on individual cases. Be that as it may, there are many cases of improved school achievement and more constructive behavior when the child's self-image has been improved.

Unfortunately, the school itself sometimes contributes to the destruction of a child's self-esteem. A youngster may come to school from a happy home, one that has made the child feel good about himself or herself. In school the child may be bullied by other children, or teased; or may encounter difficulty in learning to read; or may experience failure in a variety of ways. This lack of success in school may cause the child's parents to be disappointed in his or her performance, and this may be conveyed to the child either unintentionally or overtly. Experiences such as these can, and often do, have a devastating effect on the child's sense of personal worth. A child with these experiences is almost certain to have problems in social relations; indeed, it would be remarkable if he or she did not. The importance of successful, confidence-building experiences is stressed repeatedly in educational and psychological literature. For example, Sears and Sherman have the following to say on this matter:

> Through meeting tasks that are challenging to them children learn to cope with the real world. Self-concepts of competence

in work emerge gradually, enabling the child to meet subsequent challenges with a calm confidence. Children who do not acquire a sense of competence become dissatisfied with themselves, unfriendly to those around them, resistant to authority, and perhaps rebellious against society. Studies of delinquents have shown that in almost every case the school was unable to give the individual a sense of competence; he then tried to maintain a sort of self-esteem by antisocial means.[2]

This pattern, so well stated by Sears and Sherman, is documented by a substantial amount of research and by the observations and experiences of untold numbers of teachers. What can the teacher do, then, to build in children this feeling of confidence and competence that is so vital to good self-images?

It is imperative that the teacher establish a social climate and a classroom environment where children learn to feel good about themselves. It should be a place where people are more valued than things, schedules, assignments, or guppies. It must be a place where everyone counts for something. Whether or not they have learning problems, as almost everyone does at some time, is beside the point. This should have nothing to do with making children feel that they are *worthy human beings*. Human beings of any age, but most especially children, should not have to prove their worth.

Healthy self-images develop in *caring* environments that help children build backlogs of success experiences. Self-images are destroyed in environments where children get the impression that no one really cares about them, and where they experience constant failure. Also it is doubtful whether children can perceive of themselves positively if they do not have a personal liking for the teacher, or if they feel the teacher does not like them.

It is the teacher, therefore, who sets the good emotional climate of the classroom, the climate that facilitates social interaction based on trust, respect, and integrity. Although this is achieved mainly by example, children do need to have systematic instruction in social skills. This would include:

1. Ordinary conventions and courtesies associated with social discourse.

---

[2] Pauline S. Sears and Vivian S. Sherman, *In Pursuit of Self-Esteem: Case Studies of Eight Elementary School Children* (Belmont, Cal.: Wadsworth Publishing Co., Inc., 1964), p. 3.

2. Sensitivity to the problems and feelings of others; seeing situations from another's point of view.

3. Listening to what others have to say.

4. Developing an awareness of the consequences of large or small group behavior on individuals, i.e., the effects of cliques, pressure on individuals to conform to group norms, the excluding of certain children from group activities, and others.

5. Achieving an understanding of why people behave the way they do.

6. Becoming aware that social interaction involves decision making and choice, and that the choices one makes often carry with them consequences that affect other people.

SKILLS OF COOPERATIVE GROUP EFFORTS

Being able to contribute in a constructive way to a group task is an essential skill in school, and in life outside of school. Most of what the child will do in life will be in cooperation with other people. Consequently, the social values of education are of inestimable importance.

The usual assumption is that people learn group-work skills by experience; that is, by participating in group efforts. Although this of course is true, it overlooks the fact that learning group-work skills can be greatly enhanced through instruction. It is not enough simply to provide the opportunity to work in small groups and committees; the teacher must also instruct children in how to function in those roles associated with group cooperative efforts. This can best be accomplished by demonstrating through role playing how individuals function in small groups. From these demonstrations, standards can be generated that can then be used in evaluating the performance of groups.

It is hard to imagine how one could learn to work cooperatively in a group by working in isolation. If group-work skills are to be developed, there must be many planned classroom activities that involve children working together. Not all of these efforts will be successful; this is to be expected, because in the process of learning, one makes mistakes. The advantage of the school environment is that mistakes can be made without resulting in disastrous consequences. In this respect, in-school experiences are different from those outside of school. Learning to work independently is important, too, but this is not the format in which group-work skills are developed.

The skills that need to be taught and learned in connection with group efforts are these:

1. Contributing to group planning (providing suggestions, evaluating proposals, suggesting alternatives, compromising on points of difference).
2. Defining problems (raising questions, suggesting which questions are relevant, respecting views of others).
3. Organizing to achieve a defined task (deciding on a plan of action, suggesting subtasks, suggesting specific assignments, deciding on what materials will be needed).
4. Working as a committee member (knowing and carrying out specific responsibilities, assisting with planning, cooperating and working with others rather than in isolation, supporting the leadership of the chairperson, working responsibly toward the achievement of group goals).
5. Assuming leadership of groups (developing plans cooperatively with group members, respecting the suggestions and contributions of group members, moving the group toward the achievement of its goals, delegating responsibility as needed, serving as spokesperson for the group, maintaining democratic rather than autocratic relationships with group members).

Instruction in group-work skills needs to take place over a long period of time. The teacher may single out one small subskill and concentrate attention on it when it applies particularly well to the work of the class. Standards for group work can and *should* be developed cooperatively with the children. These can be posted and used as criteria for evaluating the work of the groups.

When applying these skills it is usually a mistake to begin by dividing an entire elementary school class into small subgroups. Children are not ready for this degree of independence; they have not developed the maturity to be entirely self-directed. It is better to begin with one small group that is given a specific task—with clear directions. The group should be closely supervised by the teacher. The remainder of the class can be kept intact at this point. Gradually, all of the children can be members of such small groups, at which time two or more small groups can be at work simultaneously. In time, the teacher can have the entire class working productively in small groups. Group-work skills need to be evaluated frequently, and children should be provided with generous praise when their efforts have been successful.

CONFLICT RESOLUTION

Jason is waiting in line at the drinking fountain when Eric comes along and tries to nudge his way ahead of him. Jason tries to close the gap with his body; Eric pushes him out of the way. Jason pushes back; Eric strikes him—and the altercation has escalated into a fullblown fight. A teacher is called. The boys are separated, perhaps led off to the principal's office, and some attempt is made to resolve the matter. It may be that the issue is settled at that point, or it may be that the conflict continues, perhaps resulting in an after-school fight on the way home. Incidents involving two pupils or groups of pupils are fairly common in schools, and are usually unpleasant for all concerned when they happen. Because dominance relationships are so widespread throughout nature, including human beings, there is really no way that conflict can be avoided entirely. There is rarely a social relationship where conflict is wholly absent. This applies whether we are considering national and international issues or examining social relationships on a face-to-face basis within families, in neighborhoods, or on the school playground.

There are three ways the elementary school teacher should be prepared to deal with conflict situations. Each is discussed briefly.

1. *Establish classroom conditions that minimize the possibility of conflict and that encourage harmonious social relations.*

Why is it that some classrooms are characterized by a higher level of hostility and aggression than others? To answer this question we must examine the conditions within classrooms that give rise to such behavior.

Perhaps the most powerful force affecting classroom climate are statements made by the teacher. If the teacher uses a preponderance of negative and directive statements, the level of tension and hostility in the classroom will be elevated. This is predictable, and it has been demonstrated in human-relations laboratories hundreds of times. One of the most effective ways to reduce hostility and aggression in groups is to increase the number of positive, constructive statements made by the teacher, and eliminate those that are negative, directive, and critical.

Hostility and aggression also escalate when children are under great pressure to work rapidly, or when they are required to do more than they are able to in the time provided. This can be generalized: Any procedure that continually frustrates children is likely to reflect itself in aggression and conflict. Those who cannot perform satisfactorily under tension-producing conditions are likely to turn on others when venting their hostilities. A conflict on the playground may be the result of frustrations built up in the classroom. A more comfortable and relaxed instructional pace, coupled with realistically achievable requirements, can go a long way in reducing the possibility of interpersonal conflicts.

The classroom atmosphere can be more conducive to improved human relations if competitive situations are kept in proper perspective. Competition can be wholesome to the productive output of a group, providing it does not get out of hand. Children need to engage in fair competition and to learn the appropriate behavior associated with winning and losing. When children engage in competitive sports and games, the meaning of good sportsmanship is one of the important lessons they should learn. Good sportsmanship is a part of the American tradition. The classroom, of course, is not a sports arena, but it can be a place where competitiveness is handled with an attitude of fairness and goodwill. When classroom competition becomes intense, with some pupils lording it over others, there is likely to be hostility leading to conflict. Cooperative group efforts by the class can do much to reduce the ill effects of competition, and can teach children values associated with consideration for others.

2. *Resolve interpersonal conflicts immediately, but plan for longer range solutions to the problem.*

When there are conflicts between individual children or between groups of children, the teacher must intervene immediately. That may take care of the problem for the moment, but some type of longer-range corrective measures should be undertaken. When a fight is stopped in the lunchroom, the teacher may be treating the symptoms rather than the causes of conflict. Very often the teacher begins by asking who is responsible. Of course, the children blame each other. ("He hit me first," says one. "But he started it by swiping the ball," says the other.) After some discussion the children apologize to each other, shake hands, and the matter seems to be settled. When there have been injured feelings, however, this is not a satisfactory settlement of the issue. It does little good to force an apology from a youngster, or to have them shake hands, unless something is done about the conditions that brought about the conflict in the first place. An exploration of these conflicts will often show that both children are contending for something of value, whether it is approval by classmates, peer leadership roles, positions on athletic teams, or the favor of a high-status classmate.

3. *Provide instruction on conflict and conflict resolution.*

Much of our work with conflict in the elementary school might be described as little more than *moral injunctions* against conflict. "Good" children do not fight, quarrel, or bully others. They show proper respect and consideration for others. They are kind to each other. They are admonished to "turn the other cheek" rather than to strike back at someone who has offended them. Although there may be some need for this kind of instruction ar early levels, overall these approaches have not proven to be effective strategies for dealing with conflict. Some children and adults continue to fight, quarrel, and bully each other; they do not show respect and consideration for others—in spite of valiant efforts by the home, church, and school. We still read about ill-tempered persons who hurt or even kill others as a result of conflicts over trivial matters—someone honks his horn because the car ahead did not move quickly enough when the light turned green; someone makes an obscene gesture at someone else; or someone tries to bypass others while standing in line with a child waiting to see Santa Claus. In each of these three cases an individual was killed as a result of the ensuing altercation. The six to seven hours a day that American children spend watching television undoubtedly adds little to their desire, or ability, to resolve conflicts rationally.

Perhaps more productive strategies should involve analysis of conflict situations, an exploration of the values that are at issue, and the development of an appreciation of the affective dimension of conflicts. An important part of this teaching must concern itself with *coping* behavior. One must learn that it is not always possible to have one's own way; neither can an individual always allow himself or herself to be trampled on. Moreover, pupils need to learn what constitutes appropriate behavior when confronted with conflict situations.

Instruction in conflict resolution involves three important elements. The first is the identification of all the *facts* of the case. Who did what to whom, when, how many times, with what consequences? The second is the identification of the *issues* involved. Why is there a problem? What is the source of the conflict? How, and why, are the facts perceived and interpreted differently? And the third is the definition of all *possible decisions* that can be made regarding a resolution of the situation, along with the ensuing consequences of each decision. By using this model in studying cases of conflict, children will learn that usually one party is not wholly wrong and the other wholly right; the issue involves value choices between options, both of which may be right.

In applying this model to the study of conflict resolution, cases may be devised by the teacher, relying on real-life conflict experiences of children. Simulation games and role playing are particularly well suited for instruction in conflict resolution.

Study Questions and Activities

1. Teachers often use workbooks to provide "drill and practice" for children in such skills as are associated with language arts and mathematics. What advantages and disadvantages are there in reinforcing skills in this way?

2. Provide an example of a skill that could have been learned *incorrectly* in the early grades. How would this adversely affect the child's subsequent learning? Why are these skills so difficult to relearn in their correct form?

3. What are the advantages of teaching some skills in the content fields (i.e., subject matter), such as science, social studies, health, and mathematics?

4. Sometimes in learning a skill the child makes rapid initial progress but then shows no evidence of progress for weeks or months. What reasons can you give to explain this inability to show improvement?

5. Why is it that individuals who are highly skilled at what they do,

such as professional athletes, artists, musicians, and dancers, continue to work with their teachers?

6. Why are behavioral objectives well suited for use in teaching skills?

7. Does one learn a skill through drill and practice, or does one develop greater efficiency through drill and practice of a skill that has *already* been learned? Discuss. Does this tell you something about the place of drill and practice in the *sequence* of learning skills?

For Further Professional Study

ASCD *Educational Leadership,* **39** (Oct. 1981). This issue contains eleven articles dealing with teaching thinking skills.

Beyer, Barry K. "Common Sense about Teaching Thinking Skills." *Educational Leadership,* **41** (Nov. 1983), 44–48.

Brown, Jerry L. "On Teaching Thinking Skills in the Elementary and Middle School." *Phi Delta Kappan,* **64** (June 1983), 709–714.

Hennings, Dorothy Grant. *Teaching Communication and Reading Skills in the Content Areas.* Bloomington, Ind.: Phi Delta Kappa, 1982.

Pendergrass, R. A., and A. Maureen McDonough. "Teaching Thinking Skills: Helping Teachers Meet a Growing Demand." *Education,* **103** (Winter 1982), 186–189.

Shaftel, Fannie R., and George Shaftel. *Role Playing in the Curriculum.* 2d ed. Englewood Cliffs, N.J.: Prentice-Hall, Inc., 1982.

Teaching Facts, Concepts, and Generalizations

10

THE QUALIFIED AND COMPETENT TEACHER . . .

1. Understands the nature of facts, concepts, and generalizations and their importance in learning.
2. Is able to apply appropriate procedures in teaching for informational outcomes.
3. Uses conceptual approaches in organizing the teaching of substantive material in the content fields.

Performance Criteria

As a result of the serious study of this chapter, the student should be able to . . .

1. Provide examples of basic concepts and generalizations from various school subjects.
2. Describe basic principles of conceptual teaching and show by example how each would be applied in a subject and grade level of his or her choice.
3. Show by an example the difference between inductive and deductive teaching of concepts.
4. Show by an example how subject matter, skills, and affective learning are interrelated.
5. Demonstrate the ability to teach a concept to a group of children or a peer group, applying the principles of conceptual teaching described in no. 2, above.

Human beings have the remarkable capacity to reconstruct imaginatively situations previously experienced, as well as to invent new ones, by using intellectual processes and conceptual tools. To illustrate, read the following selection and, as you do, consciously try to visualize what is being described:

> From the viewpoint at Windy Ridge, one gets some sense of the awesome disaster that was visited on this spot five years ago. At 8:39 A.M. on Sunday, May 18, 1980, the volcano that had been dormant since 1857 erupted with such force that it blew 1,300 feet off the mountaintop. The effect was one of indescribable devastation. Huge trees that forested the area were suddenly stripped of their foliage and were scattered about like matchsticks. An avalanche of ice, mud, rock, and volcanic debris came tumbling down the mountain with a

thunderous roar and buried everything in its path. A once placid resort lake disappeared in an instant. The temperature in the vicinity of the summit exceeded 900 degrees Fahrenheit, producing a natural holocaust. In moments, a steam and ash plume rose 70,000 feet above the crater. By nightfall an ash blizzard extended 300 miles to the northeast of the site, giving residents an erie feeling of darkness and disaster. Today the once pristine peak, reputed to have been one of the most symmetrical in the entire world, lay gray and barren, exposing its oblong wound to the world. But that everlasting cycle of life and death takes form within the crater as the forces of nature are at work once again, building a new dome that may one day grace this proud mountain's crest.

1. Having read the selection, would you be able to describe the disaster site to someone else?
2. How do you think your description would be different if you had been in the vicinity of the eruption on the day of the disaster?

Even though the description might be more vivid and accurate if one had been a witness to this phenomenon, one can, nonetheless, gain both a knowledge and feeling of the force that was released there simply by reading about it. In reading the selection, one can reconstruct in one's mind what it must have been like to have been in the blast area on that fateful day. As we mature and build a backlog of experiences, we extend our understanding of key ideas or *concepts* that we rely on to give meaning to the reality around us. Thus, we do not always have to work with real objects in solving problems and in gaining meaning from new encounters. We do that "in our head" by calling on our past experiences.

Young children would not likely be able to visualize the reality just described because they would not know the meaning of *volcano, avalanche, holocaust, summit, crater,* and several other concepts used in the paragraph. It is doubtful that many who read this passage have experienced on a firsthand basis a place exactly like the one described. Yet most adults would have no problem visualizing the reality depicted and would conclude that it is Mount Saint Helens that is being described. This is so because the reader is familiar with the basic facts and ideas necessary to construct the situation in his or her mind. Many prior firsthand and vicarious life experiences have contributed to one's ability to derive meaning from a passage such as this. Because firsthand experiences are prerequisite to the understanding of concepts, it follows that teachers will need to make experience building an important part of teaching concepts to children.

The Relationship Among Facts, Concepts, and Generalizations

The relationship among facts, concepts, and generalizations is often represented by using a pyramid-shaped diagram. Facts, being the most numerous, are placed at the base of the pyramid, concepts at midrange, and generalizations at the apex. The logic of this abstraction is that facts (i.e., individually experienced perceptions of reality) are combined into categories of related meaning to form concepts. Concepts, then, are used to form generalizations that show the relationship between and among related concepts. To a point, there is merit in representing the structural relationship among facts, concepts, and generalizations in this way.

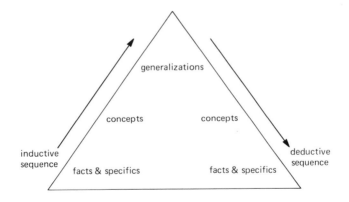

Much of the literature on teaching and learning of cognitive components regards facts and specifics disdainfully. Such expressions as "mere facts" or "facts simply require recall" appear frequently in professional books and in journal articles. Presumably the reason for such comments is to encourage the teacher to be concerned with broader, more significant learning outcomes. Unfortunately, such references may be construed to mean that facts and specifics are unimportant, and that this can lead to ineffective teaching of concepts and generalizations. Facts and specifics are not only important, they are essential requirements for the development of meaningful concepts and generalizations. None of the various strategies for concept development claims that facts and specifics are unimportant. Without exception, these strategies urge that specifics, growing out of direct, firsthand experiences, be used for understanding concepts.

It is often stated that facts are soon forgotten, whereas concepts and generalizations are remembered longer. This is only partly true. Many facts and specifics are quickly forgotten, but *some* are remembered for a lifetime. It is further claimed that where facts are remembered for a long time, there is opportunity for frequent review and reinforcement. This also is only partly true. For example, it is not uncommon for veterans to recall their military service numbers fifty years or more after they were in the service, with hardly any review in the interim. Persons in their seventies can often recite poems they memorized when they were in the elementary school. It is claimed, further, that such facts are remembered for a long time when they are *over-learned,* but this is not necessarily the case either. Sometimes a single experience or exposure to a specific bit of information will be remembered for a lifetime. For instance, an individual might remember the exact day and hour that he shook the hand of the then President John F. Kennedy. We must conclude, therefore, that there are many exceptions to commonly accepted generalizations about how facts are learned and how long they are retained.

We do not discourage overemphasis on facts because they are unimportant or cannot be remembered, but because of their *limited* usefulness and their overwhelming number. Very simply, there is too much specific information to be able to remember it all. Also, there is little need to remember vast amounts of specific information. Reference works and information-retrieval devices can provide adequate data storage for us. Naturally those specifics and facts that we need and use frequently ought to be learned so they can be instantly recalled. One should not have to consult a science reference book each time one needs to know that water freezes at 32°F. and boils at 212°F.

Facts and specifics are more functional and more easily recalled if they are learned in relationship to some overarching concept.

The concept becomes a category in which specific facts can be placed. This may not always be practical and feasible, in which case facts deemed to be important must simply be taught directly and learned. For example, a young child does not need to have a well-developed understanding of such concepts as voltage, electrical current, circuits, and conduction to learn the fact that if one places a metal object into the receptacle of an electric outlet one is likely to be severely injured or even killed.

Conceptual teaching means teaching for meaning. Therefore any teaching strategy selected must be one that promotes meaningful learning. Herein lies the chief difference between factual learning and conceptual learning. Factual learning is sharply limited in the extent to which it can or even needs to be given depth of meaning. Factual learning can be and often is achieved by associating a specific bit of information with the verbal symbol used to label it. For example, the symbol $\times$ in mathematics is the symbol indicating that two values are to be multiplied as, 4×5. How much time needs to be spent making such a fact ($\times$) meaningful? Hardly any at all; it is simply memorized as a fact.[1] Some facts can and should be made meaningful whenever possible, as for example, in learning the symbol for hundredweight, cwt. Mathematical facts such as those of multiplication, addition, subtraction, and division can and should be made meaningful.

The Nature of Concepts

Mental images, which are identified by terms such as *volcano, avalanche, holocaust, summit, crater,* are referred to as *concepts.* One does not know their full meaning by learning a definition of them, because their meanings are expansive, open ended. Understanding concepts depends to a large extent on one's experience, and therefore it is not ever possible to learn all there is to know about many concepts. There are always new variations, new horizons, additional refinements that extend the meaning with increased experience.

Specific concepts have qualities, or *attributes,* that distinguish

---

[1] We are here talking only about the sign $\times$; *not* the relationship 4×5, which, of course, should be learned meaningfully.

them from other concepts. A rectangle has attributes that are different from those of a triangle or a circle. The attributes give a rectangle its "rectangle-ness." For example, in order to have "rectangle-ness" a figure must be an enclosed plane figure having four sides, and the sides must connect to form four right angles. It does not matter whether it is large or small, whether it is drawn on colored paper or white, whether the lines are wide or narrow—none of these qualities has anything to do with making a figure a rectangle. Moreover, what this figure is *called* has nothing to do with altering its attributes. It could just as well be called an "oogaloo" and still be "an enclosed plane figure having four sides that connect to form four right angles." It just happens that long ago it was decided that such a figure would be called a rectangle—not an altogether illogical choice of labels.

Labels simplify discourse in that one does not have to recite all of the attributes of a concept each time one refers to it. We simply use the word label, in this case *rectangle*, and we understand that what is meant is "an enclosed plane figure having four sides that connect to form four right angles." Concepts and the word labels used to identify them are sometimes confused. The story is told of the child who said, *"Pig* is a good name for a pig because it is such a dirty animal!" This confusion illustrates the substitution of a label for a concept.

Just because a youngster is able to use the word or phrase that represents a concept, it cannot be assumed that the concept is understood. Obviously, there is little problem with a simple concept such as "rectangle." A rectangle has few attributes, and it is a concept that can easily be made concrete. We could, for example, have the child draw one. But when in social studies we deal with abstract concepts such as authority, justice, and culture; or transpiration, photosynthesis, and life cycle in science, the matter of differentiating between knowledge of the concept and using its label is not so simple.

Concepts are important in teaching and learning because they constitute the basic structure of a field of knowledge. Concepts are used to form theories and generalizations in fields of knowledge and, therefore, serve as the keystones to the understanding of these broad principles and laws. In recent years programs in mathematics, science, and social studies have, almost without exception, organized their curricula around key concepts in those fields. Examples of key concepts from each of these fields are given on pages 298–299.

Concept Development

Concepts, as we have already noted, are ideas that are heavily loaded with meaning and are expressed as words or phrases. Concepts are often referred to as having *depth* and *dimensions,* underscoring their potential for meaning. Strategies for teaching concepts, therefore, must take these characteristics into account.

Strategy One

One way to develop concepts is to use a listing-grouping-labeling sequence. Imagine a primary-grade class engaged in a unit on their local community. The teacher might ask the question, "If we went on a walk through the community, what would we find there?" Pupils would respond with such items as these: houses, supermarket, barber shop, buses, cars, bicycles, trucks, bakery, bank, insurance office, drugstore, beauty salon, gasoline station, fire station, police station, churches, park, jewelry store, motorcycle, telephone booth, newspaper stand, clothing store, variety store, parking lot, department store, library, post office, apartment houses, doctors' offices, hospital, school, playground.

After having listed as many specific items as possible, children are asked to see if they can group them. That is, the things that seem to go together should be placed together. This involves identification of some common elements that serve as the basis for the grouping. It is in this process that conceptual formation takes place. The items might be grouped as follows:

cars	flower shop	insurance office
buses	bakery	fire station
bicycles	drugstore	police station
gasoline stations	jewelry store	hospital
motorcycle	clothing store	doctor's office
parking lot	variety store	
trucks	department store	post office
	supermarket	telephone booth
barber shop		newspaper stand
beauty salon	houses	
bank	apartment houses	
church		

school   park
library   playground

The next step in the process is to have the children give a name or a label to each of the groups. For example, the following names might be appropriate for the groups defined.

transportation   *retail stores*   *protective services*
personal services   *homes*   *communication*
education   *recreation*

This example is a good illustration of what happens in concept formation. We make countless numbers of individual perceptions of reality in our day-to-day living. We group these perceptions in ways that place related ones together, and we give these categories labels. The object of concept teaching, therefore, is to get related specific *instances* or *examples* of concepts together in categories, and to get nonrelated ones out. For example, placing "gasoline stations" in the "homes" group would be incorrect and, therefore, a *misconception.*

In the foregoing example, the following procedures were used:

1. The teacher had the children *list* as many items as they could think of that were associated with the subject. They were responding to the question, "If we went on a walk through the community, what would we find there?" They had to be able to *differentiate* what they would see on a walk through the community as opposed to what they would see on a walk in the forest.

2. They were then asked to *group* those items that seemed to belong together. This necessitated *identifying common properties.* They had to respond to the question, "What belongs together?" They had to decide on criteria to apply in deciding what items belong together.

3. They then had to *label* each group. Here they were responding to the question, "What would you call these groups?"

Strategy Two

Let us examine another procedure that represents a somewhat different approach to concept development. We will select an example from science: *the lever.* This concept is related to a larger concept, *simple machines.* These concepts are almost always a part of the elementary school science program.

In everyday life the lever is one of the most commonly used devices. The handle of a claw hammer, baseball bat, golf club, tennis racket, and a wrench are used as levers. Our arms are levers. Tools such as nutcrackers, pliers, scissors, crossbars, can openers, and nail pullers are levers. A seesaw is a lever. Any device used for prying something is probably a lever.

A lever consists of a rigid bar that can be turned about a fixed point. The point is called the *fulcrum.* In the operation of the lever there is a *weight* to be moved and a *force* applied to do the moving. The *distance* between the weight to be moved and the fulcrum is called the *weight arm.* The distance between the fulcrum and the force to be applied is called the *force arm.* Thus, *weight, force, weight arm,* and *force arm* are subconcepts of the main concept, *lever.*

In developing the concept *lever* and its related subconcepts, the teacher provides the learners with numerous direct experiences with levers. For example, with a 1" × 4" board three or four feet long to serve as a lever, and a brick to serve as a fulcrum, the learners can experience directly the principles involved in the operation of a lever. With a stack of books as the weight, it can be demonstrated that the amount of force needed varies with the length of the weight arm and the force arm. If the playground has a teeter-totter, the teacher can demonstrate how one child can lift two or more children simply by placing them at the right position on opposite sides of the fulcrum. A small child can lift the teacher, who is much heavier, by using a short weight arm and a longer force arm in a Type A lever. (See Figure 1, below.) As children are involved in these activities, they begin to identify certain ideas and principles relating to levers. These statements made by the pupils can be used as working hypotheses to be tested in other settings. For example,

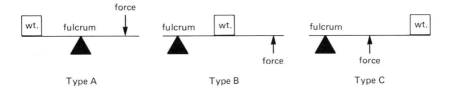

Type A   Type B   Type C

Figure 1. *Essential parts of a lever in three different configurations.*

(Courtesy of Patricia A. Conrard.)

Handling real objects often makes complex concepts meaningful to young children. Provide examples of a few concepts whose meaning would be enhanced through the use of concrete objects.

children may conclude that "the longer the lever, the less force is needed." The teacher can help clarify this generalization by having children explore further to learn that what they really mean is that in a Type A lever, "when the distance from the fulcrum to the force is longer than the distance from the fulcrum to the weight, the amount of force needed is reduced." This

294

can be refined further by noting that "force needed is reduced when the force arm is longer than the weight arm in levers where the weight and force are on opposite sides of the fulcrum."

After some of the basic terminology, subconcepts, and elementary principles of levers are introduced through direct experiences, the teacher extends the experience base of pupils by providing other examples. For instance, the teacher might bring to class—or have children bring to class—ice tongs, nutcrackers, pliers, scissors, a shovel, a wrench, a claw hammer, a can opener, and similar lever devices. On each of these, the children could be asked to identify the fulcrum, the weight arm, and the force arm. They could be asked to explain how the lever principle operates in each case. Depending on the maturity of the learners, the teacher might even refine the lever concept by developing the precise mathematical relationship between the weight and force as related to the length of the weight arm and force arm.

As we examine the procedure just described, we find that it involves the following principles:

1. Learners are provided extended, direct, firsthand exploratory experiences with the concept.
2. Essential terms and subconcepts are defined and their meanings developed as the need for such definitions and meanings emerges in the learner's process of study.
3. Learners are encouraged to make statements of principles that seem to explain the main concept, based on their observations and firsthand experiences.
4. These statements are then tested, rejected, and/or confirmed by observing new examples of the concept in operation.
5. The statements are refined through extended firsthand experiences, thereby expanding the meaning of the main concept.

The procedure as outlined is widely used in the development of science, mathematics, and social studies concepts. It involves back and forth intellectual movement, from direct observation to hypothesis making, to hypothesis testing back to direct observation. A concept such as *lever* has no meaning unless it is used in a descriptive or functional statement. Such statements are really generalizations. Children should be encouraged to make such statements and then use them as hypotheses to be tested. We see, therefore, that in the development of substantive meanings, concepts and generalizations are very closely related.

WHAT WOULD YOU DO?

Mr. Hendricks was conducting a unit entitled "Healthful Living" with his fourth-grade class. In the process he wanted to develop the concept *nutrition*. He remembered two principles of concept development discussed in his methods class in college.

"Learners are provided extended, firsthand exploratory experiences with the concept."

and . . .

"Learners are encouraged to make statements of principles that seem to explain the main concept, based on their observations and firsthand experiences."

1. If you were Mr. Hendricks, what "firsthand exploratory experiences" would you provide these fourth graders?
2. What statements of principles can you think of that would "seem to explain the main concept?"
3. What subconcepts would be important to develop in connection with the main concept *nutrition?*

Strategy Three

The two examples of concept development cited are both based on inquiry procedures. The children were to a considerable extent involved in discovering the meaning of the concepts. Although the meaning of concepts is never *given* to the learner by the teacher, there are more direct ways of teaching concepts than the two examples just discussed. These more direct approaches also make use of inquiry, but rely less on the discovery of meanings by pupils. Let us examine one such procedure.

Let us say that a middle-grade class was studying a science unit on animal life, and the teacher wanted to introduce and teach the concept *crustaceans*. The teacher might explain that there is one group of animals called crustaceans, write the word (concept label) on a chalkboard, and explain that the class was now going to learn how to identify crustaceans. The teacher goes on to say that in order to be a crustacean, an animal must have these characteristics:

1. a hard outer shell
2. jointed legs
3. antennae that serve as feelers

The teacher then shows the class a plastic model of a lobster and tells it that this is a typical crustacean. The class is shown that this animal meets the requirements of having (1) a hard outer shell, (2) jointed legs, and (3) antennae that serve as feelers. The teacher points these out and lets them touch and feel the model crustacean themselves. They tap the outer shell lightly with their pencils, confirming the fact that it is, indeed, hard. They move the plastic legs to see what "jointed" legs mean and how the legs work. They touch the huge pincers that are formed by one pair of legs. They are amazed at the length of the antennae. As this is taking place, the teacher has the children contrast the characteristics of this animal with animals they are familiar with in everyday living, such as dogs, cats, and horses. In this way nonexamples of crustaceans are presented. They have now experienced both examples and nonexamples of the concept.

The teacher proceeds to use other visual aids. A plastic crab is displayed, and the class is asked if it is a crustacean. It is established that the crab has all the attributes, and is indeed a crustacean. The children then examine a plastic turtle. Although the turtle has a hard outer shell, it does not meet the other requirements. The same applies to an armadillo. A shrimp, however, does meet the requirements. A sand dollar does not. At this point the teacher asks the children to identify one example and one nonexample of a crustacean for the next day's lesson, and be able to tell why it is or is not a crustacean. Following this series of lessons, the teacher will want to evaluate the class's understanding of the concept. It should be able to identify instances and noninstances of crustaceans from pictures, models, or live specimens.

In this last example of concept development, the following procedures were used:

The teacher

1. identified the symbol (word) for the concept.
2. provided the major attributes of the concept.

3. provided an example that illustrated the specific attributes of the concept.

4. provided a nonexample of the concept.

5. presented examples and nonexamples, had the learners identify major attributes, and explain why each was or was not an example of the concept.

6. encouraged children to find examples and nonexamples on their own, as a follow-up exercise.

7. evaluated whether or not learners could identify examples and nonexamples.

A SAMPLING OF BASIC CONCEPTS FROM VARIOUS SCHOOL SUBJECTS

Mathematics

Set	Factor	Ratio
Decimal	Per Cent	Place Value
Scales	Regrouping	Natural Numbers
Numeral	Zero	Common Denominator
Area	Subset	Measurement
Volume	Prime Number	Whole Numbers
Fraction	Point	Rational Number
Cardinal Number	Average	Number System

Science

Air	Ecosystem	Energy
Atmosphere	Gases	Adaptation
Force	Soil	Climate
Atom	Motion	Living Things
Liquid	Inertia	Life Cycle
Friction	Matter	Magnetism
Electricity	Molecules	Plant Kingdom
Gravity	Light Year	Boiling Point

Social Studies

Justice	Resources	Power
Responsibility	Production	Social Change
Social Class	Conflict	Modernization
Division of Labor	Money	Culture
Imperialism	Urban Life	Needs and Wants
Labor	Freedom	Colonization
Authority	Distribution	Habitat
Property	Institutions	Exchange

Language Arts

Phonics	Diction	Sentence
Communication	Poetry	Speech
Usage	Syllable	Punctuation
Grammar	Novel	Paragraph
Composition	Play	Modifier
Main Idea	Short Story	Vocabulary
Context	Language	Antonym
Contraction	Linguistics	Synonym

The Nature of Generalizations

Elementary school teachers often ask children questions such as these:

1. Can you tell us in one sentence what we have learned about a shopping center today? (grade 2)
2. Who can think of a sentence that explains how goods and people move in and out of a community? (grade 3)
3. Who can think of a statement that tells what characteristics are important in defining a region? (grade 4)
4. Will someone make a statement that tells how farming practices changed during this period? (grade 5)
5. What would you say is the relationship between an individual and the culture in which the person lives? (grade 6)

When questions of this type are asked, the teacher expects the pupil to respond by making a summarizing or concluding statement. One-word answers will not be adequate. In each case the question calls for a statement that explains a *relationship*. Let us examine some possible responses to the foregoing questions.

1. A shopping center helps people get the goods and services they need.
2. Goods and people are moved in and out of a community by a connected transportation system.
3. In any region there must be one characteristic that is found in the whole area.

4. During this period the use of horses decreased, the use of power machinery increased, farm population decreased, and production increased.

5. One's way of life is learned from one's culture.

Notice that in each case the response consists of (1) a declarative statement that (2) expresses a relationship between two or more concepts. We refer to such statements as *generalizations*. Along with concepts, generalizations have become important in recent years in planning and implementing instruction.

As is apparent from the foregoing response examples, generalizations vary in their degree of abstraction and complexity. To further illustrate this characteristic, notice the difference in abstractness and complexity of these two generalizations from science:

> Objects made of iron are attracted by magnets.
> The magnetism of a substance is due to the magnetic qualities of the electrons in its atoms and to the arrangement of its atoms.

Because concepts are combined to form generalizations, it is sometimes mistakenly presumed that generalizations are more difficult to understand than concepts. The illustration presented here clearly shows this *not* the case. There are simple and complex generalizations, just as there are simple and complex concepts. At early levels in school, children will be learning the meaning of relatively simple variations of concepts and will be making concluding statements that are simple generalizations. As the youngsters grow in maturity the concepts and generalizations with which they work will correspondingly increase in abstractness and complexity. A few examples of generalizations from social studies, science, mathematics, and language arts follow.

A SAMPLING OF REPRESENTATIVE GENERALIZATIONS FROM VARIOUS SCHOOL SUBJECTS

Social Studies

> The physical environment affects the way people live.
> People fulfill most of their common needs and desires in the community in which they live.

The unequal distribution of natural resources makes trade between states, regions, and nations necessary.

Successive or continuing occupance by groups of people, as well as natural processes and forces, have resulted in a changed and changing landscape in our state.

Many tools and new equipment make work in the home easier.

Places on the earth have a distinctiveness about them that makes them different from any other place.

The global location of a nation or a region contributes to its importance in international affairs.

Science

Life exists almost everywhere on earth.

Living things are built of basic units called cells.

Air is a mixture of nitrogen, oxygen, water vapor, carbon dioxide, other gases, and dust.

Air is essential for life.

Animals and plants depend on each other in many different ways.

Some resources such as soil, vegetation, animal life, and fresh water are renewable.

Machines make work easier.

A fuse is the weakest link in the electrical circuit.

Mathematics

A set is a collection or group of objects that are known as the members, or elements, of the set.

A given symbol must have a name, a design, an order, and a value.

The area of a rectangular plane surface can be found by multiplying the length by the width.

When the same quantity is added or subtracted to both quantities of an equation, the equality of the quantities remains the same.

In order to add or subtract fractions, each must be reduced to a common denominator.

Language Arts

Language consists of sound patterns, words, structure, and a system of word arrangement.

Many words are formed by combining other words.

Capital letters are used at the beginning of sentences, for all proper nouns, and for each line of poetry.

In forming the plural of most nouns, add *s* or *es*.

In contracted words, the apostrophe is placed where letters are omitted.

Developing Generalizations

A declarative statement is the most common form of expressing a generalization, although other forms may be used, too, as for example, a formula, $a + b = b + a$. Actually, it is not the *statement* but the *relationship* that constitutes the generalization. This is an important distinction in teaching because a learner may be able to verbalize a generalization without understanding the relationship it expresses. Nor is the ability to express a generalization necessarily an indication that the individual will behave in accordance with the content of it. Every teacher knows that pupils are often able to cite rules of grammar without being able to speak or write correctly.

In order to teach generalizations, one must (1) understand the concepts involved and (2) discover anew or verify the asserted relationships between and among them. This can only be accomplished by having learners experience the relationships in several instances. No one has ever been able to develop an understanding of a generalization on the basis of a single case. This would be logically impossible.

There are four types of generalizations commonly taught in the elementary school. They can be illustrated by the following examples:

1. A primary-grade class has been studying the movement of goods and people in its community. The teacher asks the pupils to think of a concluding sentence that tells some-

thing about the need for different kinds of transportation in the community. After some cuing by the teacher, the group concludes that "The community needs many different kinds of transportation to move goods and people."

This is an example of a *descriptive* generalization. It describes in summary form a relationship that has evolved as a part of the instructional process. Other examples of descriptive generalizations are these:

Everyone is a consumer, but only some persons are producers.
Our environment consists of both living and nonliving things.
There is a constant ratio between the radius of a circle and its circumference.
People spend their lives in some type of society.

2. A class has been conducting a series of experiments on plant life. It has controlled variables such as heat, light, moisture, and soil. It has worked with several plants. Some plants have lived; others have died. The concluding generalization is that "A plant needs a proper amount of heat, sunlight, air, water, and good soil in order to grow."

This is an example of a *cause and effect* generalization. If something happens in one part of the relationship, it will have an effect on something else. Other examples of cause and effect generalizations are these:

Improved tools can make possible increased production.
When people do not buy goods, the workers who produce them may become unemployed.
Metals expand when they are heated.

3. A news article spurred the class discussion of equality of opportunity. It came just at the time when the class was studying American ideals and the great documents of freedom. References were made to specific provisions of the Bill of Rights and to other Amendments to the Constitution. The class concluded that "Practices that discriminate because of race and religion go against what we believe is right in this country."

This is an example of a *value principle* expressed as a generalization.

Most ethical-guidelines statements are of this type. Other examples are these:

> One should place the general welfare over one's own when a choice between them is necessary.
>
> Business and professional affairs must be conducted in accordance with ethical principles.
>
> Freedom, as expressed in the Bill of Rights, is a cherished value in the United States.
>
> Everyone is required by conscience to treat fellow human being with compassion and humaneness.

> 4. A sixth-grade class has been engaged in a study of ways of living in various cultures around the world. In each case the pupils see how people have built their cultures, and at the same time how profoundly these people are affected by their cultures. This leads the class, with careful teacher guidance, to the generalization that "Human beings build their culture, but culture builds human beings."

This is an example of a *law* or *principle* based on a vast amount of research and abstract knowledge. Curriculum directors and textbook authors have used generalizations of this level of abstraction as their organizing frameworks for social studies, science, and mathematics curriculum documents and textbooks. Other examples are these:

> All languages have a grammatical structure, but few grammatical relations are common to all languages.
>
> Matter is not destroyed; it changes in form.
>
> The art, music, architecture, food, clothing, sports, and customs of a people help to produce a national identity.
>
> Language is a system of arbitrary vocal symbols that permits human communication.
>
> In any society, consumers outnumber producers of goods and services.

These examples of the four types of generalizations emerged in settings that should be familiar to most adults, because they are so commonly used in schools. In each case the pupils had extensive experience with the basic concepts involved, and were already mindful of many of the relationships that prevailed. All that was needed was the formal statement concluding or summarizing the relationship. In most cases, relationships are not suddenly perceived in a brilliant flash of insight. Quite the contrary. A great deal of preliminary groundwork was prepared by the teacher to make it possible for the children to "see" the relationship. To allow them to just muddle around on their own, hoping they will stumble on a complex relationship, is not the way generalizations are developed. A better procedure would be to have the teacher do the following:

1. Make sure the children understand the major concepts involved in the relationship.
2. Encourage them to make statements or propositions linking two or more concepts.
3. Encourage them to combine statements into ever larger, more encompassing propositions that relate the concepts to each other.
4. Test the validity of the assertions by relating them to experiences and observations.
5. Test the validity of the assertions by applying them to new situations.

The procedures described thus far follow what amounts to an *inductive sequence* of instruction. The generalizations emerged as a natural extension of the inquiry into concepts and their relationships. It is also possible to develop an understanding of generalizations by using them as working hypotheses that can be verified, confirmed, or rejected. When the validity of generalizations is developed through a *deductive process*, two approaches may be used, demonstration or verification.

In teaching a generalization through demonstration, the object is to show the learner the validity of the assertion. Neither the learner nor the teacher sets out to test the truthfulness of the statement. For example, take the generalization, "The earth along with its moon revolves around the sun every 365 days, while the earth rotates on its axis every 24 hours." The motions of these heavenly bodies are well documented and must be accepted on the basis of sound scientific evidence. A generalization such as this one can, therefore, be demonstrated without questioning its validity. A piece of equipment, such as a planetarium, is helpful in showing the relationships expressed in this generalization. Similarly, the generalization, "The volume of a rectangular figure can be found by multiplying its length by its width by

(Courtesy of Patricia A. Conrard.)

The joy of teaching is never more real than when children express wonderment or excitement about learning. Identify four or five lesson topics that would give children the kind of learning satisfaction shown in this photograph.

its height," can be demonstrated through the manipulation of one-inch size cubes. These can be arranged in layers and counted, thus showing the relationship embodied in the generalization. This could, and probably should, be followed with the learners demonstrating the generalization themselves. In using demonstration procedures to teach generalizations, it is important to observe the following:

1. The generalization should be stated and the basic concepts understood.
2. The nature of the relationship expressed by the statement should be made explicit.
3. The application of the generalization in operation should be presented, if possible, in several different applications (cases or instances).

4. The learners should replicate the demonstration, explaining the relationship involved.

5. The learners should provide additional examples or instances of generalizations.

A somewhat different procedure is involved if the generalization is regarded as an hypothesis to be verified or rejected. It should be emphasized that both options—verification and/or rejection—can and should be used. For example, superstitious beliefs are forms of generalizations that can be tested and will probably be rejected.

The verification of generalizations for school purposes relies on scientific procedures. This means that the assertion is stated and a search is begun to find examples that show the statement to be true or false. Examples must be of so high a calibre that independent, objective observers would agree that what is observed is, indeed, an instance or case of the relationship. The evidence supporting many generalizations has to come from secondary sources. It is not possible for learners to personally verify many generalizations, historical and some scientific principles being obvious examples.

SENSING RELATIONSHIPS

For each of the following sets of concepts, form a generalization that expresses a relationship among them.

Set I	river, heat, light, generator, electricity
Set II	fiction, characters, life styles, modern times
Set III	human groups, families, basic needs, survival
Set IV	web of life, living things, animals, plants
Set V	holidays, seasonal, culture, social roles
Set VI	tools, workers, unemployment, production

Inductive and Deductive Sequencing

The serious study of teaching and learning has always concerned itself with the question of whether it is more productive to provide instruction that goes from the specific to the general or from the general to the specific. Whatever mode of teaching is selected, the teacher will be making important decisions concerning the sequence to be followed. Let us examine each of these briefly.

Inductive Sequencing

Inductive sequencing refers to the process of going from specific examples to a rule, a generalization, or a broad principle. For example, suppose in a social studies lesson the teacher wanted to develop the idea that "money (a medium of exchange) serves as a convenient way of exchanging goods and services." The idea as expressed here is a generalization. In inductive teaching it would come near the *end* of the teaching or presentation sequence. In other words, the teacher would engage the children in a series of activities and experiences that would provide them with a broad exposure to the exchange of goods and services. Perhaps this would begin with examples of bartering. The children would see the difficulty in establishing a standard of value that would be acceptable to everyone. That is, if one person has goat skins and another has a horse, and they want to exchange these goods, who decides how many goat skins are equal to the value of a horse? One way to do this would be to convert both to a third item, whose value is established and acceptable to both parties. Suppose such an item were bushels of wheat. Then, if a goat skin is worth one bushel of wheat and a horse one hundred bushels, it would require one hundred goat skins to effect an exchange for the horse. But bushels of wheat as a medium of exchange have obvious disadvantages. These could be discussed by the class and other alternatives suggested. Without going into all the details of a lesson of this type, it is clear that the discussion of specific examples will lead to the use of money, and that children can thus be brought to the idea that "money serves as a convenient way of exchanging goods and services."

Examples from other areas of the curriculum could be cited to show the inductive or example-rule sequence. In mathematics a child can be shown several groups of similar items and be led to the principle that "a set can be thought of as a group of things or ideas that are precisely defined." In science, the teacher can provide several examples of the interdependent relationships between plants and animals in the cycle of life, and have pupils conclude from this exploration that "animals and plants depend on each other in many different ways." In spelling, the teacher can show several instances of adding the *ing* suffix to words ending with the letter *e,* such as bite-biting, strike-striking, write-writing. Children then learn the rule: the use of this suffix with words ending with *e,* when preceded by a single consonant, necessitates dropping the *e* before adding the *ing.*

It is clear that inductive sequences favor discovery learning. Often teachers are advised to provide a sufficient number of examples so that learners can discover the relationship for themselves. Partly for this reason, it is sometimes mistakenly assumed that discovery learning and inquiry learning must involve inductive sequencing of teaching. This is not necessarily the case. As a matter of fact, a conclusion based on an inductive search might quite properly be considered a *tentative* hypothesis, subject to further testing by a deductive process, as we shall see.

Deductive Sequencing

Deductive sequencing reverses the procedure just described. In this case, the teaching sequence moves from a rule, generalization, or principle to specific examples. Teaching is planned in a way that introduces learners directly to the rule, generalization, or principle. They are then expected to search for examples or instances of it. It can provide inquiry or discovery aspects if the given rule, generalization, or principle is accepted as a *working* hypothesis. Learners can then gather data to prove or disprove it.

Deductive sequencing is a common form of teaching. It has been subjected to a fair amount of criticism in recent years because it is associated with traditional telling and recitation teaching procedures. An obvious limitation of deductive sequencing is that the learner may commit the rule or generalization to memory and be able to reproduce it for examination purposes, yet have no familiarity with the basic concepts and supporting details that give depth of meaning to such statements. For example, a child may be able to recite "money is a convenient means of exchanging goods and services," but may not be able to support such a statement with examples and nonexamples.

Commentary

Great claims have been made for the virtues of inductive sequencing, and as already noted, much criticism has been leveled

---

WHICH IS WHICH?

The following sketches suggest that the teacher may be using either an inductive or a deductive sequence in teaching. Study each one and tell whether you think inductive or deductive sequencing is being used.

1. The teacher explains the rules of a game about to be played by the children in a P.E. class.

2. In a reading lesson, children have learned about key sentences in paragraph reading. Now the teacher has them read new material to identify key sentences.

3. The class has been studying "Batteries and Bulbs" in a science lesson. The children have had extended firsthand experiences with bulbs, batteries, wires, and switches. Near the end of the lesson, the teacher asks, "What conditions have to be present for us to have a complete electrical circuit?"

4. In the social studies unit on the supermarket, the teacher says to the class, "Suppose we took a walk through a supermarket, what would we see? You tell me and I will write what you say on the board."

5. The teacher says, "Be sure you study carefully the part called 'Hints for Better Spelling,' on page 23. Those rules will be helpful to you in spelling words correctly."

6. In a lesson on safety, the teacher says, "This large study print shows people doing fifteen things that are unsafe. How many can you find?"

7. Each child has written a short news story, and the teacher says, "I will write two standards for your papers on the chalkboard. Before handing in your news story, please check to see that it meets these two standards."

8. "We have talked about several examples," says the teacher. "Now who can state a rule that summarizes what we have said?"

---

against deductive sequencing. Because the development of thinking has emerged as a major goal of instruction, it is believed that inductive sequencing is more consistent with the use of intellectual processes associated with reflective thought. Such claims, however, most often represent beliefs or opinions rather than research-based findings. After an extensive review of the literature on this subject, Branch concluded that "Research on the effect of inductive or deductive sequencing of instruction while voluminous, has failed to produce consistent results favoring either sequencing."[2] The research does suggest, however, that deductively sequenced instruction facilitates immediate retention and inductively sequenced instruction enhances greater transfer of learning and delayed retention. The tentative nature of these findings is indicated by the caution exercised by researchers in reporting them. The use of qualifiers such as "there may be a tendency," "it seems to be that," and "there appears to be relatively" characterizes much of the literature dealing with this subject.

Because of the equivocal findings relating to these processes, the teacher is well advised to develop teaching strategies that involve both deductive and inductive sequencing. Although traditional teaching may have relied too heavily on deductive procedures, perhaps present-day strategies give more credence to inductive sequencing than can be justified on the basis of research evidence. The two sequences involve different thought processes, and for this reason alone the child should have experience with both. Inductive procedures tend to be more time consuming than deductive strategies. Consequently, where efficiency of instruction is an important consideration, perhaps deductive strategies should be used.

Study Questions and Activities

1. "Verbalism" is the practice of using words without knowing their meaning. Why is concept learning particularly susceptible to verbalism? Suggest some things a teacher could do to help combat verbalism by learners.

2. Webster's *New Universal Dictionary of the English Language,* unabridged, provides eighty-seven meanings for the common word label *run.* What does this suggest about having children provide one-sentence definitions of concepts?

---

[2] Robert C. Branch, "The Interaction of Cognitive Style with the Instructional Variables of Sequencing and Manipulation to Effect Achievement of Elementary Mathematics." Unpublished doctoral dissertation, University of Washington, Seattle, 1973, p. 1.

3. Some specialists have said that a teacher does not "give" the meaning of a concept to learners; that learners must develop those meanings themselves. What implications do you see in this for the role of the teacher in helping children develop concepts?

4. Limited conceptions are called stereotypes. Describe teaching practices that help to overcome stereotyped ideas of common concepts.

5. Identify some *mis*conceptions you have experienced in your own life. Reflect on how you formed them and suggest what might have been done to help you form more accurate understandings of those concepts.

6. Sometimes one encounters a teacher of unquestioned competence as a scholar who is unable to explain his or her subject to others. In the context of the ideas presented in this chapter, what might such a teacher do to overcome this difficulty?

7. Explain how class discussions can help in elaborating the meanings of concepts and generalizations. What conditions in the classroom must prevail if discussions are to have this purpose?

8. Contrast the role of *learner experience* in learning skills as compared with learning concepts. What teaching implications are there in this difference?

For Further Professional Study

Broudy, Harry S. "What Knowledge Is of Most Worth?" *The Elementary School Journal,* **82** (May 1982), 574–578.

Galyean, Beverly-Colleene. "Guided Imagery in the Curriculum." *Educational Leadership,* **40** (March 1983), 54–58.

Kaltsounis, Theodore. "Developing Concepts and Generalizations Through Inquiry," Chapter 4, *Teaching Social Studies in the Elementary School.* Englewood Cliffs, N. J.: Prentice-Hall, Inc., 1979, pp. 80–109.

Koeller, Shirley. "Concept Building Through Vocabulary Development." *The Elementary School Journal* (November 1981), 137–141.

Shepherd, Gene D., and William B. Ragan. *Modern Elementary School Curriculum.* 6th ed. New York: Holt, Rinehart and Winston, Inc., 1982, Part II.

Tennyson, R. D., and O. Park. "The Teaching of Concepts: A Review of Instructional Design Research Literature." *Review of Educational Research,* **50** (Spring 1980), 55–70.

Walsh, Huber M. "Working with Concepts," Chapter 3, *Introducing the Young Child to the Social World.* New York: Macmillan Publishing Company, 1980.

11

Affective Learning in the Elementary School

THE QUALIFIED AND COMPETENT TEACHER . . .

1. Has a sensitivity to the affective dimension of all learning.
2. Involves children in choice making and decision making.
3. Establishes a classroom environment that reflects the general values embraced by this society.

Performance Criteria

As a result of the serious study of this chapter, the student should be able to . . .

1. Provide specific examples of general values and be able to explain how these differ from personal values.
2. Describe characteristics of a classroom that enhance affective learnings.
3. Describe basic principles of affective learning and show by example how each would be applied to a grade of his or her choice.
4. Demonstrate the ability to conduct a lesson in one or more of the arts by doing so with a group of children or with a peer group.

Cognitive learning, as we have seen in Chapter 10, is that which deals with knowledge and knowing, and focuses on learning facts, concepts, and generalizations associated with the subject matter of science, mathematics, and social studies. Affective learning, on the other hand, deals with attitudes, values, and feelings, and focuses on the aesthetics, arts, and humanities. For purposes of study and analysis, this dichotomy between cognitive and affective is a convenient one. In reality, however, the two go hand in hand, and must be considered together. It is difficult to imagine, for instance, how a child could learn mathematics without developing some feelings about that subject. The same could be said about any subject or skill studied. In the discussion that follows, therefore, we stress the interrelatedness of the cognitive and the affective—the affairs of the head and those of the heart—rather than their separateness.

The school experience is a powerful force in shaping the affective development of children. They learn to like school or dislike it. They develop and extend their value system in school. They grow to feel good about certain encounters and certain people, or they are repulsed by them. Most of these feelings they will carry around with them as part of their affective baggage, so to speak, for the rest of their lives. The school experience, moreover, has a strong impact on the creative expression of children. School can excite and nurture the imaginative and creative abilities of children or it can stifle them.

Movements to improve the schools often work to the disadvantage of the arts and aesthetic components of the curriculum. Reformers invariably direct their attention to the basic academic subjects and skills, and in so doing, may take resources or even instructional time from the humanities and the arts. This is unfortunate, especially at the elementary school level, because it is at this time in the child's life when it is particularly appropriate to develop the sensitivities and to build the technical skills that the arts and humanities require. It is easy to interest a primary-grade child in a poem, a play, a dance, or a piece of art. Moreover, such an interest, if well-established early in life, stays with the child, becoming a permanent part of his or her intellectual and cultural life.

The curriculum imbalance that is unfavorable to the arts and humanities has long been recognized by many educators and laypersons. Even so, it is not likely that this inequity will be redressed in the foreseeable future. The problem has to do with the setting of priorities for education; deciding what is most important for children to learn. Clearly, the mood of the nation has been and continues to be one that favors academics rather than the arts. Historically, the only arts programs that have received enthusiastic support in the curriculum at *any* level have been those that relate to industrial employment.

Priorities for public school programs are an extension of the general values of the larger society. To strive, to work hard for a better standard of living, for a good income, and for material advantages is an important part of the American tradition, one that runs deep in the character of Americans. In a great many ways, this quality has reflected itself in what Americans value. They usually admire one who has overcome great obstacles to achieve material and economic success. This quality also expresses itself in what is valued in the school curriculum. Typically, those subjects and skills that are related to, or instrumental in, achieving economic advantage are the ones most highly prized. Thus, it is clear why reading, writing, mathematics, and science are assigned high priority in the curriculum. These are "useful" subjects and skills. They help the learner to become a productive person. The arts, literature, drama, and aesthetics

Most children, like the one in this photograph, look forward to school with enthusiasm. Too often this initial enthusiasm diminishes as the child moves through the grades. How can children's books, stories, creative dramatics, puppetry, music, and other creative art activities be used in sustaining a high level of interest and enthusiasm for learning?

(Courtesy of Terri Malinowski.)

are not "useful" in this framework of values. It is not surprising, therefore, that these components of the curriculum are given a low priority. Indeed, in many schools very little is done with them at all.

The industrial technology in the second half of the twentieth century is changing economic and social conditions to the extent that this traditional set of priorities must be challenged. People do not have to spend most of their waking hours earning a living. It appears that such concepts as the four-day week and a guaranteed annual wage will become realities. Larger numbers of workers are electing early retirement. Increasingly, machines are doing the work. Consequently, people now have and will continue to have more and more time for themselves. But what are they to do with this leisure time? Serious questions are being asked as to whether people can actually cope with an environment of affluence over a long period of time. Many believe that loneliness is the overwhelming problem of modern life.

How do these realities relate to the work of the elementary school teacher? As school districts reduce the number of special teachers and supervisors in the arts, as has been happening in recent years, the responsibility for teaching these subjects rests increasingly with the regular classroom teacher. This can have a number of advantages in encouraging creativity throughout the day and integrating the arts in the curriculum. It also means that the quality of the arts program will depend on the talent and motivation of individual teachers, a situation that is not likely to produce arts programs of consistent high quality. Teachers can work with each other in trading off teaching those subjects in which each has strength. In any case, it is important to recognize that, outside the home, it is the elementary school classroom teacher who has most to do with the early nurturing of aesthetic sensitivities of the children. It is the teacher who helps children learn to respond aesthetically to their surroundings.

The Affective Environment

We usually associate affective learning with the humanities— art, music, literature, and drama. There is little to be gained, however, in providing a formal curriculum in these subjects unless the total classroom and school reflect a sensitive concern for affective learning. What is required, first of all, is an environment in which people are more highly valued than things and procedures. Any practice that contributes to the erosion of the self-image and self-esteem of individuals must be open to question. This is of vital importance in promoting affective learning because self-esteem is so easily threatened whenever creative self-expression is involved. A thoughtless remark by a teacher may do permanent damage to a child's willingness to participate in any form of creative art—be it music, drama, literature, painting and art, or creative writing. Pupil growth in the affective area requires, above all, risk-free environment.

A "risk-free" classroom environment is one in which the child can take the support of the teacher for granted. Individual children do not have to demonstrate their worth in order to know that their teacher is their advocate. Moreover, each child knows that the teacher will provide a shield to protect him or her from the ridicule of classmates. Children know intuitively that they

---

REMINISCENCES

What experiences do adults remember of their elementary school years? The reading groups? The math lessons? Science experiments? Plays? Pageants? Holiday programs? Or would it be those fictional characters, Ismail, Omak, Juanita, and Juan, who graced the pages of the social studies texts? One can speculate only that what is remembered are experiences that are heavily weighted with affect. Experiences that were particularly enjoyed or those that were especially disliked have a better chance of remaining on long-term deposit in one's memory bank than those that were affectively neutral.

1. What activities and experiences of your own elementary school days stand out in your memory? Were they affectively toned?

2. If funding reductions require cutbacks in curriculum offerings, what can be done at the school level to shelter the programs in the arts?

---

can be secure in trying out new ideas and suggesting alternatives without fearing destructive criticism or other penalties if the ideas do not succeed. The teacher provides a safety net to encourage children to use their creative imaginations. The relationship between the teacher and the children does not have to be informal, but it must be one in which children feel psychologically and emotionally comfortable.

In addition to the concern for affect in human relations, the physical environment of the classroom must be conducive to affective growth. Fortunately, as older school buildings are being replaced, elementary schools are shedding their dreary institutional appearance. Many of the newer schools reflect a genuine sensitivity to aesthetics. School architects are now able to design at reasonable cost educational facilities that are not only functional but aesthetically pleasing as well.

There is a great deal that individual teachers can do to enhance the aesthetic quality of their classrooms. Bulletin boards and display areas can be used to exhibit materials conveying affective messages. Often paintings and reproductions are available to the teacher on a rental basis, perhaps through the school district's instructional services center. Books, visual materials, periodicals, and recordings can be made available for pupil use within the classroom, where appropriate. These suggestions are presented simply to indicate that a teacher who is concerned about the affective quality of the physical environment can often do much to improve it, at little cost or effort. Imagination and a willingness to be concerned pay big dividends here.

The Arts Curriculum

The "arts curriculum" includes all of the many processes, media, and experiences that come under each of the generic labels *art, music, dance,* and *drama.* The essence of the arts curriculum is *beauty,* and it should contribute to the development of children in at least three ways. First, it should nurture the aesthetic sensitivities of children through planned experiences. Second, it should teach children to become more discriminating in their aesthetic development. Third, it should help children gain satisfaction and enjoyment from participating in creative expression. These goals cannot be achieved by limiting the children's experiences in the arts to the singing of patriotic songs each morning or doing drawing, coloring, cutting, and pasting on Friday afternoons or during rainy-day recesses. The arts have to occupy a position of importance in the school curriculum if their educational goals are to be achieved.

The arts come into the curriculum by being included in the daily time schedule of the classroom. During the year children should experience a balanced program of instruction in art, music, drama, and dance. It is helpful if a teacher with specialized preparation in the arts is available at least part of the time. But this is not usually the case, and it is the classroom teacher, therefore, who carries the responsibility for teaching these subjects. Oftentimes, it is possible for teachers to exchange teaching duties with each other in order to capitalize on the strengths or interests that each has. Teaching in the arts has been greatly enhanced by the availability of recordings, films, videotapes, and other media.

Although much can be done by the nonspecialist to present a rich program in the arts, it is critical for children to get needed technical instruction at appropriate times. For instance, kindergartners and first graders may paint a forest of "lollipop" trees, but there comes a time in the child's development when such

What are some of the educational values that can be derived through the use of an activity such as the one shown in this photograph?

(Courtesy of Patricia A. Conrard.)

a rendering is no longer self-satisfying. It is at such times that the child needs technical instruction that will move him or her to the next stage in expression. If such instruction is not forthcoming, the child's involvement in art diminishes. As children mature and become more self-critical, the need for specialized instruction increases in all of the art forms.

In addition to the regularly scheduled instructional periods for the arts, much can be done to integrate them in other curriculum areas. The social studies in particular provide a fertile field for teaching and learning the arts. For example, as children learn about the home and family, their community, or people in other lands and other times, they can express these learnings through various creative art forms. The folk songs of the period can add deeper meaning and feeling to the study of the Westward movement. Children can role-play to gain insights into social relations. They can participate in folk dances that come from another culture. When the emphasis is on creative expression, the inclusion of the arts in social studies generally strengthens both the social studies *and* the arts program.

There is a close link between poetry, literature, and the arts. Nowhere is this more apparent than in the use of creative dramatics, where the children respond to situations spontaneously without depending on a script or stage properties to keep them in role. Using a story or a poem as the basis for the dramatic episode, the children can represent the mood, feelings, and actions of the principal characters. Closely related is the use of pantomime and puppets, both of which are excellent art forms for use with elementary schoolchildren.

The arts curriculum would not be complete without providing generous opportunities for children to express their thoughts and feelings through one or more of the sensory modalities. These voluntary activities have no purpose other than to provide an outlet for spontaneous, creative self-expression and to gain personal satisfaction from doing so. When the child is free to engage in an art experience, secure in the knowledge that those efforts will not be ridiculed, such involvement can be a powerful and positive influence in shaping his or her attitudes not only toward the arts but toward learning in general. Additionally, in such creative endeavors, the child will be participating in one of the most ancient preoccupations of human beings, that of representing and communicating feelings and thoughts symbolically.

Music, painting, dramatics, dance, singing, drawing, pageants, plays, and similar activities included in the arts curriculum are long-time favorites of children. Given an appropriate setting and

---

DO THINGS LIKE THIS STILL HAPPEN IN SCHOOLS?

Sarah was a sensitive child, seven years of age and in the second grade. Her year and a half in school had gone well for her. She was learning how to read and write, and she participated in class projects as actively as most children. She liked being in school. In "singing" she belted out her songs with a good, loud voice. One day during the singing lesson her teacher said, "Sarah please don't sing so loudly. We can hardly hear the other boys and girls." Sarah was embarrassed and hurt by the teacher's insensitive remark. It was at that point that Sarah stopped singing. She is now a woman more than sixty years of age, and to this day does not sing.

1. Would every child have reacted to the teacher's remark in this same way?

2. Can you provide examples from your own experiences of children being "put down" by a teacher?

---

encouragement, children love to express their creative impulses through the manipulation of sound, form, texture, and color. In the process, they learn to perceive their environment from new and richer perspectives. In spite of the fact that the arts have always been given short shrift in school programs, participation in the arts constitutes some of the most cherished memories of the elementary school for many adults.

Values and Teaching

Values are elements in the human personality that determine what an individual perceives as important and unimportant, what he or she thinks is worth striving for, what is believed to be right and wrong. One's values may be inferred from what the individual does and how he or she behaves—what motivates a person, what his or her attitudes are, what interests and aspirations are apparent, what concerns are expressed, and what one believes. Values may be defined as internalized guides to human behavior.

From early Colonial times to the present, it has been understood that elementary schools have a shared responsibility for the moral development of pupils. This being the case, it can be said that values education must be an essential component of the school program because (1) one's value orientation is basic to choice making and decision making; (2) harmonious social life requires commitment to common core values shared by individuals in society; and (3) the behavior of individuals is ultimately determined not only by what they *know* but perhaps more importantly by what they *believe.*

Whenever society experiences a breakdown in social control—such as a riot, a demonstration that got out of hand, an unauthorized work stoppage, a student walkout, or a violent crime, we are reminded once again how much we rely on individual citizens to conduct themselves in responsible ways. We go about the business of ordinary living in our neighborhoods, communities, at our places of employment, at recreational centers, and in other social settings with the full expectation that the persons with whom we associate will conduct themselves in predictable and, for the most part, trustworthy and honorable ways. Although we take reasonable precautions, we really do not expect to be mugged, robbed, raped, cheated, or lied to, or to have our homes burglarized or our reputations slandered. We assume that most people will do what we perceive to be "right."

It is often said that one cannot legislate morality, and that a law that is perceived to be unjust cannot be enforced. These observations, based on centuries of experience, tell us that in the matter of personal and group behavior, there must be a willingness to comply with whatever standards are established. External force and police power may be effective in keeping a few unwilling offenders in line, or even large numbers of people for short periods of time, but in the long run, external measures to force compliance are not effective in enforcing behavior that is not acceptable to the group. Consequently, societies get willing compliance by socializing their members into behavior patterns that cause most people to believe that they *should* behave the way the group expects them to behave. This means that individuals must internalize the values that are important to that society, and as a result, they will conduct their lives in accordance with those values.

SOURCES OF VALUES

All indications are that one's value orientations take shape fairly early in life. Children learn the values that guide their lives from the adults who are close to them. Their parents and family, of course, are prime sources of personal values, as are other significant adults. This might include neighbors, religious leaders, authority figures in the community, and certainly teachers in the elementary grades.

The child does not learn personal values entirely from human beings with whom he or she is closely associated. The media encountered are also important mechanisms in values education. Children may be involved in several hours of television viewing each week, and what they see and hear shapes their values. Magazines, newspapers, pictures, and advertisements help tell what is important and what is not; what is good and what is bad. Significantly, in this cluster of value transmitters are also instructional materials the children use in school, particularly textbooks. The content and illustrations of textbooks have a profound effect on children's values, if we are to believe the research that has been done on this subject.

Textbook content and illustrations can have an impact on the values of readers in numerous direct, as well as subtle, ways. Does it make any difference if males are always shown in positions of greater prestige than females? In the case of social studies texts, does it make any difference that some books deal with controversial issues as if there really *is* consensus on these issues? Does it make any difference if important aspects of our nation's history are not included in the text, such as sensitive matters dealing with racism and sexism? Does it make any difference if a child is never required to consider various conflicting aspects of a problem, never required to do creative thinking on problems, or is always asked to search for the "right" answer? Many authorities think all of these issues, and many more like them, *do* make a very great difference in the value orientation of the child. Moreover, the research tends to support this view.

But what right does the school or the textbook author have to promote certain values? Besides, assuming they have such a right, *what* values are to be promoted? The issues suggested by these questions are often the cause of much controversy between parents and schools. Either the schools are promoting values not shared by the parents, or the school is failing to promote certain values deemed to be important by the parents. This has caused cautious (and often fainthearted) school teachers to assume an alleged neutral position on the values question.

To claim neutrality in teaching values is not a realistic position. For example, even a decision to *avoid* a sensitive, controversial issue in the classroom is an expression of a value. By so doing, the teacher is valuing social harmony, possibly even his or her job, more highly than value placed on the educational outcomes of the controversial lesson. This is not meant to suggest that the teacher should or should not make one choice or the other in such a case. We mention this only to show that value preferences are always present in teaching, and cannot be avoided. A hundred times a day the teacher makes decisions that are values-based—what questions to ask, what questions to avoid, who should be called on to respond, what is to be read, how much time is to be spent on a topic, what films to use, who to invite as a resource person, what materials to avoid. Similarly, the textbook author makes hundreds of decisions about what topics to include, which ones to emphasize, what study questions to ask, how many pages to devote to certain historical periods, and so on. Whether or not the school and the textbook author have the *right* to promote certain values is really beside the point, because the promotion of values cannot be avoided in either schools or textbooks.

WHAT CAN *YOU* DO ABOUT IT?

To what extent do classroom situations contribute to stealing, lying, cheating, aggression, hostility, and lack of consideration for others? Many think they contribute very substantially. Consider the following situations:

1. A teacher leaves loose change lying around on her desk during the school day.
2. A teacher stores her purse containing money in an unlocked and easily accessible closet in the classroom.
3. Assignments are unreasonably excessive, with embarrassing consequences for noncompletion.
4. Testing situations are poorly or carelessly supervised.
5. A child or children fear drastic consequences if it is found that they have been involved in an infraction of school rules.
6. The classroom atmosphere is one of high tension and anxiety; pupils are constantly edgy, easily irritated.
7. There are many competitive situations, where children are pitted against each other, and are such that pupils enjoy excelling or "beating" their classmates.
8. The teacher makes an excessive number of negative and destructively critical statements.
9. There are few opportunities to relax and enjoy social interaction.
10. The children fail to establish attitudes of respect for the belongings of others or careless storage of personal items, making it easy for them to use and take things (innocently or intentionally) that belong to others.

1. What would you predict to be the consequences of each of the situations described?
2. Do situations of the type described encourage dishonest or inconsiderate behavior even at the college level?

GENERAL VALUES AND PERSONAL VALUES

In order to know *which* values are to be promoted, it is necessary to differentiate between *general* values and *personal* values. General values may be defined as the ethical and moral guidelines that are embraced by this society. They are identified in the great historical documents of the republic. They are defined in the laws of the land. They have been clarified by court decisions. They are a part of our religious heritages. They are universally accepted as the keystones of social morality, and the woof and warp of the fabric of our national character. They are sometimes alluded to in a humorous way as representing "God, country, and motherhood"—meaning that they are so generally pervasive and so abstract that they are acceptable to everyone. Freedom, equality, the right to life, liberty, and the pursuit of happiness, honesty, truthfulness, fair play, good sportsmanship are a few examples of *general* values.

Ordinarily the school and the textbook author encounter few if any problems in promoting general values. Indeed, they are required to do so by the education codes of most states. It is important for the teacher to recognize the presence of general values in the curriculum, and to understand that communities throughout the country expect citizens to know and to embrace them.

As we move from *general* values to *personal* values, we encounter quite different conditions for teaching and learning. Personal values are those ethical and moral guidelines that individuals internalize to guide their personal lives. In this society, where freedom of conscience is a highly prized general value, personal values must be individually derived. Personal values are the interpretations and applications of general values that each individual human being makes. For example, the school may promote honesty as a general abstract value, but precisely how an individual behaves in situations that involve honesty is for the person alone to decide. Thus, what may be interpreted as honest behavior by one individual might be viewed as social insensitivity by someone else. What one individual may perceive as a consuming and rewarding hobby may be seen as a waste of time by someone else. One person's interpretation of freedom is what the next sees as soft-headed liberalism.

What often happens is that personal values are taught as if they were general values, or even as if they were cognitive learnings. For example, the value *loyalty* (a general value) may be

(Courtesy of Mary Wilbert Smith.)

What experiences do adults remember of their elementary school years? Evidence indicates that those that were particularly enjoyed are ones that are most often remembered. What is there about the situation in this photograph that suggests an enjoyable experience for these children?

taught as though there is only one way to behave if one is loyal: being totally and unquestioningly obedient. The concept of "loyal opposition" would be unacceptable to this interpretation of loyalty, yet it is a well-established principle in both American and British political life. Or, to take another example. Suppose fourth graders were studying city life. A great deal of information about cities and city life may be included. Several general values may also be stressed, such as the need for sanitation, concern for the environment, the pleasure of aesthetically pleasing surroundings, and others. But the child may be asked, "Do you like the idea of a Megalopolis?" Or the child may be shown a city dwelling of the future and be asked, "How do you like it?" These are good examples of questions that help children analyze their own personal values. How can one tell someone else what he or she should like or dislike? How can one claim that there is a "right" answer to such questions? Yet these are important questions, because sooner or later everyone will need to sort out the things one likes and those one dislikes. Children need to be thinking about their preferences—not only what they are, but why they choose them.

Children need frequent opportunities to examine their value choices in a nonthreatening environment such as the classroom. They need to try their ideas out on each other. None of this will get very far if the teacher is looking for "correct" answers from the children to questions dealing with personal values, or allows the responses to be ridiculed because they happen to be different from others in the group. Personal values are just that—personal, private matters. Some personal values should only be thought about, not shared with anyone else, least of all one's classmates.

With children in the primary grades, it is difficult to distinguish between general and personal values. The examples used to explain a general value are likely to be personalized by the youngsters in developing their own value framework. For example, in the first grade such general values associated with family life as affection, security, and caring for others are often apparent. The child will interpret these in terms of his or her own family. How the child personalizes these values will, of course, depend on how consistent they are with the realities of his or her own life. At these early levels children need many examples of behavior based on general values. Otherwise, they would have no way of knowing what behavior society expects, i.e., behavior that results in reward, and that which results in punishment.

Even at this level, however, the teacher should allow generously for simple choice making, because this provides children with opportunities for expressing value preferences.

VALUING AND VALUE CLARIFICATION

As children move into the middle and upper grades, more can be done in differentiating between general and personal value development. At this level, children should become more actively involved in the *valuing* process. This process involves the identification and analysis of value components of problems and issues, making personal choices and commitments, understanding the consequences of value choices, and acting in accordance with value preferences. Valuing exercises of this type, when properly handled, may provide children with opportunities to think about and clarify their own values, and to explore the extent of their own commitment to particular values.

The teacher is cautioned against the indiscriminate use of value clarification exercises. The procedures are deceptively simple but may carry a powerful emotional and psychological impact.

Valuing strategies that explore the child's interior psychological space may be defended on the basis of value clarification but may in fact be violating the person's privacy. Responsible advocates of value clarification go to great lengths in explaining to teachers that participants in value clarification must always have the choice of participating or not. Yet with all of us, and with young children in particular, the social pressure to participate is often so compelling that the individual is not really able to exercise a choice. A teacher who is exercising responsible judgment will not place a child in a position of having to make such a difficult decision.

Value clarification gets into difficulty when it takes on the characteristics of group therapy. In the process, children are involved in "exploring" basic beliefs that guide their lives. This almost certainly leads the discussion in the direction of religious values, precepts, and beliefs that children have learned at home or in their church. Of course, this results in parental objection. When value clarification enters the private lives of children to the extent described here, the teacher has far exceeded the ethical, and perhaps even the legal, parameters of the curriculum of the public school classroom.

ACTIONS SPEAK LOUDER THAN WORDS

The following is a list of values that to some degree are embraced by large numbers of Americans:

Justice	Individual liberty
Competitiveness	Industriousness
Independence (personal)	Consideration for others
Productive output	Time conservation

1. Can you think of examples of specific classroom practices that support and reinforce these values?

2. Can you think of examples of classroom and administrative practices that contradict these values?

3. Which of these values most frequently reflect themselves in classroom practices? Is this consistent with what schools claim to be emphasizing?

Moral Education

Conventional approaches to moral and value education have defined moral behavior in terms of specific virtues and discrete character traits. The assumption is that one is honest or not, responsible or irresponsible, truthful or deceitful, self-directed or dependent, self-controlled or impulsive, and so on. The strategies used to teach these traits were almost entirely expository and catechetical. Such *direct* instruction took the form of reading stories that had strong moral messages. In these case studies, violators of the moral code were dealt with most harshly; crime definitely did not pay. Other teaching methods made use of moral codes, creeds, oaths, and injunctions calling for ethical behavior. These direct methods of instruction were the accepted way to teach moral behavior until the early part of this century, at which time questions were raised about the validity of the assumption that verbal behavior is a correlate of action, that knowing means doing.

The maturing of the professional fields of education and psychology, along with research on human behavior, brought a rejection of these approaches to moral education. The classic studies of Hartshorne and May conducted at Columbia University from 1928 to 1930 had a profound effect on moral education in the public schools.[1] These studies reported that moral character was little influenced by the usual ethical instruction as it is conducted in the schools. They concluded that character education and religious education had little if any influence on moral behavior as measured by objective tests of honesty, service, altruism, and self-control. These studies found that children could not be divided into two groups, those who cheat and those who do not. Whether one cheated or not evidently depended on the risk of being caught. There were situational variables in certain classrooms that seemed to encourage or discourage dishonest behavior.

These studies and their findings were widely cited in educational and psychological literature, and there is no question that this resulted in a turning away from moral education by the schools. If school instruction is powerless to influence moral behavior, why should it be concerned with moral education at all? Although there has been no research that challenges the basic findings of the Hartshorne and May studies, there are indications that somewhat different approaches to moral education may be productive in bringing about behavior change.

We are recommending that *indirect* methods of instruction be used in conducting moral education. When indirect methods are used, moral education becomes a part of the entire work and life of the school day. Children are expected to practice on a firsthand basis consideration for others, for example. They learn what it means to take individual responsibility for actions and to deal with others honestly by living in accordance with these virtues. Through biographies and the study of the lives of historical figures, they gain a sense of appreciation of others and an awareness of what human characteristics this society values. Moral education is not a subject to be studied twenty—or however many—minutes each day, but is an integral part of the total school experience for children. This is well summarized by Professor Jeanne Pietig:

---

[1] Hugh Hartshorne and Mark A. May, *Studies in Deceit* (New York: Macmillan Publishing Co., Inc., 1928).

Moral education, like morality itself, is multifaceted. It involves much more than moral reasoning, much more than clarifying values, and much more than instilling discipline in students. Perhaps John Dewey still offers elementary school teachers the most sensible way for teaching values to students; he emphasized that education is an intrinsically moral enterprise, and he interpreted the ethical responsibility of the school in the broadest and freest spirit.[2]

Study Questions and Activities

1. What reasons can you give for the erosion of the arts in the school curriculum in recent years?

2. Should education in the arts in the elementary school consist only of pleasurable "do your own thing" activities, or should it include disciplined approaches similar to those of artists? Provide a rationale for your response.

3. What are some of the contributions of children's literature, dramatics, music, puppetry, and dance to the overall goals of American education?

4. Some specialists have claimed that affective learnings tend to be "caught" rather than "taught." Provide specific suggestions as to what a teacher might do to facilitate this process.

5. What reasons can you give to explain why teachers often encounter difficulty with parents when they involve children in value clarification?

6. Provide specific suggestions of ways a teacher might make the classroom learning environment more aesthetically pleasing to children.

7. The text authors favor indirect strategies for teaching values. Does this mean that there is no place for the discussion and analysis of issues that are based on certain values or that there is no place in the classroom for the discussion of and analysis of the meaning of specific values? Explain.

---

[2] Jeanne Pietig, "Values and Morality in Early 20th Century Elementary Schools: A Perspective," *Social Education* 47 (April 1983), 265.

For Further Professional Study

ASCD *Educational Leadership,* **39** (April 1982). This issue contains twelve articles dealing with affective education.

Daniels, Elva S. "Great American Work Songs." *Instructor,* **93** (March 1983), 55–63.

Frost, Joe L. "Free to Be: The Arts and Child Development." *Childhood Education,* **57** (Nov.–Dec. 1980), 66–71.

Hansen-Krening, Nancy. *Competency and Creativity in Language Arts: A Multiethnic Focus.* Reading, Mass.: Addison-Wesley Publishing Co., Inc., 1979.

Marrow, Lesley Mandel, and Carol Simon Weinstein. "Increasing Children's Use of Literature through Program and Physical Design Changes." *The Elementary School Journal,* **83** (Nov. 1982), 131–137.

Maxwell, William. "Games Children Play." *Educational Leadership,* **40** (March 1983), 38–41.

Mills, Beth Solow. "Imagination: The Connection Between Writing and Play." *Educational Leadership,* **40** (March 1983), 50–53.

Rubin, Louis. "Artistry in Teaching." *Educational Leadership,* **40** (Jan. 1983), 44–49.

Shallcross, Doris J. *Teaching Creative Behavior: How to Teach Creativity to Children of All Ages.* Englewood Cliffs, N. J.: Prentice-Hall, Inc., 1981.

Szekely, George E. "Art Partnership Network: A Supportive Program for Artistically Gifted Children." *The Elementary School Journal,* **83** (Sept. 1982), 59–60.

Professional Development of the Elementary School Teacher

THE QUALIFIED AND COMPETENT TEACHER . . .

1. Recognizes the importance of professional development throughout a career.

2. Is knowledgeable about the societal and professional impacts on the teaching profession.

3. Takes advantage of the opportunities for professional development.

Performance Criteria

As a result of the serious study of this chapter, the student should be able to . . .

1. Analyze the role of teacher organizations in the professional development of teachers.

2. Describe the opportunities for professional development that result from membership in professional associations.

3. Describe the opportunities for professional development programs for inservice education, certification, advanced degrees, continued education, and career-branching specializations.

The public's attention to *the teacher as a professional person* was heightened during 1983 as a result of the report, *A Nation at Risk: The Imperative for Educational Reform.*[1] The report, which was critical of teachers, met with mixed reactions in the public and professional sectors. Some critics called for *merit pay* for teachers— paying teachers according to the extent their learners achieve, whereas others asserted that an "across the board" salary increase for all teachers was the key to better quality. These points of view, among a host of other proposed solutions, must be dealt with in the coming years. An objective appraisal is difficult because of the diverse roles society expects the teacher to perform.

Some believe that the life of a teacher is a relatively easy one, and until recent years, the occupational restraints felt by teachers were somewhat less rigorous than those imposed on members of most other occupations. The reasons for this belief— many would prefer to call it a myth—seem to bear up rather well when certain facts are considered. These facts show that

---

[1] *A Nation at Risk: The Imperative for Educational Reform.* Report of the National Commission on Excellence in Education (Washington, D. C.: U. S. Department of Education, 1983).

(1) admission to teacher education, in terms of entry requirements, is easier than that of most other professions; (2) the amount of coursework devoted exclusively to professional education is very low—a national average of about 13 per cent of the total coursework required for a baccalaureate degree; (3) reentry into the profession usually requires no special preparation other than locating and securing a teaching position; (4) requirements for keeping current in professional knowledge and attendant skills are loosely coordinated; and (5) fringe benefits, including a work year of approximately 185 days, are provided.

Many would argue that these conditions are more than offset by several counterbalancing factors: (1) teaching, psychologically speaking, is a high-stress occupation; (2) possibilities for professional promotion within the teaching ranks are limited and usually are confined to "advancement" to an administrative position; and (3) the teaching profession is subject to the caprice and whims of a voting public insofar as decision making and job security are concerned.

These pros and cons relative to the merits of the profession are sufficient to suggest that perhaps teaching does not qualify as a true profession; however, the vast majority of educators insist that teaching is a profession and should be so designated. They frequently base their claim for this distinction on the fact that education has certain characteristics that are similar to those associated with the medical profession. Both professions provide essential service to society, and each group requires a specialized body of knowledge for its practitioners. Both professions have national organizations—The American Medical Association and the National Education Association and the American Federation of Teachers. A training period, followed by a certification or licensing requirement, is imposed on practitioners of each group. Both groups also promote professional standards and protect the welfare of their members.

Although these claims are reassuring, most educators would probably agree that education has much to accomplish before it can match the uniformity of standards and professional rewards enjoyed by the medical profession.

We believe the teaching profession must make a serious effort to establish its professional image. This best can be done by recognizing the teaching profession as a long-term career that requires continual development on the teacher's part. We believe also that preservice teachers need to give serious thought to the teaching profession as an enduring career at the onset of their program. The selection of the teaching level, academic field, and other aspects of the preparatory phase become choices that, when made early, with a long-term career in mind, can serve to make teaching a fulfilling occupation.

Professional development has many dimensions that can be explored and enjoyed by the elementary school teacher. Chief among these are opportunities provided by participation in teacher organizations and professional associations, pursuit of a continued education, and a variety of career-branching opportunities within the profession..

The Impact of Teacher Organizations on Professional Development

Elementary and secondary school teachers have two major teacher organizations that represent their interests, the National Education Association (NEA) and the American Federation of Teachers (AFT). These two teacher organizations have achieved power and influence at the local, state, and national levels. They have lobbyists who represent their respective views in the legislative bodies of the government. They endorse political candidates for office and take stands on various social and economic issues. These organizations have done much to promote the teaching profession as a force to be reckoned with in decisions concerning public policy. As a result, teachers have come to realize that political power in a democracy is developed and applied largely through organized groups. The concept of organized political involvement by teachers in their own behalf is viewed by some people, however, as unethical. This viewpoint is based on the notion that public school teachers, as employees of the state, should not engage in such organized political activities. Teachers, however, tend to view political activity as a legitimate means to achieve their objectives. Since World War II they have turned in ever-increasing numbers to *teacher organizations* as the vehicle for the realization of their goals. They view a strong teacher organization as a necessity for their professional advancement and as a vital linkage between the profession and the public.

341

For a professional group to have credibility it must be well organized and have the majority of the group it represents as its members. In the field of medicine such an organization is the American Medical Association. The American Bar Association is the prime organization for lawyers. Dentists recognize the American Dental Association as their professional organization. Thus, in the major professions, the majority delegate their individual authority to the organized parent group whose leaders exert a collective authority on their behalf.

THE NATIONAL EDUCATION ASSOCIATION (NEA)

The NEA is the larger of the two teacher organizations with approximately 1,600,800 members in 1983. The NEA grew out of the National Teachers Association established in 1857. The name of this organization was changed to NEA in 1879. The organization serves members who are located largely in suburban and rural areas. Its membership constitutes about one half of the nation's teachers.

The NEA offers numerous services to teachers. In addition to working toward better salaries and improved working conditions, the NEA has established:

1. a code of ethics and a bill of rights for teachers.
2. a national liability program.
3. a legal services program for defense.
4. a research program.
5. a political action program.

The organization has a constitution and a set of bylaws for the governance of its activities. NEA governance offers numerous possibilities for teacher participation at the local, state, and national levels. The Representative Assembly is the primary legislative body. Policy making is conducted by this group. The assembly meets annually and acts on resolutions and proposals that have originated at the local level and in most instances have received endorsement at state-level representative assemblies. Leadership of the NEA is conducted by the board of directors, the president, and the executive committee, all of whom have been elected by the members of the association. A professional career-type staff is employed to conduct the daily affairs of the association. The executive director is responsible for the organization and management of the professional staff.

The NEA has grown away from its once close affiliation with school administrator members. There are various reasons for this estrangement; however, the NEA's adoption of such strategies as teacher strikes to obtain benefits for teachers has widened the gap between administrators and teachers.

The National Education Association's programs directly reflect its goals and objectives. A major objective is to promote excellence in education. Another objective is to promote research that responds to classroom teachers' problems, and a third objective is to provide information systems that support the individual teacher's professional practice. To this end two publications are provided each member. *Today's Education* addresses curriculum and instruction topics, and the *NEA Reporter* covers professional and Association developments. Additional publications, such as various research reports and topic-specific memoranda, are available for sale to members. Direct services of a professional nature also are available to members on request. Additional personal benefits for members include computer job location service, educational travel opportunities, low cost medical plans, group insurance, annuities, and reduced cost purchase plans.

For preservice teachers the NEA sponsors the Student NEA found on numerous college campuses. It offers student members many of the benefits available to members of the parent organization.

THE AMERICAN FEDERATION OF TEACHERS (AFT)

The AFT was founded in 1916 and was granted affiliation with the American Federation of Labor that year. Today it is an affiliate of the American Federation of Labor and Congress of Industrial Organizations (AFL-CIO). Most of its approximately five hundred eighty thousand members reside in large cities where labor unions are strong.

The AFT resembles the NEA in many aspects of its organization, purposes, and services. It has a constitution and bylaws for the governance and conduct of its business. It operates through local affiliate groups, area councils, and state federations. The AFT conducts a biennial national meeting of its delegates. Its administrative organization includes a president, various vice-presidents, and an executive council. It has various departments and several councils. These departments and councils offer a variety of services to members as well as helping them to improve their salaries and working conditions.

The services include the promotion of collective bargaining for teachers and other educational staff employees, research on teacher stress and on the education of handicapped children, and various other educational topics and issues. The organization lobbies for legislation that would enhance the educational profession. It presents an annual Human Rights Award and bestows grants in the education and labor arenas. These services parallel, in general, the kinds of services provided by the NEA, including legal counsel and defense and protection against unfair disciplinary or dismissal actions. The AFT publishes the journals *American Educator* and *American Teacher*.

The Impact of Professional Associations on Professional Development

The professional development of the elementary school teacher is greatly enhanced as a result of enrichment opportunities offered by numerous *professional associations.* These associations are devoted to the promotion of excellence in teaching and to improvement of curriculum. They have a scholarly orientation, a characteristic that sets them apart from the larger, politically oriented teacher organizations such as the AFT and the NEA. We believe that the career teacher should be aware of these associations and participate in one that is relevant to his or her teaching interest. These groups conduct a variety of professional activities as well as publish journals, yearbooks, bulletins, and miscellaneous reports that enable the teacher to keep abreast of developments in academic areas.

Professional association conventions/meetings bring teachers together from across the nation. At these meetings recognized leaders speak and report on research and development. Publishers display books and materials in attractive exhibits. Teachers have opportunities to make new acquaintances, share ideas, serve on committees that meet at convention time, and to mingle with persons who have a high level of professional commitment. All of these activities create a rich atmosphere for professional development.

A sampling of several professional associations that offer career enrichment possibilities for elementary school teachers includes:

1. *Association for Childhood Education International* (ACEI), 3615 Wisconsin Ave. N. W., Washington, D. C. 20016. The association is for teachers, parents, and others who are interested in good education for children from infancy through early adolescence. Publications include the journal *Childhood Education,* bulletins, and bibliographies. Approximately eleven thousand members belong to the association. Annual conventions are held.

2. *Association for Supervision and Curriculum Development* (ASCD), 225 N. Washington St., Alexandria, Virginia 22314. An association for professionals who are interested in curriculum and supervision. Membership includes supervisors, curriculum coordinators, curriculum consultants, curriculum directors, professors of education, classroom teachers, school administrators, and others who are interested in curriculum. The association has approximately thirty-five thousand members. Publications include a journal, *Educational Leadership,* a yearbook, and miscellaneous monographs. Annual convention/meetings are held.

3. *International Reading Association* (IRA), 800 Barksdale Road, Newark, Delaware 19711. The purpose of the association is to stimulate research and to disseminate knowledge about reading. The membership is comprised of individuals who teach or supervise reading at all school levels. Publications include the *Journal of Reading, Reading Teacher, Reading Today,* and the *Reading Research Quarterly.* There are approximately forty-one thousand members. An annual convention is held.

4. *National Association for the Education of Young Children* (NAEYC), 1834 Connecticut Ave. N. W., Washington, D. C. 20009. The association is for teachers and directors of nursery schools, day-care centers, and other groups having similar programs for young children. Publications include the journal *Young Children,* books, and monographs. Approximately thirty-six thousand members belong to the association. Annual conventions are conducted.

5. *National Council for the Social Studies* (NCSS), 3501 Newark St., Washington, D. C. 20016. The purpose of the council is to promote the improvement of teaching social studies in the nation's schools. Publications include the journal *Social Education* and numerous monographs. Approximately seventeen thousand members belong to the council. Annual conventions are conducted.

6. *National Council of Teachers of English* (NCTE), 1111 Kenyon Road, Urbana, Illinois 61801. The council is for teachers of English at all levels. Publications include the journals *English Journal* and *College English.* There are approximately ninety thousand members. An annual convention is held.

7. *National Council of Teachers of Mathematics* (NCTM), 1906 Association Drive, Reston, Virginia 22091. The council is for teachers of mathematics at all levels. Publications include the journals *Mathematics Teacher, Arithmetic Teacher,* a yearbook, and other monographs. The council has approximately fifty-seven thousand members. The organization meets in an annual convention.

8. *National Science Teachers Association* (NSTA), 1742 Connecticut Avenue, N. W., Washington, D. C. 20009. The association is for science teachers at all levels. Publications include the journals *The Science Teacher* and *Science and Children,* and other monographs. There are approximately forty-two thousand members. An annual convention is conducted.

9. *Phi Delta Kappa* (PDK), Eighth Street and Union Avenue, Bloomington, Indiana 47401. A professional, honorary fraternity in education. Publications include the journal *Phi Delta Kappan.* Membership is approximately one hundred nineteen thousand professionals. The association conducts biennial conventions.

10. *Pi Lambda Theta,* 4101 E. Third Street, Bloomington, Indiana 47401. A professional honorary association in education. Publications include a quarterly journal *Educational Horizons.* Committees include one on the status of women. There are approximately fourteen thousand members. A biennial convention is held.

Many professional associations have a student membership for preservice teachers. This courtesy offers preservice teachers an excellent opportunity to affiliate with a professional group early in their career.[2]

Opportunities for Professional Development at the Local Level

The certification of teachers usually occurs upon completion of a four-year professional training program and a baccalaureate degree. As a consequence of such a tightly packed program, the education of teachers is considered to be only partially completed on receiving the degree and an initial teaching certificate. The majority of states recognize this limitation by requiring teachers to take postbaccalaureate work prior to receiving a permanent or continuing certificate.[3] In many instances this additional coursework is completed as part of a fifth-year requirement. This is a common practice in many states, and usually is based on the condition that the fifth year of training is to be completed only after the teacher has demonstrated successful teaching experience.

The beginning teacher should acquire a clear understanding of the state requirements for coursework beyond the baccalaureate degree. These requirements differ from state to state. The Teacher Education Office or the Graduate Advisory Office in Colleges of Education has this information. It can also be obtained from any State Department of Education certification office. The information is usually available also in the certification or personnel offices of local school districts.

Certification requirements often are misunderstood by teachers, which results in coursework taken that is not relevant for certification purposes or, even worse, failure to take courses that are required. The beginning teacher should seek responsible advice at the outset, before any coursework for certification is

---

[2] For a comprehensive list and description of professional associations see Denise S. Akey, ed., *18th. Edition, Encyclopedia of Associations, Volume 1: Part I and II. National Organizations of the U. S.* (Detroit: Gale Research Company, 1984).
[3] These certificates are variously referred to as Standard Certificates, Continuing Certificates, Life Certificates, and Permanent Certificates.

undertaken. It is advisable for the teacher to obtain a written evaluation of needed coursework in order to have an official documentation.

The combination of coursework for permanent certification and advanced degree attainment is an attractive possibility that is overlooked by many beginning teachers. The total number of credits required when these goals are combined in one program is usually only slightly greater, if at all, than that required for only one of them. Forty-five quarter credits[4] generally are required for both. Frequently teachers who have completed required coursework for the permanent certificate discover too late that they could have been pursuing work for a master's degree at the same time. Teachers should recognize that they must be admitted to a graduate program *prior* to taking courses that are to be applied to an advanced degree. Usually coursework taken before admittance to a graduate program is not approved for inclusion in such a program. For these reasons, as well as to ensure proper guidance, the beginning teacher should seek official advice at the earliest possible time.

The professional development of teachers is thus assured, up to a point, following the preservice training period. After the receipt of the permanent certificate, however, subsequent professional development of the teacher is an individual matter. The successful teacher is knowledgeable about the many opportunities for career enhancement and has the dedication to participate in activities that are available.

The possibility for professional development of teachers has never been as good as it is today. This fortunate situation is the result of recent impacts on the profession, including those created by the increasing public interest in quality teaching, the growing power of teacher organizations, and the programs and activities offered by professional associations.

For many years teachers were simply expected to do a competent job in teaching the children assigned to their classrooms. School administrators, by and large, were expected to take care of the management and conduct of the school, as well as the larger questions concerning teacher welfare. As a consequence, salary policies, working conditions, curriculum development, evaluation of teaching, and inservice education were administrative prerogatives. Today teacher decision making and participa-

---

[4] Quarter credits can be converted to semester credits by reducing them by one third; e.g., forty-five quarter credits equal thirty semester credits.

tion are common in all those activities. With this ever-growing number of teacher activities has come a corresponding increase in opportunities for professional development for teachers. The career teacher should recognize these activities as opportunities not only for professional development but as possibilities that contribute to a fuller personal life as well.

INSERVICE EDUCATION ACTIVITIES

The 1970s was the decade of "inservice education." The decline of public school enrollments along with the resulting oversupply of teachers caused a shift in attention from preservice education to education at the inservice level. As a result, elementary teachers as well as their colleagues in the secondary schools were confronted with a puzzling array of offerings designed to provide inservice education. The inservice movement, however, suffered as a result of the confusion surrounding the governance of the various offerings and the wide divergence of quality control that was applied. Anything from a course in backpacking to a scholarly college offering in "Recent Interpretations of the American Revolution" was thus considered to be appropriate inservice education.

The situation was confused even more by the competitive atmosphere in which various agencies and institutions offered inservice courses for college credit. Private corporations entered the picture with "packaged courses" in various aspects of teaching and learning. These courses were sometimes sponsored by institutions of higher education for college credit. Nonaccredited educational agencies also offered course credits in activities based on "effective ways to teach" or "newer ways to discipline," adding to an already confused situation. The National Education Association, through its state associations, endorsed inservice courses for teachers—a development that represented a sharp break from its historical dependence on teacher education institutions to select and provide courses for career teachers.

The career teacher in many instances was caught in the middle of a growing confrontation between teacher organizations and teacher education institutions in a struggle for control in the governance of inservice education. This dilemma sometimes manifested itself in the teacher's frustration in discovering that credits earned in an inservice course offered by an agency at the district level was not acceptable in a master's degree program at the university. The confrontation between teacher organizations and teacher education institutions also produced a propaganda campaign to confuse the teacher still further. Teachers received circulars advertising a given teacher organization inservice course as being "practical" rather than "theoretical." The unfortunate result of this labeling was an acceptance on the part of many teachers of the belief that college courses were too theoretical to have any value for the inservice teacher. This power struggle with its negative consequences shows few signs of abatement at the present time. As a result, a promising avenue for professional development is weakened.

Any attempt to create divisiveness in the teaching profession is unfortunate. The responsibility for the competitive climate that exists at the inservice education level between teacher organizations and teacher education institutions must be addressed by both groups in an honest effort to build better relationships. A workable definition of inservice education must be provided in order for professional unity to occur. We believe that the vast array of activities now being lumped together under the inservice umbrella needs to be sorted out in order to distinguish between (1) those courses that represent continuation and extension of the teacher's development in the study of teaching and learning and (2) those courses that are intended to enable the teacher to fulfill a job-specific requirement. Konecki and Stein[5] refer to the first type as an example of "continued education—an organized program of courses or experiences leading toward a professional goal or a graduate degree, and the second type as "inservice education"—courses or experiences that meet the need of the employer and employee at the district level. This classification serves to provide the teacher with a rationale for understanding the purpose of a given course or experience. Thus, a teacher might pursue coursework or experiences that contribute to both objectives—inservice education as well as continued education activities—at various times throughout a career.

Whatever the type of professional development—inservice education or continued education—the career teacher should utilize the opportunities that each offers. The teacher who has developed a specialty in a teaching technique such as role-playing, questioning, creative dramatics, storytelling, or creative writing should take advantage of opportunities to instruct others in that

---

[5] Loretta Konecki and Alida Stein, "A Taxonomy of Professional Education." *Journal of Teacher Education,* 29 (July-August, 1978), 43.

(Courtesy of Terri Malinowski.)

Career teachers need to keep abreast of emerging developments that affect education. The teacher in this photograph has become competent in the use of the microcomputer. Name other emerging topics that require continued education on the teacher's part.

particular skill. Such opportunities are increasing as a result of expanding inservice education programs.

Staff development programs offered by school districts as a form of inservice education also offer professional development opportunities. Teachers can enroll in staff development courses designed to improve skills in such areas as communication, problem solving, computer-assisted instruction, and human relations.

The teacher who has completed a graduate degree should be alert to opportunities to teach in the evening or in summer school programs offered by teacher education institutions. Many of these institutions encourage local teachers to assist in their instructional programs and the practice contributes to the teacher's professional status as well as to the professional enrichment of his or her colleagues.

CONTINUED EDUCATION ACTIVITIES

Teachers who live near a college or university have an excellent opportunity to pursue advanced degree coursework during the school year by taking late afternoon or Saturday classes. Most institutions schedule their offerings at times that make it possible for teachers to pursue their studies while teaching full time. Summer school sessions offer teachers a chance for full-time study. For teachers who wish to enroll for summer school work only, colleges and universities usually make it possible for them to enroll without the admission procedures that apply to regular year programs. Most professional educators agree that the teaching profession needs to encourage its practitioners to continue their pursuit of knowledge beyond the baccalaureate years. Colleges and universities offer academic and education courses that make it possible for the teacher to complete an advanced degree or to satisfy requirements for an advanced certificate. In each case, the teacher usually is encouraged to continue the pursuit of knowledge beyond the baccalaureate degree.

Many educators believe that too much emphasis has been placed on the vocational aspects of teaching at the expense of scholarship. The concept of the *teacher as a scholar* has its place at all levels of education. Recent public clamor about the school's failure to teach literacy reflects a growing concern that teachers do not place sufficient value on preparing pupils with the knowledge and skills necessary for participation in a literate society. For teachers to do so they must provide role models for pupils that encourage scholarship and literacy.

School districts provide incentives for teachers to earn advanced degrees through the awarding of salary increases for completion of such degrees. Advancement on the salary schedule is also frequently attached to the number of credit hours the teacher accumulates. As a result of the recent explosion in the kinds of courses and credits being offered by outside agencies in the name of inservice education, many school districts have decided to grant salary increments only for those courses offered by accredited colleges and universities.

In any case, continued education in the pursuit of an advanced degree, or for the completion of advanced certification requirements, or that satisfies both requirements, remains a highly respected avenue for professional development.

TEACHER ORGANIZATION ACTIVITIES

At the local school district level, teacher organizations provide members with numerous opportunities to be involved in association activities. The Shoreline Education Association,[6] affiliated with the Washington Education Association and the National Education Association, provides an excellent example of these activities.

The constitution of the Shoreline Education Association establishes a governance structure that includes

1. A President, Vice-President, immediate past President, Secretary, and Treasurer. Each of these officers has prescribed responsibilities and duties required by the constitution.

2. An Executive Board, composed of the officers and designated organization members.

3. A Representative Council, consisting of the elected officers and at least one representative from each school and the Instructional Services Center. The Council is the governing body of the organization and its duties include authorizing the organization's bargaining team to negotiate with the school district on matters relating to salaries and working conditions.

The bylaws of the Shoreline Education Association establish additional groups that assist in the governance of the organization.

1. The Certificated Cabinet consists of six members appointed by the President and the Representative Council and six members appointed by the school Superintendent. The Superintendent and the President co-chair, and alternate chairing the meetings. The body serves in an advisory capacity and its goal is to improve communication between the school district and the teacher organization.

2. The Standing Committees/Commissions. There are four standing committees and five commissions. These meet at least once each month and are responsible to the Representative Council. Members are appointed by the President and are subject to ratification by the Representative Council. (These are detailed in the following nine descriptions.)

3. The Instructional and Professional Development Committee is responsible for recommending proposals involving class size, preparation time for teachers, departmentalization, curriculum and instruction, and other related concerns.

---

[6] Shoreline Education Association, 17455 68th. Ave. N. E., Suite 202, Bothell, Wa., 98011.

4. The Compliance Committee is responsible for identifying compliance deficiencies and recommending measures to remedy them.

5. The Nominations and Elections Committee is responsible for securing candidates and controlling all aspects of the elections.

6. The Public Relations Committee is responsible for recommending proposals related to community and pupil relations.

7. The Legislative (Shoreline Education Association/Political Action Commission) Commission is responsible for informing the membership about legislation, its effect on teachers; interviewing political candidates, and informing the members of their views; mobilizing members to accomplish political action and carrying out *Policy Unity of Leaders in State Education* (PULSE) programs.

8. The Bargaining Commission consists of ten members who have trained for the bargaining process. It is charged with the responsibility of bargaining with the school board.

9. The Teacher Education and Professional Standards Commission is responsible for supervising and promoting standards of teachers through various activities that enhance teacher education conditions, improved teacher certification standards, and staff evaluation procedures.

10. The Grievance Commission studies and prepares action programs for obtaining satisfactory policies and procedures for the redress of grievances brought by its members.

11. The Personnel Practices Commission is responsible for proposing recommendations concerning District personnel practices, leaves, and fringe benefits.

Many teachers extend their teaching careers in a professional way through participation in activities such as the foregoing. They require the talents of the very best teachers, those who have the professional knowledge, human relations skills, and selfless dedication to serve their profession. These qualities are essential for the intelligent leadership of the teaching profession.

TEACHER PROMOTION

Promotion of teachers within the ranks is virtually nonexistent. The traditional avenue to advancement has been promotion *out of teaching* and into an administrative or supervisory position. This is unfortunate because frequently an outstanding teacher is rewarded through promotion to a principalship, only to become an average or even a mediocre administrator. The temptation of a higher salary is a powerful incentive for a teacher to aspire to an administrative position. The qualifications for each position are quite different; however, the traditional practice of promoting a teacher to an administrative position continues to flourish on the assumption that "a good teacher should be a good administrator."

The absence of a promotion system for teachers also removes what could be a powerful incentive for professional development. Attempts to establish a promotion system usually have been resisted by teacher organizations. They believe that a hierarchy would be created within the teaching ranks. This would result in a group of teachers who could easily conceive of themselves as an *elite* within the teaching profession.

Efforts to establish a promotion system have tended to follow three approaches: (1) recognition of master teachers, (2) merit pay, and (3) differentiated staffing. The Master Teacher plan is based on an evaluation system that includes criteria for outstanding teaching. A panel of judges, including teachers, evaluates each candidate. The master teacher recognition usually results in a higher salary for the teacher and may sometimes entail additional responsibilities.

The Merit Pay plan provides for salary increases for teachers who meet specific criteria such as leadership and teaching effectiveness. The granting of merit pay is usually determined by a panel or a committee.

Differentiated staffing has been attempted more frequently in secondary education than at the elementary school level. Even so, the concept is appropriate for the elementary school. Team teaching is the common mechanism for implementing the differentiated staffing plan. The team is usually led by a teacher leader who receives a higher salary than the other team members. Sometimes the team also includes teacher aides who are on a lower salary schedule than those team members who are certified teachers. The plan has many advantages, one of which is the assignment of teachers to perform in those areas where they are strongest and where their specific interests lie. The major difficulty associated with the plan lies in obtaining personnel who have the diversity of competencies and interests necessary to establish balanced teaching teams. Screening, selection, and classification

(Courtesy of Kay F. Engelsen.)

The responsibility of the teacher extends beyond the classroom. Here we see a group of teachers, administrators, and laypersons working together to promote a levy issue to support local schools. Give other examples of extra-classroom activities that fall within the scope of an elementary school teacher's responsibility.

of teachers for assignment also present problems that school district administrators are reluctant to assume.

The absence of teacher promotion constitutes a serious deficit in professional development opportunities. The promotion of teachers to administrative positions also is characterized by still another problem in our society—sexism. The number of women teachers who are promoted to administrative positions has been very small. Recent federal legislation, such as the provisions contained in Title IX, may correct this situation through the opening of existing administrative positions to women. Until the profession is willing to reward the qualified and competent teacher through some kind of recognition within the ranks, teachers will continue to be regarded as underlings in a hierarchical system headed by administrators. This only contributes to the misunderstanding between the two groups.

Career-Branching Opportunities in Education

Career-branching opportunities for teachers are increasing. They are the result of the growing complexity of our social and political structure that is demanding a diversity of professional roles in education. These roles frequently are attractive opportunities for elementary school teachers who wish to specialize in an educational role that provides an essential service for classroom teachers.

The following are examples of professional roles that offer possibilities for career-branching for the elementary school teacher.

1. School Administrator

The elementary school principal is the most frequent example of this role. Urban school districts often employ assistant principals for the larger elementary schools. Administrative positions, of course, exist at higher levels, such as the superintendent, assistant superintendent, personnel manager, business manager, or research director.

2. Librarian

This is an important position at all levels of instruction in local school districts. The larger elementary schools frequently have a school librarian assigned on a full-time basis.

3. Instructional Resources Specialist

This position often includes responsibilities for the coordination of instructional resources for the K–12 program. Possibilities for the instructional resources specialist to produce instructional programs that are disseminated by means of school television are available in some school districts.

4. Subject Area or Grade-Level Consultant

The large school districts frequently have full-time consultant positions in various subject areas, such as art, music, physical education, mathematics, science, social studies, language arts, or reading. Many smaller districts employ part-time consultants for this purpose. These persons may teach part time in order to round out a full-time assignment.

Consultants are sometimes classified according to elementary or secondary education, and in such instances have a comprehensive responsibility for various school subjects. In certain instances, the consultant also supervises teachers in the various subject areas or grade levels.

In addition to the foregoing professional roles, there are also career-branching possibilities contained in the various specialized referral services that are made available to elementary school teachers. These include:[7]

1. Communication Disorders Specialist

This specialist provides diagnostic, therapeutic, and consultant services for children who are handicapped by language, speech and/or hearing disorders. He or she is usually assigned to several elementary schools and serves pupils on a rotating basis.

2. School Counselor

The counselor provides individual and group guidance services for children with personal, social, or educational problems. The position also requires that the counselor have knowledge of career development information and educational assessment and testing.

3. Occupational Therapist

The school occupational therapist works with children who have disabilities that impair their ability to cope with ordinary tasks of living. These disabilities may be caused by deficits in development, such as physical injury or illness, or other psychological or social problems.

---

[7] Descriptions of the responsibilities of these specialized roles are adapted from *Washington Administrative Code: Professional Preparation Certification Requirements,* Chapter 180–79. Olympia, Wa.: Office of State Superintendent of Public Instruction, 1979.

4. Physical Therapist

The physical therapist serves children who require relief from a physical disability or pain, and/or restoration of motor function. The specialist seeks to assist the child to achieve maximum performance within the limits of the disability. Assessment and diagnosis of the pupil's disability and prescription of treatment are primary responsibilities of this position.

5. School Psychologist

This role requires the specialist to conduct academic and intellectual assessment and diagnosis (including administration and interpretation of individual intelligence tests); make behavioral observations and analyses; counsel children and interview parents, teachers, and others relevant to the situation; develop remedial programs for children; and conduct research and evaluation relative to pupil-related matters.

6. Reading Resource Specialist

The reading resource specialist provides numerous services for children and school personnel. These include serving as a diagnostician, advisor, consultant, and trainer of school personnel who work with the reading program. Specifically, the specialist must be able to demonstrate knowledge and techniques of teaching reading; compare various approaches to teaching reading; interpret research data; conduct diagnosis of pupils' reading difficulties; plan and implement reading programs; and conduct staff development training programs.

7. School Nurse

The school nurse works with children and their families on health matters. He or she develops a school health program and responds to the individual pupil's health problems. A major responsibility is the development of a school atmosphere that promotes sound health practices.

8. Social Worker

The social worker assigned to schools assists children and their families in resolving social adjustment problems. Knowledge of human development and the social structure is necessary for the successful performance of this role. The social worker also must have knowledge and skill in interviewing children in an individual or family setting; working with family members; and in providing assistance to family, educational and other personnel related to the problem. Knowledge and use of referral agencies for the child and/or the family are necessary in order to accommodate the problems that are frequently encountered.

The enactment of PL 94–142, the *Education for All Handicapped Children Act,* will necessitate additional professional roles necessary for the assistance of teachers who are to provide for mildly handicapped children in their classroom instruction. These are yet to be defined in most instances beyond the utilization of teacher aides and the various specialists who work with handicapped children. We believe, however, that there will be a need for additional support persons once the mainstreaming of mildly handicapped pupils in regular classrooms becomes a reality across the nation.

Bilingual education programs as well as instructional programs in English as a second language offer career-branching opportunities. The growing emphasis on computer-assisted instruction promises to provide an additional avenue. Thus, there are numerous opportunities for the elementary school teacher who wishes to become a specialist.

On the other hand, beginning teachers who plan to devote a career to classroom teaching should be encouraged to do so because the foundation of elementary school education depends on a solid group of dedicated teachers. We hope that the ideas presented in this chapter will contribute substantially to the professional development of the career teacher as well as to the career of the teacher who wishes to serve the profession in a specialized role.

Study Questions and Activities

1. The text emphasizes that planning for professional development should begin early in the elementary school teacher's career. With this point in mind, what are your career goals for ten years from now?

2. Compare the goals and objectives of the American Federation of Teachers (AFT) and the National Education Association (NEA). Do you have a preference for one of these organizations? If so, why?

3. Interview three teachers about their views on the two major teacher organizations identified in Study Activity number 2. How do their views compare with your own?

4. The text describes several professional associations. Identify the ones that offer possibilities for *your* professional development.

5. Visit a library and examine several of the publications of the professional associations presented in the text. Describe the publications according to their value in helping you to be a good teacher.

6. Contact the administrator in charge of staff development in a local school district to ascertain the opportunities for professional development available to elementary school teachers. Which of these appeal to you? Why?

7. What are the certification requirements for a continuing or permanent teaching certificate in your state?

8. There are various proposals for the determination of teacher merit, such as merit pay based on performance as well as various career-ladder incentives. Which of the current plans do you favor? Why?

For Further Professional Study

Armstrong, David G., Kenneth T. Henson, and Tom V. Savage. *Education: An Introduction.* New York: Macmillan Publishing Company, Inc., 1981, Chaps. 12, 13, 14.

Burrello, Leonard C., and Tim Orbaugh. "Reducing the Discrepancy Between the Known and the Unknown in Inservice Education." *Phi Delta Kappan,* **63** (Feb. 1982), 385–388.

Fimian, Michael J. "What Is Teacher Stress?" *The Clearing House,* **56** (Nov. 1982), 101–105.

Foxley, Cecelia H. "Sex Equity in Education: Some Gains, Problems and Future Needs." *Journal of Teacher Education,* **33** (Sept.–Oct. 1982), 6–9.

Goodlad, John I. *A Place Called School: Prospects for the Future.* New York: McGraw-Hill Book Company, 1984, Chaps. 6, 9, 10.

Gulek, Gerald L. *Education and Schooling in America.* Englewood Cliffs, N. J.: Prentice-Hall, Inc., 1983, Chaps. 19, 20, 21.

Jarolimek, John. *The Schools in Contemporary Society: An Analysis of Social Currents, Issues, and Forces.* New York: Macmillan Publishing Company, Inc., 1981, Chap. 10.

Joyce, Bruce, and Michael McKibbin. "Teacher Growth States and School Environments." *Educational Leadership,* **40** (Nov. 1982), 36–41.

Orlosky, Donald E., ed. *Introduction to Education.* Columbus, Ohio: Charles E. Merrill Publishing Company, 1982, Chap. 14.

Scherer, Marge. "Merit Pay: The Great Debate." *Instructor,* **93** (Oct. 1983), 22–25, 159.

Wilsey, Cathy, and Joellen Killion. "Making Staff Development Programs Work." *Educational Leadership,* **40** (Oct. 1982), 36, 38, 43.

Index

A

Academic learning time, 51
Accountability, 59, 73–74, 150
Achievement, examinations, 20
Acland, Henry, 40
Active teachers, 52
Affective domain, 109–110
Affective learning
  as related to cognitive learning, 317
  definition of, 317
  environment, 320–322
  as a school experience, 317–320
Age-grading, discussed, 10–12
Akey, Denise S., 347
American Federation of Teachers
  (AFT), 340, 341, 343–344
Anderson, L., 243
Anderson, Linda M., 61
Armstrong, David G., 361
Arts curriculum, 322–325

B

Bane, Mary Jo, 40
Banks, James A., 35

Bany, Mary A., 230
Basic skills
  importance of, 6–7, 42
  the three Rs, 258–263
Beck, I. L., 210
Behavior problems, as related to class-
  room management, 226–230
Best, Raphaela, 35
Beyer, Barry K., 282
Bickel, William E., 61
Bilingual education
  discussed, 29–31
  legislation, 30
Birnie, Barbara, 95
Birch, Jack W., 155
Blankenship, Colleen, 210
Bloom, Benjamin S., 108, 109, 187
Blumenfeld, Phyllis C., 145
Bolster, Arthur S., Jr., 145
Brain research and school learning,
  33–34
Branch, Robert C., 311
Brophy, Jere E., 50, 118, 151, 210,
  243
Broudy, Harry S., 312
Brown, James W., 211

363